A Year with the Saints

Written and illustrated
by Calej

With heartfelt gratitude to God I dedicate this book to the Holy Family and my loving husband Patrick.

TABLE OF CONTENTS

INTRODUCTION

The saints are priceless gifts to humanity. Their lives show us that we are not alone in our struggles. We have heavenly friends who can be our role models to inspire us in our life journey.

This book is meant to introduce us to some of the greatest people who have walked the earth. Through their great love for God, they have selflessly given themselves so that we may also trod upon the narrow path that leads to our true home.

Each day of the year has feast days for many different saints so we encourage you to use this book only as a springboard for additional study.

Depending on the country, feast days may be different.

May you grow closer to our Lord through these stories and find your own patron saint. We are made for heaven and the saints are suitable guides for those of us who wish to get there.

JANUARY

SAINT JOSEPH MARY TOMASI
PATRON OF THE LITURGY

In 17th-century Sicily was born a young lad named Joseph who loved the Holy Mass. As a young child, he would dress up according to the liturgical colors of the day and would often worship God through singing the psalms in Gregorian chant.

Joseph was born into a noble family - wealthy in both spiritual and material riches. In time, four of his sisters became nuns and his parents joined the religious life as soon as all the children were grown.

He longed to serve God so at the age of 15, he gave away his inheritance and joined the Theatines. He was an excellent student of Philosophy, Theology and several languages. He was ordained in his early twenties.

Father Joseph immersed himself in his work for the Church. He often taught catechism to children and wrote much about the liturgy. In today's modern world, priests and deacons use Father Joseph's Liturgy of the Hours for their daily prayers. His great knowledge, as well as his exemplary virtues of humility and charity led Pope Clement XI to make him a cardinal.

Today, January 1st is his feast day. Saint Joseph Mary Tomasi, patron of the liturgy, please pray for us!

SAINT BASIL THE GREAT
PATRON OF MONKS

"The Word calls us to repentance, crying out: 'Come to me, all you who labor and are heavily burdened and I will refresh you' (Matthew 11:28). There is, then, a way to salvation if we are willing to follow it" - from a letter by Saint Basil the Great

Saint Basil was born in ancient Turkey in the 4th century. He came from a very virtuous and holy family. Both his parents and 4 of his siblings were all proclaimed saints by the Catholic church.

He was a nobleman who became known for his generosity in helping those in need during a time of famine.

He was a gifted speaker who grew in popularity. So as not to become proud, Basil renounced all his wealth and joined the monastery. Soon he was establishing monasteries all over. He is considered the founder of Eastern monasticism.

He is a Greek Doctor of the church and one of the Church Fathers and the patron of monks.

Today, January 2nd is his feast day. Saint Basil, please pray for us!

· ENOCH THE PATRIARCH ·

Of the many saints mentioned in the Bible, Enoch was one of those who lived a very long time. It is hard to believe but it is written there that Enoch lived until he was 365 years old. His father Jared was said to have lived up to age 962!

He was a descendant of Seth and an ancestor of Noah. When he reached 65 years old, he became a father to Methuselah. He also had other sons and daughters.

Enoch lived a life in accordance with God's will. At the end of his life, God took him to heaven and he had a happy death.

"Enoch pleased the Lord, and was taken up; he was an example of repentance to all generations." - Sirach 44:15

Today, January 4th is his feast day. Saint Enoch, please pray for us!

SAINT ELIZABETH ANN SETON
PATRON OF THOSE
RIDICULED FOR THEIR PIETY

Elizabeth was born into high society during the late 18th century. Her father was a doctor and their Episcopalian family lived in New York. When she was only 3 years old, her mother died. After only a year, her younger sister also passed away.

When she was 19 years old, she married William Magee Seton who was a rich businessman. They had 5 children together.

Alas, after around 10 years, the business failed and William died of tuberculosis. Elizabeth was left in a dire predicament in having to care for their young children all by herself.

It was during this time that a belief in the real presence of Jesus Christ in the Eucharist stirred in her heart. She converted to Catholicism despite this creating a rift with her in-laws. She supported her children and ensured their education by opening a school in Boston.

She is the patron of those ridiculed for their piety and widows. She is also an intercessor for those with in-law problems and against the death of parents and children.

Today, January 4th is her feast day. Saint Elizabeth Ann Seton, please pray for us!

In 1833, John was waiting to be ordained. There were so many priests in the area and the bishop got sick, so this was unavoidably delayed.

At the time, there was a great need in America for priests due to the enormous influx of immigrants. John, inspired by the Holy Spirit, came to minister to them. Given the choice to live in the city or in the countryside, he chose to go to the remote rural area where living conditions were more difficult.

Once there, he set out to work on an unfinished church. When that was done, he visited the many different farms whose inhabitants came from all around the world. Fluent in 12 languages, he was able to unite everyone to the faith.

Finally, he was ordained in Maryland in 1841 with the Redemptorists. All in all, he was able to establish 50 churches, and even began to build a cathedral. He was responsible for opening almost 100 schools and his diocese grew from 500 to 9,000.

He was a writer, catechist, and the first American man and bishop to be canonized. Today, January 5th is his feast day. Saint John Neumann, please pray for us!

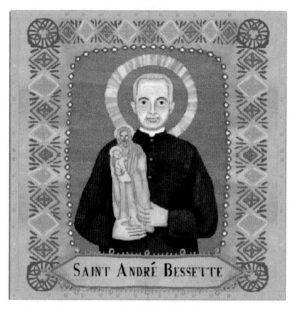

SAINT ANDRÉ BESSETTE

"Some day, Saint Joseph will be honored on Mount Royal," whispered the 25-year-old Andre Bessette. The young man spent much of his nights in prayer facing the open window overlooking the mountain. On his window sill stood a small statue of Saint Joseph.

Andre's simple background in the past was that of a farmhand, shoemaker, baker, blacksmith, and factory employee. In order to serve the Lord, he became the doorkeeper and sacristan at the Congregation of the Holy Cross. Throughout his work day, he encountered many sick people. Due to his history of poor health, he had a special concern for them. He ministered to each one by rubbing the oil from the church lamp onto the sick parts of their bodies, and soon, their diseases were healed!

Word of the miracles spread throughout Canada and 80,000 letters a year arrived asking for healing prayers. Due to the growing number of visitors, church officials wished to purchase the area to build a chapel but the owners would not sell. It was only when Andre planted Saint Joseph medals on Mount Royal's peak did the owners agree to sell. This started the practice of asking Saint Joseph's prayers when buying and selling a home.

When Saint Andre died, a million people attended his funeral.

Today, January 6th is his feast day. Saint Andre Bessette, please pray for us!

11

"May the God of love and peace set your hearts at rest and speed you on your journey: may he meanwhile shelter you from disturbance by others in the hidden recesses of His love" - Saint Raymond of Peñafort

In the 12th century lived a nobleman in Peñafort, Catalonia, Spain. He was an attorney who later entered religious life as a Dominican priest. He was so wise that he counseled kings and queens. He was known as a great confessor.

One amazing story happened when he was with the King of Aragon on the island of Majorca.

He was encouraging the king to give up a particular sin which the king was having difficulty with. Earning the king's ire, he refused the saint's request to return to Barcelona. Since it was urgent that he leave, Saint Raymond then used his trusty cloak, laid it over the waters and hastily sailed back over the sea to reach his destination!

He is the patron saint of attorneys, barristers, lawyers, canonists and medical record librarians.

Today, January 7th is his feast day. Saint Raymond, please pray for us!

SAINT GUDULE
OF BRUSSELS
PATRON OF SINGLE WOMEN

In the year 650 in Hamme, Brabant was born Gudule. She was the daughter of a count and great-niece of Emperor Pepin.

She grew up surrounded by many pious and holy people. Her mother was Saint Amalburga And her siblings were Saint Pharaildis of Ghent, Saint Reineldis, and Saint Emebert of Cambrai. Her aunt, Saint Gertrude of Nivelle taught her in the ways of God.

Gudule loved to pray and attend holy Mass. She would start her day by walking to church before sunrise with a candle to light her way. It is said that the devil kept blowing away the flame from her candle but then the flame would not fail to re-ignite again and again.

During the bitter cold of January, a flower blooms,called the "tremella deliquescens", or "Sinte Goulds lampken" (Saint Gudula's lantern) reminding us that even in the harshest circumstances, our faith can still grow.

She is the patron of single laywomen.

Today, January 8th is her feast day. Saint Gudule, please pray for us!

BLESSED PAULINE-MARIE JARICOT
PATRON OF THE POOR

Pauline-Marie Jericot was not your typical teenager in 18th-century France. She was born to a family of aristocrats but she lived an extremely simple life. She desired to live single-heartedly for God and to never marry.

She formed a group of like-minded young women who wanted to make reparations for the sins committed against God. Theyx became known as the Réparatrices du Sacré-Coeur de Jésus-Christ.

Together, the girls raised money for missionary work and helped others to draw closer to God through praying the Rosary and meditating on Christ's passion. In 1826, she established the Association of the Living Rosary.

When she contracted a heart ailment, she asked for the intercession of Saint Philomena and was soon healed! She then shared her miracle story throughout the country and helped spread a devotion to the saint.

After Pauline-Marie's death, those who knew her piety asked her for prayers. A little girl who fell into a coma after choking on food was perfectly restored to health through Pauline-Marie's prayers. This led to her being proclaimed a saint of the Catholic Church. She is the patron of the poor.

Today, January 9th is her feast day. Saint Pauline-Marie Jericot, please pray for us!

BLESSED ADÈLE DE BATZ DE TRENQUELLÉON
PATRON OF THE DAUGHTERS OF MARY IMMACULATE

In 16 countries around the world is found an organization called the Daughters of Mary Immaculate (Marianist Sisters). Their faith communities do a great many things in service of the Church.

The call for such a group started in the heart of a young French noble woman named Adèle de Batz de Trenquelléon. When she received a marriage proposal, she refused it as God wanted her to live out her vocation as a nun. Others who had the same inclinations readily joined her and they began tending to the poor and sick. They generously gave what they could and provided educational and spiritual nourishment to the people.

Adèle was a good friend of Saint Émilie de Rodat and they wrote each other regularly.

Though she died when she was only 38 years old, her legacy of charitable service endures to this day.

She is the patron saint of Daughters of Mary Immaculate.

Today, January 10th is her feast day. Blessed Adèle de Batz de Trenquelléon, please pray for us!

SAINT VITALIS OF GAZA
PATRON OF PROSTITUTES

"Judge nothing before the time, until the Lord come, who both will bring to light the hidden things of darkness, and will make manifest the counsels of the heart." - Saint Vitalis

Much like Jesus and the Samaritan woman at the well, Saint Vitalis encouraged others towards growing in the virtue of purity.

He was a monk and hermit living in 7th-century Gaza who at the age of 60 traveled to Alexandria, Egypt. There, he worked as a laborer by day and missionary by night. At the end of each day, he used his daily earnings to pay for time with one of the local prostitutes.

During the night, he prayed over them and preached about the love of God. This daily routine was able to convert many of them to turn away from their worldly sins of the flesh to embrace a chaste way of life.

One day, a pimp decided to kill him because his mission was reducing the earnings of the brothel.

He is the patron of prostitutes and day laborers.

Today, January 11th is his feast day. Saint Vitalis of Gaza, please pray for us!

SAINT MARGUERITE BOURGEOUS
PATRON AGAINST THE DEATH OF PARENTS

In 17th-century Aube, France lived a family with twelve children. The parents were devout Christians but they died while their children were still young. The sixth child was Marguerite and she immediately started raising her siblings in place of her parents. When they had matured, Marguerite prayerfully discerned her future path.

At the time, the governor of Montreal, Canada was looking for teachers for the New World and invited Marguerite to join them. She generously gave away all she owned to her siblings and sailed away to Canada.

There was much to do in her newfound home. Their group of volunteer teachers began constructing a chapel and a school. They not only taught the faith but also livelihood skills to the people. These enabled them to survive when the food was scarce. In time, she was able to convince other women to join the mission and they formed the first sisters of the Congregation of Notre Dame.

Her prayers are invoked against the death of parents and poverty. She is also the patron of people rejected from entering religious orders.

Today, January 12th is her feast day. Saint Marguerite Bourgeous, please pray for us!

St. Hilary
OF POITIERS
PATRON OF STUDENTS

"When I look at your heavens, according to my own lights, with these weak eyes of mine, I am certain with reservation that they are your heavens. The stars circle in the heavens, reappear year after year, each with a function and service to fulfill. And though I do not understand them, I know that you, O God, are in them." - Saint Hilary

Saint Hilary was raised in a pagan family and did not know much about God. He started reading the Bible and was converted by the time he finished reading the New Testament. He lived his newfound faith so well that he was appointed a bishop.

He began to write many books to explain Christianity to unbelievers and many of them were converted.

If you are having trouble with your schoolwork, St. Hilary of Poitiers is your go-to saint. He can also help pray for you if you've had a snake bite or have rheumatism. He is also the patron of mothers and children who are learning how to walk. His feast day is today, January 13th. Saint Hilary of Poitiers, please pray for us!

SAINT FELIX OF NOLA
PATRON OF THOSE WITH EYE AILMENTS

Felix was a Syrian soldier who settled in Nola, Italy in the 3rd century. When his father passed away, he sold all his belongings and donated the proceeds to the poor so he could be ordained and serve the church.

The emperor banned the practice of the Christian faith so Felix was apprehended and tortured. Afterward, Felix came to the rescue of his sick bishop by hiding him in an abandoned dwelling.

They would have been found out if it had not been for a spider that quickly spun a web over the doorway to their hiding place. This fooled the guards into thinking that no one was there.

He is the patron of those suffering from eye ailments and domestic animals. He is also invoked against lies, perjury and false witness.

Today, January 14th is his feast day. Saint Felix of Nola, please pray for us!

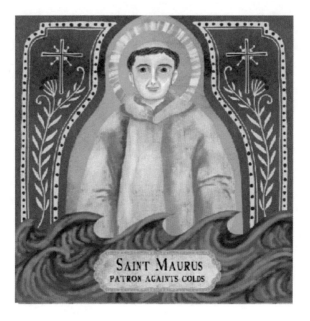

SAINT MAURUS
PATRON AGAINTS COLDS

Saint Maurus was a Benedictine monk living in 6th-century Rome, Italy. At the age of 12, he was already a student of Saint Benedict of Nursia.

One day, Saint Placid, his fellow monk was in danger of drowning. Saint Maurus sprang into action to save him. People were aghast when they saw the saint walking on the water to reach Saint Placid and carry him out of the water.

He was known to heal various illnesses through his prayers and stories abound wherein he raised the dead back to life!

When Saint Benedict died, Saint Maurus saw a vision of him walking up a street that led to heaven.

He is the patron saint against colds, gout, goiter, rheumatism, and hoarseness. He is also the intercessor of candlemakers, cobblers, shoemakers, coppersmiths, porters, tailors and tinkers.

Today, January 15th is his feast day. Saint Maurus, please pray for us!

SAINT JOSEPH VAZ
PATRON OF THE ARCHDIOCESE
OF GOA AND DAMÃO, INDIA

Saint Joseph Vaz was a preacher and confessor in 17th-century Sri Lanka. His heart longed to serve the Catholics in Ceylon where they hadn't had any priests for 50 years and the people were being persecuted by the Dutch. While waiting to be sent there, he ministered to the poor and sick and ransomed Christian slaves until the time that he could go to Ceylon.

Under the guise of a laborer, he held Masses at night. Eventually, he was arrested and jailed. In prison, he learned the local language and began converting the inmates. Then, a severe drought occurred and though the Buddhist monks prayed fervently for rain, no rain came. Fr. Joseph was called and he built an altar at the town center and prayed. A downpour ensued and yet Fr. Joseph remained dry. Afterward, the king freed him.

During his service at the Diocese of Mangalore, some evil men sought to murder him at the top of the hill. Just when they were about to attack, a brilliant light shone and water gushed forth from all around the saint, frightening his assailants away.

He is the patron of the archdiocese of Goa and Damão, India.

Today, January 16th is his feast day. Saint Joseph Vaz, please pray for us!

St. ANTHONY
OF THE DESERT
PATRON OF FARMERS

"For the one who loves his neighbor loves God, and the one who loves God, loves his own soul." - Saint Anthony of the Desert

Born of a wealthy family, he gave away most of his money after hearing the story of the rich, young man at Holy Mass. He became a lone hermit for 80 years! Who among us could live in a tomblike cave and eat bread and water for even just a day? He did this for the most part of his 105-year-long life. His life witness brought many to God and to follow his example, living a life of poverty and simplicity.

"God is gathering us out of all regions till he can make resurrection of our own hearts from the very earth, and teach us that we are all of one substance, and members of one another. For the one who loves his neighbor loves God, and the one who loves God, loves his own soul." - Saint Anthony of the Desert

He is the patron of farmers and he is also the intercessor of monks.

Today, January 17th is his feast day. Saint Anthony of the desert, please pray for us!

Saint Margaret of Hungary
PATRON OF PRAYER AND FASTING

Margaret was born in 13th-century Hungary to the royal family. She was the eighth of 10 children. Because Hungary was under the rule of the Mongol dynasty, they promised to consecrate one of their children to God if they were liberated from the foreign rulers.

When the Mongols left, Margarets parents fulfilled their vows and entrusted her to the care of the Dominican nuns. The young Margaret grew to love her faith and spent much of her time in deep prayer.

She grew to love Christ so much that she imitated Him as a suffering servant, choosing to do the most lowliest chores in the convent. To intensify her prayers, she offered up sacrifices like wearing a hairshirt or wearing shoes spiked with nails. She lived in perpetual virginity and refused to get married including the time when her father wished for her to wed King Ottokar II of Bohemia.

Margaret died when she was only 28 years old but was soon proclaimed a saint after her passing. Many miracles occurred attributed to her intercession including someone who was raised back to life.

She is the patron of prayer and fasting. Today, January 18 is her feast day, Saint Margaret of Hungary, please pray for us

23

Pope Fabian
Patron Saint of Rome

Imagine living on your farm one day and then being Pope the next! This is what happened to the 20th Pope of the Catholic Church, Pope Fabian. It was because when the Church needed the next pope, a dove landed on Fabian's head.

The dove for many Christians symbolizes the Holy Spirit so they saw this as a sign from God that Fabian was their man!

He lived in a time of persecution of believers so Pope Fabian was martyred for his faith.

He is the patron saint of Rome. He was a great administrator so those working in this field would probably benefit greatly from his prayers as well.

Today, January 19th is his feast day. Pope Fabian, please pray for us!

Saint Sebastian
Patron Saint of Athletes

Saint Sebastian's life was of humble service to God and to His people. He became a soldier to be able to assist the Christians who were being jailed for their faith. He encouraged them to remain steadfast in their beliefs even if it meant martyrdom. In so doing, he converted the other prisoners, jailer and risked his own life.

Eventually, he was found out and was put to death by Emperor Diocletian. He was blindfolded, tied and hit with so many arrows so as to become "an urchin as full of pricks" as instructed.

Despite the bloody end planned for him by the Emperor, St. Sebastian did not die! He was found by a holy woman, Irene who nursed him back to health. Once he was strong enough, he could have fled and escaped but instead he went back to the emperor because he desired that the emperor become a Christian.

The emperor got angry and for the second time, sentenced him to die by being beaten by clubs. Saint Sebastian's intercession was known to have helped heal many during the bubonic plague in the 14th century.

Today, January 20th is his feast day. St. Sebastian, please pray for us!

For a young girl of 12 or 13, Saint Agnes led an exemplary life. Known for being a great beauty, she was not vain but lived a simple, chaste and holy life. Many men wished to marry her but she wanted to live only for God.

Since Christianity was illegal in Rome at the time, she was sentenced to be beheaded and Saint Agnes readily accepted her fate. In fact, she encouraged the executioner to hurry it up so she could meet Jesus.

After her death, the daughter of Emperor Constantine (the first emperor who converted to Christianity) had leprosy and prayed at the grave of Saint Agnes. She was soon miraculously healed! After that, the emperor had a church built over Saint Agnes' tomb.

Saint Agnes is the patron of young girls and also the intercessor for engaged couples, those seeking to live a pure life, victims of rape, gardeners and girl scouts.

Today, January 21st is her feast day. Saint Agnes, please pray for us!

22 JANUARY

Saint Vincent
of Saragossa

Saint Vincent of Saragossa, Spain only had to throw the Holy Bible into the fire to save his life but out of His love for God, he did not. He endured the cruel torments of his torturers so as to be faithful until the very end.

It was the late 3rd century and one was mandated to burn incense to Roman gods. Saint Vincent refused and was scourged like our Lord, stretched on the rack, burnt, lacerated with iron hooks, and thrown on glass shards. Through it all, he was at peace and his heroic witness immediately converted one of his jailers.

Today, January 22nd, on his feast day, let us strive not to complain about our daily struggles and hardships and instead pray to God for strength. We can offer up whatever is troubling us for others who are suffering. We can ask Saint Vincent to pray for us to have joy as he did in the midst of all our difficulties.

Saint Vincent of Saragossa, please pray for us!

BLESSED BENEDETTA BIANCHI PORRO

Bianchi was born in Forli, Italy in 1936. She was a bright and cheerful child despite being afflicted with poliomyelitis at an early age. She couldn't use her left leg and constantly needed a brace to prevent the deformation of her spine. The doctors did not know what to call her mysterious disease.

She kept a diary since she was 5 years old and this became a record of her strong faith amidst all her worsening health. As a teen, her hearing became impaired. She decided to take up medicine and she was able to diagnose her illness as Recklinghausen Disease-Neuro-Fibromatosis.

Surgery after surgery only made things worse for her as she experienced paralysis of her nervous system. She couldn't practice medicine as she lost her sense of touch, taste and smell on top of her deafness. Eventually she could no longer walk and lost her sight completely.

Due to her holy virtues and fortitude, her sick room became a place of inspiration and refuge for others. On a trip to Lourdes, she received the grace of total surrender to God and acceptance of her sickness - not desiring to have anything changed in her life.

Today, January 23rd is her feast day. Blessed Benedetta Bianchi Porro, please pray for us!

Saint Francis de Sales
PATRON OF AUTHORS & EDUCATORS

"He who preaches with love, preaches effectively." - Saint Francis de Sales

Born near Geneva in 1567, France to a wealthy family, St. Francis was known to have brought as many as 40,000 lapsed Catholics back home to the Church. He was known to have written to his flock, leaving explanations about Christian doctrine under the front doors of homes. His book, "Introduction to the Devout Life" has helped many to become great saints themselves like Saint Francis.

"Do not fear what may happen tomorrow; the same understanding Father who cares for you today will take care of you then and every day." Saint Francis de Sales

He is the intercessor of writers, journalists, educators, authors and the deaf.

Today, January 24th is his feast day. Saint Francis de Sales, please pray for us!

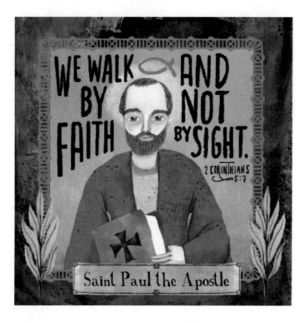

Saint Paul the Apostle

One thing you can say of Saint Paul is that he was full of zeal. At one point, he was the worst enemy of Christians. He would do anything to stop them. He thought he was doing good. But on the road to Damascus, Jesus literally stopped him in his tracks and made him see the light! The light that was too bright blinded St. Paul. That light was Jesus Himself!

Our Lord saw the heart of St. Paul and turned his zeal to fight and defend Christians instead of attacking them.

God can see what strengths we possess and guide us so that we use these for true good. He can use us as He used St. Paul.

Today, January 25th, on the feast of his conversion, let us say a prayer for all evangelists and missionaries and that we may also be used by God to bring the light of His truth to the world.

Saint Paul the Apostle, please pray for us!

SAINTS TIMOTHY
AND TITUS

Today, January 26, the Church honors 2 great saints mentioned in the Bible, Saints Timothy and Titus. Their names are familiar to everyone who has read the New Testament.

Both of these saints became bishops of the early Church. They did their part in sharing the Good News to the world by accompanying and serving Saint Paul and all the Christian communities they lived amongst.

Saint Timothy lived to a ripe old age of 80 and died a martyr's death while the circumstances of Saint Titus' passing is unknown.

If you have a painful stomach, you can ask Saint Timothy to pray for you. He was the first bishop of Ephesus (in Turkey).

Since Saint Titus was the first bishop ordained there, he is the Patron Saint of Crete.

Today, January 26th is their feast day. Saints Timothy and Titus, please pray for us!

St. Angela Merici
Patron of the Sick

Today's saint is no stranger to hardship. Being too poor to send his children to school, her father Giovanni told them stories from the Bible and the "Golden Legend" book about the lives of the saints. Then, their loving home was shattered as both her parents and older sister died within a short span of time and left Angela and her brothers orphaned at an early age.

Despite being the youngest of 5 siblings, Angela took care of her brothers as best as she could, preparing their food and caring for their farm in Dezensano, in Northern Italy.

She lived a holy life of service and vowed to remain single for God her whole life. As a young woman, she became a Third Order Franciscan, wearing a simple habit every day. She was known to rush to the aid of the sick and whoever was in need.

She is usually depicted as a traveler because she spent six months on an arduous pilgrimage to the Holy Land. If you are sick, handicapped, missing your deceased parents, or physically challenged, you can ask Saint Angela to pray for you.

Today, January 27th is her feast day. Saint Angela Merici, please pray for us!

St. Thomas Aquinas
Angelic Doctor of the Church

Thomas was born in 1225 in the town of Aquino in central Italy. He was quiet and reserved so his fellow students gave him the mean nickname, "the Dumb Ox." His teacher, the future Saint Albert the Great, set them right by saying, ""You call him the Dumb Ox, but in his teaching he will one day produce such a bellowing that it will be heard throughout the world."

Indeed, he shines bright as one of the greatest minds the world has ever known. As a young 26-year-old Dominican priest, the Pope conferred on him the title of "Master of Theology. The Church hails him not only as one of the doctors of the Church but as "Angelic Doctor, Common Doctor and Universal Doctor. His Summa Theologica is the most widely known of his writings and brings clarity and understanding to all who wish to delve more fully into Divine Truth.

Despite being one of the greatest intellectuals, he was a humble man. He is the patron of students, Catholic schools, booksellers, chastity, theologians, scholars, publishers, apologists, and his prayers are especially effective against storms.

Today, January 27th is his feast day. Saint Thomas Aquinas, please pray for us!

St. Sarbelius & St. Barbea

Saints Sarbelius and Barbea's lives and ultimately, their deaths bound them together in history as strong witnesses of Christianity.

The pair lived in 2nd century Edessa, Mesopotamia, an ancient city located in modern-day Turkey. At the time, Sarbelius was a pagan high priest offering sacrifices to idols. Through the persistence and witness of holy Saint Barsimaios, the bishop of Edessa, he was converted. He soon shared his newfound belief with his sister Bebaia (Barbea) and both of them were baptized into the faith.

Being a Christian meant death under the Roman Emperor Trajan. St. Sarbelius' conversion became known to all so he was incarcerated for 2 months and repeatedly tortured but he never recanted his faith. Those that saw him say that he was at peace during the awful torments as if he was already in heaven even while being burnt with hot irons.

Barbea professed her faith while she stood over his body so she was also martyred where she stood. The siblings were buried together in the tomb of the Bishop Abselamus.

Today, January 29th is their feast day. Saints Sarbelius and Barbea, please pray for us!

Saint Aldegunais
PATRON OF CANCER

Belgian-born Saint Aldegunais (633-January 30, 684) is one known to be a powerful intercessor for many things. She is the patron saint against cancer, fever, headaches, pain, ulcers, wounds, childhood diseases and sudden death. She is also the patron of children learning to walk.

She was the daughter of holy parents who are both canonized saints of the Catholic Church; Saint Walbert and Saint Bertila. Virtue was contagious in their family as her sister and aunt were also saints - Saint Waldetrudis and Saint Madalberta. They belonged to the royal family of Merovingians.

Saint Aldegunais was the abbess of a Benedictine monastery in the desert of Malbode.

Today January 30th is her feast day. Saint Aldegunais, please pray for us!

"Do not lose any time. Do good, do all the good you can and you will never regret doing it." - Saint John Bosco

The young John was born to a poor family and his father died when he was only 2 years old. He had to support the family by working as a shepherd and farmhand like his father until the age of 12. Though his mother was loving and caring to her 3 sons, she could not really provide them with a good education. John learned how to live well through church sermons and life experiences.

At 9 years old, John had a life-changing dream. He saw some rough boys cussing which made John mad. Jesus appeared to him saying, "Conquer the hearts of these, your friends, not with violence but with charity. Begin at once. Teach them the evil of vice and the excellence of virtue."

Saint John Bosco, known as the "Father and Teacher of Youth", was able to raise, discipline, and support hundreds of boys as well as girls, many of who were troubled and without direction in life. He is the patron saint of apprentices, boys, editors, laborers, magicians, and students.

Today, January 31st is his feast day. Saint John Bosco, please pray for us!

FEBRUARY

Saint Brigid of Ireland

Unlike other women who wish to be beautiful, she prayed that God make her ugly and He did, but only for a time. This was so that no one would wish to marry her for she only wanted to be united to God. When she made her final vows, God restored her beauty.

Born a slave, Saint Brigid did not neglect to serve others. She was always feeding the poor and helping the sick. She once gave all their master's stored dairy to someone in need and then prayed that their stock would be replenished - and it was! The more she gave away, the more it multiplied! One story goes that when she gave water to a thirsty stranger, the water turned into milk! She was known for her holy and generous nature as she believed and said that, "Christ dwells in every creature". She was later given her freedom by the Christian king of Leinster when she gave away his jeweled sword to a beggar, saying that "her merit before God is greater than ours."

She is the patron saint of Ireland, newborn babies, fugitives, children whose parents are not married, dairymaids, cattle, midwives, Irish nuns, scholars, the poor and travelers.

Today, February 1st is her feast day. Saint Brigid, please pray for us!

Saint Catherine of Ricci
Patron of the Sick

One could describe the life of Saint Catherine of Ricci, as having one foot on earth, and one in heaven. Like her patron saint Catherine of Siena, Saint Catherine would be seen wearing a Coral ring when she was meditating on our Lord. The ring would disappear after her prayers.

This Dominican nun was an advisor to people in high places and was in correspondence with the Saint of Joy, Saint Philip Neri as well as three Popes. Even at a young age, Catherine was very prayerful and would be found on her knees in a quiet nook in their home. She was most happy and peaceful when communing with God.

She had a lifelong devotion to the Passion of Christ and was often meditating on Jesus' sufferings. To offer up sacrifice for the souls in Purgatory, she would fast, pray, and wear a sharp iron chain on her neck (under her habit where no one would know about it). She experienced the special grace of the stigmata too.

She is the patron saint of the sick as she cared for them during her time in the convent. Today, February 2nd is her feast day. Saint Catherine of Ricci, please pray for us!

3
FEBRUARY

SAINT BLASE
Patron of Illnesses
of the Throat

Despite being led off to prison for being a Christian, Saint Blase stopped on the way to pray for a boy suffering from a fishbone caught in his throat. The boy was healed on the spot! This story is why every year, the faithful come for a blessing today for illnesses of the throat.

In the 3rd century, the Black Death decimated 25 million people, almost half of Europe's population. Saint Blase was ever ready to help the sick and many were healed during this time with the help of his prayers.

He was so holy and virtuous that even animals came and listened when he preached! They came to him when they were sick and also followed what he asked of them. One story is that he helped a woman whose pig was being held captive by a wolf. Saint Blase prayed to God for the pig and soon after the wolf released it. In gratitude, the woman gave Saint Blase 2 candles to light his prison cell. He never wavered in his faith throughout the torture on metal combs until he was beheaded, bravely dying as a martyr.

Aside from throat illnesses and other diseases, he is also the patron saint for wool workers, animals, bricklayers, bakers, and farm workers.

Today, February 3rd is his feast day. Saint Blase, please pray for us!

Saint Joan de Valois
PATRON OF DIFFICULT
CIRCUMSTANCES

"I am ugly in body but I want a beautiful soul." - Saint Joan de Valois

Joan was born sickly and had a physical deformity so she was raised hidden in a chateau. She had a lifelong dream - to please God and devote each waking moment to His service. Her model was the Blessed Virgin Mary and she wanted to live as she did. At the age of 7, she was given a sense that she was going to establish a religious order before she passed away.

To advance the country politically, her father, King Louis XI married her off to Louis, Duke of Orleans at the age of 12. Despite Joan's virtuous nature, her husband treated her poorly. They had 22 long years of marriage in which Joan felt lonely and humiliated.

Once her husband was crowned as king of France, he appealed to the Pope to grant him an annulment allowing Joan to enter religious life. She confided to her confessor Fr. Gabriel-Maria about what she felt was her mission. With a lot of effort and perseverance, she founded the Franciscan order of the Annunciation 2 years before her death.

Today is her feast day, February 4th. St. Joan de Valois, please pray for us!

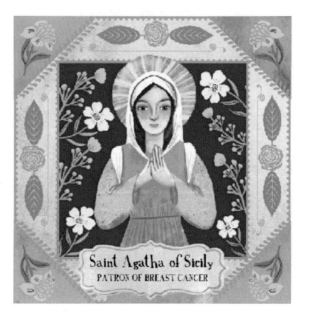

Saint Agatha of Sicily
PATRON OF BREAST CANCER

In the 3rd century, Agatha was born into a noble Italian family and was known for her beauty and wealth. Her birth was foretold to her parents before she came to be.

She wished to give her all to God, being chaste and single for life so she spurned the advances of the Roman prefect Quintanus. As his revenge, he gave the order for her arrest. On the way to prison, Agatha said, "O Jesus Christ!" she cried, as she set out on that dreaded journey, "all that I am is Thine; preserve me against the tyrant."

Saint Agatha was tortured for being a Christian. Quintanus ordered that her breasts be cut off but in a vision, Saint Peter himself came and comforted her, and her wounds were healed. When she prayed for God to take her to heaven, He granted her prayer. Her endurance in keeping the faith has given strength and inspiration to Christians for hundreds of years.

She the patron of breast cancer patients. She is also called upon in cases of natural disasters because her prayers helped stop a volcanic eruption.

Today , February 5th is her feast day. Saint Agatha, please pray for us!

"Ask Christ to help you to become happy..." - Saint Paul Miki

Today we remember the 26 martyrs of Japan who, being in violation of the edict wherein Christianity was outlawed, were executed by crucifixion in 1597.

Before their death, they were forced to march 600 miles to Nagasaki. As their judgement was read, the men sang hymns and one of the men, Paul Miki proclaimed "I am a true Japanese. The only reason for my being killed is that I have taught the doctrine of Christ. I certainly did teach the doctrine of Christ. I thank God it is for this reason I die."

Then they were hung on crosses and stabbed. Several times these brave men were asked to renounce their faith and yet not one of them chose their freedom. Saint Paul Miki, who came from a noble family, was converted to the faith by Saint Francis Xavier. His words have been passed down through generations by the hidden Christians of Japan.

The 26 saints and martyrs entered into the joys of heaven on February 5th on the feast of Saint Agatha but their feast day is today on the 6th. Saint Paul Miki and companions, please pray for us!

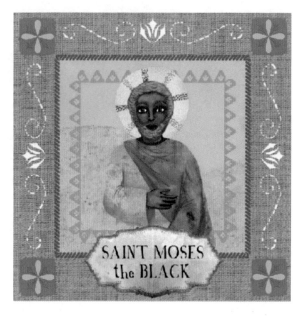

SAINT MOSES
the BLACK

The young Moses lived as an Ethiopian slave in 4th-century Egypt. He was suspected of murder and theft and so was soon sent away by his master. He turned to a life of crime, becoming the leader of a band of robbers. His strength and notoriety for violence struck fear in people's hearts at the mere mention of his name.

After many years of doing evil acts, Moses found himself hiding from the law with some monks in the desert near Alexandria. Seeing their peaceful, content, and holy lives touched Moses deeply and he experienced a deep desire to change his life and live like them. With a sincere and repentant spirit, Moses' life of transformation began and he followed all the rigors of the ascetic way of life.

One time while he was in solitary confinement, 4 robbers from his former gang came and attacked him. Moses overpowered them, tied them up and carried them to the elders of the community and asked what he was to do with them, adding that he thought that it was not good to harm them. The elders instructed him to set them free. The robbers were amazed at Moses' total change of heart. They turned away from their sinful life and wanted to live as monks as well. This is why he became the patron of Africa.

Today, February 7 is his feast day. Saint Moses, please pray for us!

Saint Josephine Bakhita
Patron Saint of Survivors
of Human Trafficking

It can be said that in the heart one can experience God without knowing His name. This was probably what Saint Josephine Bakhita meant when she said, "Seeing the sun, the moon, and the stars, I said to myself: Who could be the Master of these beautiful things? And I felt a great desire to see him, to know Him and to pay Him homage.."

Being born to a wealthy family in Sudan, she did not know hardship until one day she was kidnapped and sold into slavery. She served an extremely cruel woman who, together with her mother-in-law would beat her every day, intentionally leaving her with 114 scars for life. She was so traumatized that she even forgot her own name.

In 1883, she found herself in Venice under the care of the Canossian sisters. She was then introduced to the faith and was baptized in 1890. Through it all, Saint Josephine's harsh life did not make her bitter. She remained humble and cheerful. When she was given her freedom and entered the religious life, she said that if she met her captors, she would kneel and kiss their hands because if it were not for them, she would not have known God's love.

Today, February 8th is her feast day. St. Josephine Bakhita, please pray for us!

THE HEART IS RICH WHEN IT IS CONTENT AND IT IS ALWAYS CONTENT WHEN ITS DESIRES ARE FIXED ON GOD.

St. Michael Febres Cordero

This teacher from Ecuador was known for his gentle, prayerful, and charitable nature.

When he was a child he had difficulty walking and standing due to a foot ailment. At the age of 5, he told his family that he saw a beautiful lady in white but no one else saw her. Miraculously after that, his feet were able to walk effortlessly. At the age of 9, he was almost mauled by a wild bull but was unharmed.

He was studious and was able to publish a book when he was only 17 years old. He decided to join the La Salle religious brothers even though his father and grandmother opposed it.

Brother Michael or Miguel took good care of his students and enjoyed spending time with them. He treated them with understanding and patience and he in turn was loved and admired in the school. He organized retreats and prepared the young for first communion. He taught for 32 years.

Today, February 9th is his feast day. Saint Michael Febres Cordero, please pray for us!

SAINT SCHOLASTICA
Patron against Storms

This saintly nun loved her twin brother Benedict so much but they only met once a year. They would always talk of the things of God stirring in each other the flame of love for Him. Their last meeting was a momentous one as Scholastica did not want her brother to go. He told her that he must go back to his cell. At that, she laid her head on her hands on the table and prayed. Afterward, lightning struck, and pouring rain prevented him and his brothers from leaving until the next morning.

Just 3 days after, Benedict had a vision of his sister's soul being taken to heaven in the form of a dove. Saint Scholastica had gone to her eternal home.

Because Saint Benedict became a hermit and founded its way of life, he is known as the father of Western monasticism. The "mother" was Saint Scholastica who became the abbess of the first Benedictine nuns.

Saint Scholastica is also known as the patron of nuns, tests, reading, school, and convulsive children.

Today, February 10th is her feast day. Saint Scholastica, please pray for us!

Saint
Caedmon

Our gifts, talents, and abilities come from above. This is a truth we can find in the story of the once-shy Saint Caedmon. At celebrations, this unlettered herdsman used to steal away when he was pressed to sing. He believed that he had no talents to share.

One night though in a dream, he met a man who told him to sing and he reluctantly did. The next morning, he was a changed man. He remembered the words to the poem he sang and was able to add beautiful verses to it. His comrades immediately recognized his newfound divine ability and brought him to Hilda, the holy abbess of Whitby.

The saintly woman gave him scripture passages and Caedmon transformed these into prose. He soon entered religious life with her encouragement.

Saint Caedmon then devoted his whole life to God, writing poetry that brought clarity to deep theological concepts. He is now known as one of the greatest poets of his time. May we, like him, be able to use our God-given talents for the praise of His glory.

Today, February 11th is his feast day. Saint Caedmon, please pray for us!

Saint Eulalia
of Barcelona

Eulalia was no ordinary teenager in 4th century Spain. She was born into a wealthy and noble family and lived a comfortable life. Possessing a natural beauty, it was said that her soul was even more beautiful.

An edict outlawing Christianity was enforced by emperor Diocletian and this moved Eulalia's heart to action. In her desire to defend her brothers and sisters who were being mercilessly persecuted, she bravely approached the governor of Barcelona to stop the abuse. Knowing full well the dangers before her but inspired by the Holy Spirit, she heroically spoke compelling arguments.

God granted Eulalia the courage to stand before her captors and withstand their cruelty. She was stripped nearly naked and scourged in the blistering cold but the snow became like a cloak on her, covering her body.

They could not make Saint Eulalia recant her faith, despite the many indignities and torture. She remained a firm believer until she was executed on an X-shaped cross. This young saint has been known to have been many a Christian's ally in praying for pregnant women, seafarers, travelers, against drought, and dysentery.

Today, February 12th is her feast day. Saint Eulalia, please pray for us!

Saint Giuliana
of Turin

In 3rd-century Italy, in the northwestern town of Ivrea lived a laywoman called Giuliana.

She had a great love for her brothers and sisters of the Christian faith. It was a time of persecution of the believers so many were martyred for not worshipping pagan gods.

Though this task must not have been easy, Giuliana took it upon herself to make sure that those who had persevered until the end of their lives, being witnesses for Christ, were given proper holy burial rites.

Her act of kindness and reverence for the holy martyrs did not go unrewarded for she, herself grew in virtue through this service.

Saint Giuliana is also known as Giuliana of Ivrea. Her relics may be found at the Church of the Martyrs in Turin, Italy.

Today, February 13th is her feast day. Saint Giuliana, please pray for us!

SAINT VALENTINE

Despite all the sweet frills and frivolities that surround the celebrations that mark Valentine's day, the saint that this is named after was brave, strong, and full of zeal.

It was Rome in the 3rd century. We know that Valentine was incarcerated for being a Christian. While he was in prison, he did not keep to himself or stop serving the needs of others. His jailer had a daughter who was blind. Through Valentine's prayer, she was able to see! He signed a message to her with "from your Valentine" so the first Valentine was not at all romantic but one of friendship.

Another story is that of the saint helping soldiers get married. Since they did not allow soldiers to wed at the time, thinking this would distract them in battle, Saint Valentine married the couples in secret.

In life and in death, the kind priest gave his all to the Lord. He courageously faced a beating and was eventually beheaded for his faith.

Saint Valentine is the intercessor of sweethearts. He is also the patron saint of beekeepers and epileptics.

Today, February 14 is his feast day. Saint Valentine please pray for us!

St. Claude de la Colombière
Patron Saint of Toymakers

In 17th-century Burgundy, France lived a young man of great virtue who decided he wanted to live life as a Jesuit priest. Claude was ordained and preached with eloquence as a superior in a small Jesuit residence. There he became friends with Saint Margaret Mary Alacoque and also was her confessor. They both shared a deep devotion to the Sacred Heart of Jesus.

Father Claude had great success as a man of God, converting many people from different faiths to Catholicism.

When rumors circulated that Claude was involved in a plot to overthrow the king of France, he was imprisoned. This had detrimental results on his health. Even after his name was cleared and released, he was too weak to recover from illness.. We can ascertain though that even in his suffering, Saint Claude never lost hope in the Lord. He said, "No one has hoped in the Lord and has been confounded"

"Lord, I am in this world to show Your mercy to others..For my part, I will glorify You by making known how good You are to sinners, that Your mercy is boundless." - Saint Claude de la Colombiere

He is the patron of toymakers and turners. Today, February 15th is his feast day. Saint Claude, please pray for us!

SAINT MARUTA

This brave bishop of Syria is the friend and defender that anyone would want to have. He was a true spokesperson for Christians in the 5th century. Instead of cowering in fear for his life, and staying silent, he chose to be a true shepherd for his people.

Since the brethren were suffering oppression for their beliefs, Saint Maruta approached the king of Persia to appeal on their behalf. It so happened that the king was experiencing terrible migraines but God granted him relief through the saint's prayers.

The pagan priests did not want the king to be converted to Christianity so one of them hid under the temple floor. To king was very nearly deceived that it was a mystical voice demanding that Christians be punished - but Saint Maruta uncovered the plot and revealed this to the king.

In return, the king granted leniency to the Christians and they were able to worship in freedom. Saint Maruta was also known as a peacemaker and rebuilder of churches. He also chronicled of the martyrs and preserved their relics.

Today, February 16th is his feast day. Saint Maruta, please pray for us!

This brotherhood was miraculously called to one mission in spirit. Their response resulted in a fruitful community that is still alive today.

In the 13th century, the 7 Italian cloth tradesmen were all successful in their prospective businesses. They had another thing in common. They were all devout Christians and had a deep love for our Lord's Blessed Mother. They wished to imitate her in her being the first faithful disciple of Jesus.

They were Bonfilius, Alexis, Manettus, Amideus, Hugh, Sostene, and Buonagiunta. Each of them experienced a mystical vision of Our Lady calling them to another way of life.

From a life of wealth and prominence, the 7 noblemen discarded all their property and belongings and chose to wear simple habits - withdrawing from the world (and they never looked back). They dedicated their days to prayer and meditation on Jesus' holy sacrifice on the Cross. Through Mother Mary's eyes of sorrow, they were able to delve deeper into the mysteries of our Lord's passion.

Their peaceful, ascetic life drew many to seek out their wisdom and guidance and soon, the number of people joining them grew. With priests, friars, nuns, and lay people, their mission spread to Germany, Austria, Hungary, the Philippines, and other countries.

Today, February 17th is their feast day. 7 Holy Founders of the Servite Order, please pray for us!

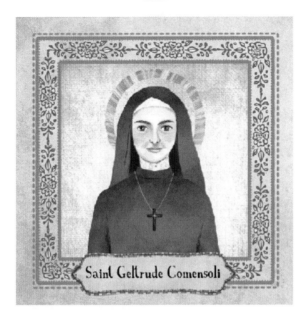

Saint Geltrude Comensoli

We often long to see miracles and yet Saint Geltrude experienced the miracle of God's presence every day. Many poor and humble people clamored for Sister Geltrude to be proclaimed a saint. They were witnesses to her charitable virtue and they wanted her life to be known to others.

In 1847, she was born a middle child in a very large family in Brescia, Italy. Her father worked in an iron forge and her mother was a seamstress.

Known as Catarina throughout her childhood, she made a promise to God at the age of 7 that she would live solely for Him. She found the greatest joy in silently talking to God and when asked what she was doing, she would say, "I am thinking".

At the age of 15, she joined the Sisters of Charity in Bergamo, Italy, and took on the name of Sister Geltrude. Her goal in life was, "Jesus, loving You and making others love You". Her ardent desire was for Jesus' presence in the most Holy Eucharist to be adored. She soon founded the Sisters of the Blessed Sacrament (Sacramentine Sisters).

Today, February 18th is her feast day. Saint Geltrude, please pray for us!

St. Lucia Yi Zhenmei

Today's saint comes from China. She was born in 1815 in Mainyang, Sichuan. She was the youngest child in the family and loved to read and learn. She was known to have been a well-behaved girl who already had a love for God at a young age. Her mother taught her how to spin and this is how she spent most of her days. This also allowed her to help her family financially.

When she joined the Paris Foreign Missions Society, Lucia knew that it became increasingly dangerous for her to be a Christian. Despite her family advising her to distance herself from missionary life, she persisted.

In 1862, the provincial administrator had the members of the mission - Zhang TienShen, Wu ShueSheng, Chen XianHeng, and Father Wen sentenced to death without a trial.

On the day of their execution, Lucia met them on the road. As she refused to renounce her Christianity, she was also martyred for the faith. She chose death rather than turn her back on God.

Today, February 19th is her feast day. Saint Lucia Yi Zhenmei, please pray for us!

St Wulfric of Haselbury

Though he was a man of the cloth, he was quite attached to worldly pursuits. He was often found partying with nobles and hunting rather than taking care of his flock. But one day, his life made a turnaround. He met a beggar and had a conversation with him. Though little is known about their conversation, Wulfric turned over a new leaf.

He started to spend his days in solitary prayer in his cold, quiet cell near the church. He submitted himself to ascetic practices such as abstaining from meat, wearing a hairshirt, and enduring freezing temperatures. He would do this as a sacrifice and penance for those he was praying for. His desire to live a godly life bore spiritual fruit as he began to prophesy. He foretold the death of King Henry I.

He was often sought out by King Stephen for advice and his prayers wrought many miracles for the people who came to him. One story was that of a mute man who was able to speak in both English and French after Saint Wulfric's prayers. Another story is of the saint cutting metal with ease using ordinary scissors. He has become one of the most influential anchorite priests of medieval times. Today, February 20th is his feast day. Saint Wulfric of Haselbury, please pray for us!

Saint Peter Damian

"Do not despair. Do not be depressed. Do not let your weakness make you impatient. Instead, let the serenity of your spirit shine through your face. Let the joy of your mind burst forth. Let words of thanks break from your lips." - Saint Peter Damian

These words seem to encapsulate the saint's life.

The young Peter knew hardship, being orphaned at an early age. He was ill-treated by an older brother who forced him to take care of the pigs. He then experienced kindness from Damian, another brother of his who was a priest. Fr. Damian took Peter under his care and provided him with a good education. The young man was so grateful that he adopted Damian as his second name.

After his studies, Peter Damian chose to enter religious life and at the age of 35, he was already in charge of leading a monastery in Fonte-Avellano, Italy. He became known to all as a holy monk who lived an austere, prayerful, and humble life. His influence grew even among the popes and he was able to institute reforms in the church.

Today, February 21st is his feast day. Saint Peter Damian, please pray for us!

Saint Margaret of Cortona
PATRON AGAINST TEMPTATION

She was called "the second Mary Magdalene". Little Margaret was born in 1247 to a farming couple in Tuscany, Italy. She lost her mother when she was 7 and her stepmother did not treat her kindly. Despite this being a great scandal during that time, she left home and lived with a nobleman named Arsenio for 9 years. She had a son with him and this period in her life caused her great grief in her later life.

Arsenio met a grim fate. He was found murdered and this event affected Margaret deeply. She took this as God's way of telling her to amend her life or her soul would be lost forever.

She showed sincere remorse by confessing her sins publicly and took refuge with the Friars Minor at Cortona. She devoted herself to caring for the sick and living only on alms. At age 30, she became a Franciscan Tertiary. She instituted a hospital and the congregation for the poor. Her son became a priest. She often preached against worldly attachments and addictions and encouraged devotion to the Holy Eucharist and our Lord's Passion. She is the patron against mental illness and sexual temptation. She is also the intercessor for the penitent, people ridiculed for their piety, single laywomen, reformed prostitutes, falsely accused, hoboes, homeless, orphans, and midwives. Today, February 21st is her feast day. Saint Margaret, please pray for us!

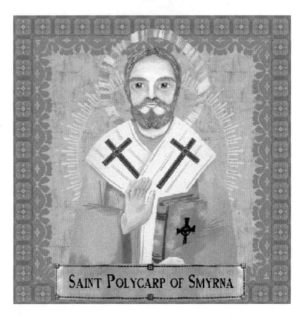

SAINT POLYCARP OF SMYRNA

Saint Polycarp's life and his writings have been a source of wisdom and courage for Christians through the centuries. He is one of only three Apostolic Fathers of the Church. This means that he was able to learn how to live the faith directly from the apostles of Jesus and handed down the teachings to believers.

The young Polycarp was converted in 80 AD by Saint John, the Beloved disciple. As a teenager, he was appointed as the bishop of Smyrna (in ancient Turkey) and pastored his flock for some 60 or 70 years.

In 107 AD, practicing Christianity became punishable by death so the officials sought to arrest him. Before his execution, the saint was granted by his captors an hour to pray and prepare his soul for death. Afterward, he served a hearty meal for all of the soldiers. He was sentenced to be burned at the stake but as the flames surrounded him, they did not harm him. Instead, a fragrant aroma miraculously arose from the fire. Just then, a soldier pierced him with a spear which was what ended his life - but from his chest where he was stabbed, emerged a dove that flew heavenward. Astoundingly, as blood from Polycarp flowed over the flames, it was able to put out the fire.

Today, February 23rd is his feast day. Saint Polycarp, please pray for us!

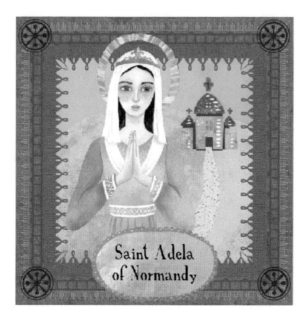

Saint Adela
of Normandy

Adela was born in 11th-century France and was the youngest daughter of William the Conqueror, the king of England. She had an excellent education, was highly intelligent and could speak several languages. She was also deeply devoted to her Christian beliefs.

As a teenager, she married Stephen, one of the richest noblemen in Europe and they had 11 children. Adela became a patron of scholars, writers, and poets. She generously supported churches and abbeys and this greatly enriched the spiritual and cultural development of the time.

So as to defend their freedom, an appeal was launched by the Pope and First Crusade began. Adela's husband was one of the first volunteers to join the battle. In the 4 years that her husband was away, Adela was left to run hundreds of estates and she managed to do this so well as to earn the title of the "heroine of the First Crusade". Sadly in 1102, Stephen died in battle.

In time, Saint Adela entered the convent and together with her son who became a bishop built hundreds of structures, chapels, and even whole villages. She used her wealth and influence to build up the Church.

Today, February 24th is her feast day. Saint Adela, please pray for us!

SAINT CAESARIUS OF NANZIANZEN
PATRON SAINT OF BACHELORS

Caesarius grew up in 4th-century Arianzus in ancient Turkey. He became a renowned physician and politician. He was raised in a holy family with Saint Gregory the Elder and Saint Nonna as parents and Saint Gorgonia and Saint Gregory as siblings.

He was well-educated in Caesaria, Cappadocia and Alexandria, Egypt. He was an excellent student in geometry and astronomy but it was in medicine that he rose to the top of his class. Since he was proficient in healing people, he grew in wealth and popularity.

He had a great many opportunities to marry noblewomen but instead chose to live as a single man. Being a man of influence, he was tasked to work in the court of the emperor. Known as "Emperor Julian the apostate", his goal was for Caesarius to turn his back on his Christian faith but this was to no avail. The saint chose to be exiled instead.

His brother, Saint Gregory attested to Caesarius as being a great man of virtue and piousness. On his deathbed, he expressly wished that all his earthly riches be distributed to the poor.

Today, February 25th is his feast day. Saint Caesarius of Nanzianzen, please pray for us!

St. Alexander of Alexandria

Alexander dedicated his life in defense of the truths we hold dear today. He could have been known for his exemplary love for the poor and virtuous works of charity but he is most honored for how he was able to preserve Church doctrine in the 4th century.

Having a pious nature since he was young, he dedicated his life fully to God as a priest and in 313 he was appointed to be the bishop of Alexandria, Egypt.

A controversy arose when a priest called Arius started teaching that there was no second person of the Trinity and that Jesus was not God. Despite gentle reprisals from Alexander, Arius continued to spread his heretical beliefs. In an effort for Arius to return to the Church, the saint excommunicated him. Arianism soon ended.

The bishop was a central figure in the Council of Nicaea in 325. He is described as "a man held in the highest honour by the people and clergy, magnificent, liberal, eloquent, just, a lover of God and man, devoted to the poor, good and sweet to all, so mortified that he never broke his fast while the sun was in the heavens." Today, February 26th is his feast day. Saint Alexander, please pray for us!

St. Gabriel of Our Lady of Sorrows
PATRON OF YOUNG PEOPLE

"Our perfection does not consist of doing extraordinary things but doing the ordinary well." - Saint Gabriel

Francesco Possenti was born into a wealthy family in Assisi, Italy in 1838. The young child grew up surrounded by grief because his mother and 4 of his siblings died within a short amount of time. Despite his terrible losses in life, the young Gabriel, as he was later called, did not rebel nor misbehave. He remained kind and good-natured to those around him.

Growing up, he was popular with the ladies, going to the theatre, hunting, and dancing. Then he became seriously ill. He then made a vow to become a priest if he got well. Upon his recovery, he returned to his old ways. The turning point in his life came when a cholera epidemic afflicted their town and a procession with an icon of the Virgin Mary was carried around. When it passed Gabriel, he heard a voice saying, "keep your promise". Thereafter dedicated his life to God and joined the Passionists. Sadly, at only 24 years old, he passed away from tuberculosis before he was ordained. He died clutching the image of Our Lady of Sorrows.

He is the patron of the youth, students, and clerics. Today, February 27th is his feast day. Saint Gabriel, pray for us!

SAINT ROMANUS OF CONDAT
PATRON OF THE MENTALLY ILL

Saint Romanus on pilgrimage found himself without shelter for the night but chanced upon the dwelling of a pair of lepers. Having no dread of the deadly disease, he asked to stay with them. For fear that the monk would get infected, the lepers tried to convince him to go away.

The saint could not be dissuaded. The story goes that he embraced the lepers and rested with them there. Lo and behold! In the morning, the lepers were found to be miraculously healed! They spread the news and the townspeople sought Saint Romanus to honor him. He in turn asked that they turn to God and be converted.

Saint Romanus of Condat is the patron saint of the mentally ill and those who are drowning.

Today February 28th is his feast day. Saint Romanus, pray for us!

MARCH

1
MARCH

Jared the Patriarch

To say that he lived a long life is an understatement. Not many of us know this Old Testament figure so it is good to reflect upon what is written about him in the Bible. He is recorded to have lived in the 5th generation after Adam and Eve.

"When Mahalalel had lived 65 years, he became the father of Jared. After he became the father of Jared, Mahalalel lived 830 years and had other sons and daughters. Altogether, Mahalalel lived a total of 895 years, and then he died.

When Jared had lived 162 years, he became the father of Enoch. After he became the father of Enoch, Jared lived 800 years and had other sons and daughters. Altogether, Jared lived a total of 962 years, and then he died." - Genesis 5:15-20

Today, March 1st is his feast day. Jared the Patriarch, pray for us!

St. Quintus the Thaumaturge

In the 3rd-century city of Phrygia (in modern-day Turkey) lived a Christian man named Quintus. He was known by all as a holy man of God who loved serving the poor. Since Christianity was banned during that time, Quintus got into trouble with the Roman emperor.

He refused to offer sacrifices to pagan idols so as a punishment, Rufus, the governor, had him tortured. Indeed, "the prayers of a righteous man availeth much," as it says in James 5:15. Through the help of Saint Quintus' intercession, Rufus, who was oppressed by an evil spirit, was freed and so in turn, he released the kind Quintus.

After some time, an earthquake hit the city, and the statues of Roman gods were destroyed. Saint Quintus was blamed for this and was called in by another official. He was again subjected to cruel torture such as the breaking of both of his legs. He never wavered in his faith.

When his captors noticed his wounds miraculously healed, they let him go. The saint then returned to his vocation of selfless care for the poor. "Thaumaturge" means "miracle worker".

Today, March 2nd is his feast day. Saint Quintus, pray for us!

"Let us open wide our hearts. It is joy which invites us. Press forward and fear nothing." - Saint Katharine Drexel

When God issued her an invitation, she gladly said yes.

If you were given $35,000 every day for the rest of your life, how would you spend it? More importantly, would you be able to give it all up for God?

That was the value of her inheritance in today's currency. She chose a life of simplicity and total service to God instead.

It is surely God's grace that allowed her to make this decision though kindness and generosity were instilled in Katharine and her sisters at a young age. Growing up, their family would regularly welcome the poorest members of their community to their home and assist them with their needs.

"Ours is the spirit of the Eucharist, the total Gift of Self."

She is the intercessor for social justice and philanthropy.

Today, March 3rd is her feast day. Saint Katharine Drexel, pray for us!

SAINT CASIMIR
PATRON OF LITHUANIA

For this young man, earthly wealth, power and acclaim were all nothing compared to heavenly treasure. Being the son of King Casimir IV of Poland and Queen Elizabeth of Austria, the young Casimir Jagiellon was no ordinary prince.

Instead of wearing fine clothes as fitting his royal status, he chose to wear simple clothing with a hairshirt underneath. He chose to be surrounded by the poor instead of rich noblemen and instead of a luxurious bed, he often spent the night on the floor, meditating on Jesus' passion. He had a deep devotion to the Blessed Virgin Mary.

Crowned king at the age of 15, he declined to marry the emperor's daughter. He firmly resolved to live as a single man so he could serve God and others more. He remained chaste until his death of tuberculosis in 1484.

After his passing, many miracles occurred through his intercession from heaven such as in the battle of Lithuania against Russia where soldiers saw an apparition of him leading them to victory.

Saint Casimir is the patron of Lithuania, Poland, kings, and bachelors.

Today, March 4th is his feast day. Saint Casimir, pray for us!

Blessed Giovanna Irrizaldi

If it is God's will that you be somewhere, He can get you there by whatever means He wishes! For the blessed Giovanna, He used her veil as a vessel to allow her to travel over air or sea.

It was not only once that this Mercedarian nun was known to have traveled by extraordinary means but it is said that angels would also carry her on their wings if she longed to be at the confessional. It is a testament to God's amazing grace as well as Blessed Giovanna's sanctity in allowing her to be a miracle worker.

In Spain during the winter of 1471, the Cadagua River was flooded and became impassable, even by boat. It was here that the saint was witnessed to have flown over to the other side.

Today, March 5th is her feast day. Blessed Giovanna Irrizaldi, pray for us!

Saint Colette
Patron for Couples Praying for a Child

Colette was born in 14th-century France, to an aging carpenter and his wife. Orphaned at 17, she stayed with the Benedictines. In time, she desired to live a consecrated life and became a Third Order Franciscan.

She was a holy nun who fasted on Fridays and who frequently meditated on Jesus' Passion. She was often in a state of heavenly ecstasy for hours after receiving Holy Communion. Like Saint Francis, she was kind and gentle to animals especially birds.

One day, Saint Colette had a vision of Saint Francis telling her to bring back the Order of Saint Clare to its original discipline and rule. This overwhelmed her but when she was suddenly struck blind and mute for a few days, these temporary disabilities encouraged her to move forward.

After many stumbling blocks and much opposition, and traveling from one convent to another (even walking barefoot), she was installed as the Superioress and established 17 convents known as the Colettines.

She is the patron of the Poor Clares, Corbie in France, those praying for children, those suffering from eye disorders, headaches, fever, servants, craftsmen, and the orphaned. Today March 6th is her feast day. Saint Colette, pray for us!

Saints Perpetua and Felicity
Patrons Against the Death of Children

The names of Saint Perpetua and Saint Felicity are forever intertwined in history. Though unrelated, they are the truest of sisters in the faith as they both forsook all for the love of Christ.

In 2nd-century Carthage, North Africa, the Roman Empire prohibited Christianity. Both of the women were imprisoned for their faith. Whereas Perpetua was wealthy and of noble birth, Felicity was a slave but they had a strong bond in that both were in the early stages of motherhood. Perpetua had just given birth and was nursing her infant while incarcerated and Felicity was pregnant when she was captured.

Perpetua's writings chronicled their experience. In an instant, they could have spared their lives and would have been released had they agreed to pay tribute to the pagan gods of Rome but they knew that their eternal home with God awaited them. They were both martyred for the faith.

Saint Perpetua is the patron of widows, mothers of deceased sons, cattle, Carthage, Tunisia and Santa Perpetua de Mogoda in Catalonia, Spain. Saint Felicity is the patron of those praying for male children and against infertility. Both saints are patrons in the aid of parents with children in danger of death, widows, and martyrs.

Today March 7th is their feast day. Saints Perpetua and Felicity, pray for us!

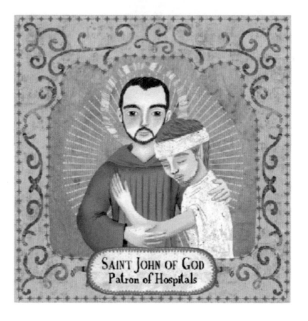

SAINT JOHN OF GOD
Patron of Hospitals

"Labour without stopping, do all the good works you can, while you still have the time." - Saint John of God

Love propelled him to give all his earnings to an impoverished family. His generosity and extreme penances were mistaken as a mental condition. He was carted off to an asylum where he received daily whipping and beating (as was the "treatment" for such cases in those days).

His experience clarified his mission "to run a hospice where the abandoned poor and those suffering from mental disorders might have refuge and that I may be able to serve them as I wish."

Soon enough, other people joined him in feeding and healing the needy. This included society's shunned like prostitutes, the homeless, unemployed, widows, and orphans. The Order of the Hospitallers began.

Many miracles marked his life. One such time was when he was found running in and out of a burning hospital carrying patients to safety. He was totally unharmed by the fire. For this reason, Saint John is the patron of firefighters. He is also the patron of hospitals, nurses, the sick, heart patients, printers, booksellers, printers, and heart patients. Today March 8th is his feast day. Saint John of God, pray for us!

9 MARCH

SAINT FRANCES OF ROME
PATRON SAINT OF MOTORISTS

"I feel as if my whole life has been one beautiful dream of purest happiness. God has given me so much in your love." These were the dying words of Lorenzo, Saint Frances' husband. Their relationship was so full of love that in their forty years together, they never had a single argument. She served her family with joy and devotion yet always found time to meditate even when she was busy with her household duties.

One time while reading the psalms, she was repeatedly called away to attend to some errand. When she'd finish, she returned to her prayers. By the fifth time, she saw that the words on her Bible were inked in gold!

Their family suffered many trials throughout the years like the death of her children and when a plague hit the city. Instead of despair, Frances helped the sick and the destitute. When her husband passed away, she was finally able to fulfill her lifelong dream of entering the religious life.

Saint Frances consulted her guardian angel often and it was said that he was ever before her lighting her way - much like the headlights of a car. This is why Saint Frances is called upon by motorists to pray for them in their travels. She is also the patron of widows and those with children who are seriously ill and in danger of death. Today March 9th is her feast day. Saint Frances of Rome, pray for us!

SAINT MARIE-EUGÉNIE DE JÉSUS

"Transform everything into praise and thanksgiving!"

Eugenie Milleret de Brou (de Bron) was born on August 26, 1817 in France. She was baptized but did not know the faith well.

Though she grew up in a well-to-do family and did not want for anything, the young woman at age 18 became dissatisfied with life. It was at Holy Mass while hearing a sermon by Fr. Henri Lacordaire that the questions that disturbed Eugenie's soul were answered.

At that moment her heart opened up to the love of God. She said, ""I was truly converted and I was seized by a longing to devote all my strength or rather all my weakness to the Church which, from that moment, I saw as alone holding the key to the knowledge and achievement of all that is good."

Eugenie found her vocation and dedicated her life to serving others. She worked tirelessly to form a teaching institute that kept monastic observances. This became what is now known in 34 countries as the Congregation of the Assumption (Religious of the Assumption, Sisters of the Assumption). Today, March 10th is her feast day. Saint Marie-Eugénie de Jésus, pray for us!

11 MARCH

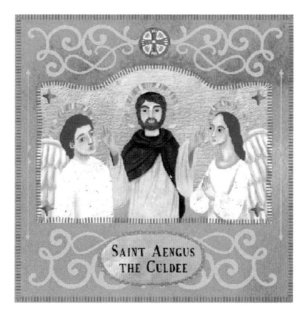

SAINT AENGUS
THE CULDEE

In 8th-century Ireland, along the banks of the river Nore, there frequented a holy monk called Aengus the Culdee. It is said that this is where he met with angels and spoke with them.

Being a hermit, he was drawn to peace and solitude. He read the whole Psalter and knelt 365 times each day. He subjected himself to daily sacrificial acts of discipline to show his reverence for God.

As his holiness attracted many, he stealed away to a monastery and together with Saint Maelruan wrote the Martyrology of Tallaght, a catalog of Irish saints, in 790.

One day when Aengus was chopping wood, he accidentally severed his left hand. That moment, the birds filled the sky with loud noises as if crying out to the heavens for help. Aengus then calmly reattached his hand and it miraculously healed on its own.

He is called the "Culdee" derived from "Ceile Dé" which means "Servant of God".

Today March 11th is his feast day. Saint Aengus the Culdee, pray for us!

SAINT SERAFINA
PATRON OF THE HANDICAPPED

To this day, March 12th is celebrated as a holiday in the medieval town of San Geminiano, Tuscany, Italy. It is the time to honor the beautiful and well-loved Saint Serafina. As a young child, Fina led a quiet life spinning in her room by day and praying long hours by night. She only left her home to go to daily Mass. Despite not having much, she gave to the poor as much as she could.

One time when Fina was walking with friends, they met a crying child. She was upset because her pitcher broke. Fina told the child to hold the broken pieces under the running water and the pitcher became whole again! At ten years old, a mysterious ailment afflicted her, making any movement painful. Instead of a bed, she chose to rest on a wooden board and there she spent the rest of her days. Paralyzed and in constant discomfort and pain, Fina was always joyful and never complained. Upon her death, the church bells rang by themselves and white violets bloomed through the surface of her wooden pallet. A fresh floral fragrance permeated throughout the home.

She is the patron saint of the handicapped, disabled, physically challenged, and spinners.

Today March 12th is her feast day. Saint Serafina, pray for us!

St. Ansovinus of Camerino
Patron for the Protection of Crops

The name Ansovinus comes from the West German word "ansus" which means "God" and "wine" which is the Old English word for "friend". Together it means "a friend of God". Indeed that is what today's saint was.

Growing up in 9th-century Camerino, a military town in Central Italy, Ansovinus entered religious life at a young age. He lived many years as a hermit and became the spiritual advisor of the Roman Emperor Louis II.

During that time, bishops were responsible for the conscription of soldiers into the imperial army so when Ansovinus was appointed the role, he accepted on the condition that his flock be exempted from this obligation.

The pious man of God had a deep love for the poor and needy. They often came to him to ask for food. When the supply from the Castel Raimondo granary ran out, Ansovinus turned to God for help. He heard the saint's prayer! Grain miraculously appeared and all the people had their fill. This is why he is invoked by farmers and gardeners.

Today, March 13th is his feast day. Saint Ansovinus, pray for us!

Saint Matilda of Saxony
Patron of Large Families

In the year 895, there once was a girl who grew up to become the Queen of Germany. Instead of lording it over her subjects, she had the kind heart of a servant. One would always find her comforting the sick, visiting the imprisoned, attending to the needs of the poor, and teaching them how to pray.

She was known throughout the land for her generosity. The kingdom's wealth was put to good use as she supported 3,000 monks, established monasteries, churches and schools.

Her husband King Henry was a charitable ruler and virtuous spouse to Matilda allowing her to freely engage in works of mercy.

Her compassionate heart was clearly born out of a deeply rooted prayer life. It is said that sometimes she would leave her husband's side in the middle of the night to pray.

She is the patron of large families, queens, second marriages, widows, the falsely accused, disappointing children, people ridiculed for their piety and invoked against the death of children.

Today, March 14th is her feast day. Saint Matilda of Saxony, pray for us!

Saint Louise de Marillac
Patron of Social Workers

Being a saint does not exempt one from disappointments in life. It was Louise's fervent wish to enter religious life but no nunnery would accept her on account of her ill health. Little did she know that God had other plans for her life and that His timing was perfect.

She became a wife, and later a widow, and throughout this period, she served God and His people by serving the poor, taking spiritual inspiration from Saint Vincent de Paul. In 1642, she founded the Daughters of Charity.

In time, God finally called her to take her vows and she served as superior in the convent for the rest of her life. She was instrumental in bringing many young souls closer to God through her example and wisdom.

"Let us truly love each other in Him, but let us love Him in each other since we are His." - Saint Louise de Marillac

She is the patron of social workers, the Vincentian Service Corps, widows, disappointing children, people rejected by religious orders and the sick. She is also invoked upon the loss of parents.

Today March 15th is her feast day. Saint Louise de Marillac, pray for us!

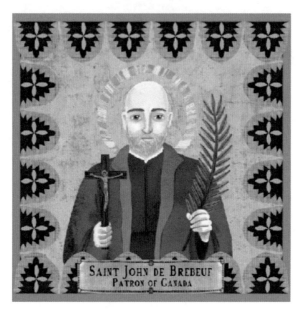

SAINT JOHN DE BREBEUF
PATRON OF CANADA

Have you ever played the game of Lacrosse? It is today's saint who named it thus since the stick used by the Indians reminded him of a bishop's crosier (la crosse).

This French Jesuit priest was not only big in size but had a big heart full of missionary zeal. He left his home in Normandy, France in 1625 to live with the Huron people in Canada.

Throughout more than a decade, he had to overcome many challenges and hardships such as learning the language and enduring the harsh climate. He did this so well that the natives gave him the name "Echon" which meant "load bearer".

Saint John paid the ultimate price, giving up his life for God when the Iroquois captured him and his brother missionary Gabriel Lalemant. Subject to all sorts of tortures, the saint did not show any sign of pain so upon his death the tribesmen ate his heart. For all his labors, heaven must have given him a hearty welcome as he taught and baptized 7,000 souls for the faith.

Today March 16th is his feast day. Saint John de Brebeuf, pray for us!

SAINT PATRICK
PATRON OF IRELAND

Saint Patrick is undoubtedly one of the greatest saints in history. His feast is widely celebrated until today.

At the age of 16, he was captured by pirates and forced to live in a rugged, pagan land steeped in superstition.

Praying a hundred times a day and a hundred times a night, a powerful transformation came upon him and he became filled with gratitude despite living in such harsh conditions. One day, he heard God's voice in his soul telling him that his boat was ready and that he needed to go back to Britain. His escape after 6 years of being a slave was a preparation for his life's mission - the conversion of a country.

After years of Catholic instruction, he was ready to go back to Ireland, this time as a bishop. What was once a place of demonic curses, spells, black magic and the worship of nature became the "Land of the Saints", true believers in the God of love. Saint Patrick's witness, prayers, and faithful missionary work brought the faith to the people of Ireland and this spread to the whole of Europe and the world.

Today, March 17th is his feast day. Saint Patrick, pray for us!

SAINT CYRIL OF JERUSALEM

When Saint Cyril was proclaimed Bishop of Jerusalem, it was as if heaven itself wished to send a sign of approval. A bright shining cross about two miles wide appeared over the place of our Lord's crucifixion. A rainbow also encircled it. Everyone marveled at such a glorious occurrence.

This heavenly sight must have given courage to Saint Cyril who stood against a grave threat to 4th-century believers. The Arian heresy was causing confusion, division, and scandal in the Church. This belief denying the divinity of Jesus could have spread if it had not been for staunch defenders like the good bishop Cyril.

It was a long drawn-out battle and throughout the 4 decades of serving as Jerusalem's pastor, Bishop Cyril was often opposed, falsely accused, and was even exiled three times.

Despite the persecution, he preached so eloquently and with great love for the people that these were always met with loud applause.

Let us pray for more faithful shepherds like the Bishop and Doctor of the Church Saint Cyril. May his shining example inspire us in our faith journey.

Today March 18th is his feast day. Saint Cyril of Jerusalem, pray for us!

BLESSED SYBILLINA BISCOSSI
PATRON SAINT OF SERVANTS

Sibyllina was orphaned at the tender age of 10. Being uneducated, she became a servant. Then, a mysterious ailment afflicted her with blindness. When the community of Dominican tertiaries took charge of her, she developed a devotion for Saint Dominic and asked his intercession for her sight to be recovered but her prayers were unanswered. Convicted that this was to be her cross in life, she fully embraced it.

Her fervent desire was to give herself fully to Christ and as a confirmation of this wish, Saint Dominic appeared to her in a vision. By the age of 15, she began life as a contemplative nun living in a small walled-up room.

Though she found her deepest joy in silent communion with our Lord, pilgrims from near and far were drawn to her holiness and many came to visit her. They came for spiritual guidance as well as for her prayers. She always tried to enflame in their hearts a deep love for the Holy Spirit.

For over 60 years, many miracles occurred due to the intercession of Blessed Sibyllina. After her death in 1367, her body was exhumed and found to be incorrupt after 487 years. She is the patron saint of maids, children whose parents are not married and invoked against the loss of parents. Today, March 19th is her feast day. Blessed Sibyllina Biscossi, pray for us.

BLESSED AMBROSE SANSEDONI OF SIENA
PATRON OF BETROTHED COUPLES

When little Ambrose was born, he was badly deformed. One day, a stranger passing through saw the child's face covered with a scarf. He told the nurse, "Do not cover that child's face. He will one day be the glory of this city." After a few days, the boy said the name of Jesus and stretched out his arms and legs. In an instant, he was healed!

He grew up to be a loving, well-behaved, and pious child. At times he preferred to pray and meditate rather than sleep. At two years old he was already interested in the lives of the saints. He often served the sick and those in need with great care. He grew to be handsome and joined the Dominicans despite the opposition of his family. There, he discovered his true calling to be a preacher.

During the 30 years of his ministry, many witnessed miraculous occurrences due to his zeal and love for God. At times when he would conduct his sermons, Blessed Ambrose would be found levitating. He seemed to be in a constant state of prayer and ecstasy. Oftentimes he was seen with a bright light and colorful birds in flight encircling him.

He is the patron saint of betrothed, engaged couples, and Siena, Italy. Today, March 20th is his feast day. Blessed Ambrose Sansedoni, pray for us!

SAINT NICHOLAS OF FLÜE
PATRON OF DIFFICULT MARRIAGES

This Swiss soldier fought with a sword in one hand and a rosary in the other. He was a beloved husband and father of 10 children but one day God called him to live a life set apart from the world.

He received a vision of a horse eating a lily (a sign of purity) and took this as a sign that he was to leave his secular life and serve the Church. With the blessing of his wife and family, he assisted in the Holy Mass every day and spent the rest of the day in meditation and prayer.

For 19 years, he subsisted only on the Holy Eucharist and did not need any other form of sustenance. Because of his piety, prophetic gifts and visions, his advice and spiritual guidance were sought out by many and his intervention even prevented a bloody civil war. Winning the respect of both Protestants and Catholics, he is called the "Father of Switzerland".

He died in the loving embrace of his wife and children.

He is the patron of difficult marriages, separated spouses, large families, councilmen, magistrates, Pontifical Swiss Guards and Switzerland.

Today, March 21st is his feast day. Saint Nicholas, pray for us!

SAINT LEA
OF ROME
PATRON OF WIDOWS

Not much is known about Saint Lea but we know from the writings of Saint Jerome that she was held in high esteem. He made special mention of her to the early Christians so there is much we can learn from her.

She was a married lady in 4th-century Rome who became widowed. Her husband left her with considerable wealth but instead of living a life of affluence, she chose to give her earthly treasures away and do menial tasks in a convent. After some years, she became its superioress.

One cannot but think of the story of the widow's mite as relayed to us by our Lord Jesus. "Truly I say to you that this poor widow has put in more than all; for all these out of their abundance have put in offerings for God, but she out of her poverty put in all the livelihood that she had." - Luke 21:1-4

She is the patron saint of widows. Today, March 22nd is her feast day. Saint Lea of Rome, pray for us!

SAINT RAFQA
PATRON OF THE SICK

Sister Rafqa spoke very little, lived simply, and loved to meditate and pray. She often received divine revelations. On the feast of the Holy Rosary, she made an unusual prayer requesting to share in Jesus' passion. She immediately experienced debilitating pain in her head that moved to her eyes. Upon the doctor's advice, she underwent eye surgery but asked not to be given anesthesia. At one point, the doctor fumbled and her eye popped out of its socket and fell to the floor. In response, she calmly pronounced a blessing on the doctor.

Despite the operation her severe headaches didn't stop but she still helped found a new monastery in Batroun, Lebanon. She eventually became totally blind and then paralyzed. When only her hands could move, she spun wool and knitted socks. Throughout this time her condition caused unbearable pain and torment and yet she never complained.

In the days before she passed away, bedridden, she asked God to grant her 1 hour of sight so she could see her friend. Her prayer was answered and she was able to see her friend clearly for an hour. When Saint Rafqa died, a bright light shone on her grave and many miraculous healings occurred as a result of her intercession. Today, March 23rd is her feast day. Saint Rafqa, Little Flower of Lebanon, pray for us!

SAINT CATHERINE OF SWEDEN
PATRON AGAINST MISCARRIAGES

Catherine was educated in a convent. She was given in marriage at age thirteen to a kind German nobleman. Together they decided to live a chaste and pure marriage much like that of the Blessed Virgin Mary and Saint Joseph. When her father died, Catherine visited her mother to go on a pilgrimage to Rome and visit the relics of saints. Shortly afterward, her own husband died and the two saintly widows spent the next 25 years praying, assisting the poor, sharing the faith, and going on pilgrimage.

Both Catherine and her mother had to deal with unwanted attention from the local young men who wished to marry them. Once, a wild stag appeared and helped Catherine drive one of the suitors away.

When her mother passed away, Catherine joined the Order of the Holy Savior (Brigittines) at Vadstena, Sweden. She soon became its abbess. There she wrote the devotional Sielinna Troëst (Consolation of the Soul). She wished to never offend God so she confessed her sins to a priest daily.

Catherine and her mother Bridget are both celebrated as saints in the Catholic Church. Saint Bridget's feast day is on July 23rd.

Today, March 24th is Saint Catherine's feast day. She is the patron against miscarriages and abortions. Saint Catherine of Sweden, pray for us!

SAINT DISMAS
PATRON OF PRISONERS

Today we remember the "Good Thief" who hung on a cross alongside our Lord Jesus. He is said to have "stolen heaven" that day when he repented from his sinful life.

An old Arabian story goes that when the Holy Family fled to Egypt, they came across a band of robbers. Instead of the thieves attacking them, they were left unharmed. This was due to one of them, the young Dismas, who convinced the others that they were special and should be left alone.

Dismas said to Jesus, "Remember me when you come into Your kingdom. Jesus answered him, "Truly I tell you, today you will be with me in paradise." Luke 23:39-43

Saint Dismas is the patron saint of prison inmates, prisoners on death row prisoners, dying people, funeral directors, repentant criminals, prison chaplains, undertakers, Przemysl, Poland and Merizo, Guam.

Today, March 25th is his feast day. Saint Dismas, pray for us!

SAINT CASTULUS OF ROME
PATRON AGAINST LIGHTNING

3rd-century Rome was an extremely dangerous place for Christians. Upon Emperor Diocletian's decree, worship was reserved for Roman gods alone. This did not deter the brave military officer Castulus from harboring Christians and even holding religious gatherings at the palace.

Along with his friend Saint Tiburtius, he brought many believers to Pope Cauis to receive the sacrament of baptism. Among those he sheltered from authorities were brother saints Mark and Marcellian. His wife Irene was the one who nursed Saint Sebastian back to health.

Eventually, Saint Castulus was apprehended when Torquatus betrayed him. He was given the chance to escape death by recanting his faith but he never wavered. As a punishment, he was buried alive in Via Labicana just outside of Rome.

He is the patron saint invoked in case of storms, lightning, blood poisoning, erysipelas (a skin infection), fever, horse theft, and wildfires. He is also the intercessor for farmers, cowherds, shepherds, Hallertau, and Moosburg an der Isar, Germany

Today, March 26th is his feast day. Saint Castulus, pray for us!

BLESSED PANACEA DE 'MUZZI OF QUARONA
PATRON OF SHEPHERDS

Sometimes we cannot help it but we are greatly disliked by certain people. In Panacea's case, it was her stepmother.

In 1378, there was a girl whose mother died shortly after she was born. She grew up in Quarona, a provincial city in northwestern Novara, Italy. This young child lived simply and as soon as could walk, she took care of the sheep. She was a kindhearted girl who loved to pray, help the sick, and do whatever good she can.

When her father re-married, the woman he chose abhorred religion. She immediately grew to hate the pious Panacea and even beat her when she was unable to finish her chores.

One day when the five-year-old Panacea had not yet come home from tending the sheep, her stepmother furiously went in search of her and found her in deep prayer on the pasture of Mount Tucri. Enraged, the woman repeatedly hit Panacea and accidentally killed her.

Blessed Panacea de 'Muzzi is the patron of shepherds and shepherdesses. Today March 27th is her feast day. Blessed Panacea de 'Muzzi, pray for us!

ST. JOSEPH SEBASTIAN PELCZAR
PATRON OF EDUCATORS

Raised by good Christian parents, the young Joseph discerned to be a priest while he was a junior in high school. In his diary he wrote, "Earth ideals fade, I see the ideal of life in dedication, and the ideal of sacrifice - in the priesthood".

After his ordination, he taught for many years, taking special care of his students. He was a friend to young people, encouraging them to draw closer to God through devotion to the Sacred Heart of Jesus, and frequent partaking of the sacraments. Despite ill health, he devoted much of his time to works of mercy such as sheltering the homeless, establishing orphanages, soup kitchens, scholarships for seminarians, and libraries. He wrote over a thousand books. Along with Blessed Klara Szczesna, he co-founded the Sister Servants of the Most Sacred Heart of Jesus, an organization for young women.

"There is no greater happiness as to be the object of love of the Merciful Heart." - Saint Joseph Sebastian Pelczar

He is the patron of educators, universities, schools, students, and the Sister Servants of the Most Sacred Heart of Jesus .Today March 28th is his feast day. Saint Joseph Sebastian Pelczar, pray for us!

SAINT SATURUS
OF AFRICA
PATRON OF THE POOR

There was once a wealthy man who lived in 5th-century Africa. He lived a comfortable life with his wife and family. He had a secure post as master of the king's household, property, and riches. He also had servants to do his bidding.

When the king returned from Italy, he enforced strict rules outlawing Christianity. Since Saturus was a devout believer, the king had him tortured in an effort to dissuade him from practicing the faith. His wife too tried to convince him to recant but he was unshaken.

He was forbidden to ever see his family, stripped of all earthly riches, and was relegated to a life of a slave cowherd and miner. He remained ever faithful to God, praying while doing his menial work for the rest of his days.

He was a friend of Saint Armogastes, a former count who suffered a similar fate. They are both patron saints of the poor.

Today March 29th is his feast day. Saint Saturus, pray for us!

SAINT SECUNDUS OF ASTI
PATRON OF MERCHANTS AND BANKERS

In the 2nd century, Secundus was a young soldier in the Roman imperial army. He was a friend of Sapricius, the city magistrate. Together they visited the Tortona and there Secundus met Saint Marcian. He was the area's first bishop and he shared the Good News with Secundus. Secundus got converted to the faith and was soon baptized in Milan.

Since belief in Jesus Christ was a serious offense punishable by death during those times, Saint Marcian was executed upon the orders of Emperor Hadrian. Despite the danger, Secundus honored Marcian by providing him with a Christian burial. After this, he traveled in haste to Asti to be with his family.

The authorities eventually caught up with him and Sapricius tried to reason with him to save his life but the courageous Secundus chose to meet his Lord in death rather than deny Him in life. He was then tortured and beheaded.

Aside from being the intercessor for merchants and bankers, he is the patron saint of Asti, Italy. Today his feast day March 30th is the day he received his eternal reward. Saint Secundus, pray for us!

SAINT BALBINA OF ROME
PATRON OF THROAT DISEASES

Balbina lived in 2nd-century Rome. She was afflicted with a large goiter. Her father Quirinus was a government official in charge of the imprisonment of Christians. In his custody were Hermes and Pope Alexander I whom he kept heavily guarded in separate prison cells.

Quirinus habitually visited Hermes and encouraged him to worship the pagan gods of Rome. Hermes could not be moved for he was a devout Christian. He kept telling Quirinus to talk to Pope Alexander I instead.

One day, Quirinus was amazed to find the two men in the same prison. Hermes told him that God enabled this miracle to happen. Quirinus said that he would become a Christian if God healed his daughter Balbina. The pope instructed him to bring her to his prison cell. When Balbina arrived, she started kissing the chains of the pope who told her, "You shall not kiss these chains, but go out and find St. Peter's chains. Once you've found them, kiss them with devotion and you will soon be well."

Balbina hastily did so and she was immediately cured. Soon after, she and her parents got baptized. Quirinus had the pope and Hermes released and pardoned. Saint Balbina is the patron saint of throat diseases. Today, March 31st is her feast day. Saint Balbina of Rome, pray for us!

APRIL

1
APRIL

SAINT MARY OF EGYPT
PATRON OF CHASTITY

Mary was a beautiful but spoilt child who ran away to Alexandria when she was only 12 years old. There she lived a life of dissipation as a dancer, singer, and prostitute. In her 30's, she traveled to the Holy Land hoping to tempt pilgrims into paying for her services.

She wanted to enter the Church of the Holy Sepulchre on the feast of the Exaltation of the Cross but somehow she an invisible force barred her from coming in. In that instant, she realized her need to repent.

She asked the Blessed Virgin Mary to pray for her and promised to leave her worldly life. Afterward, she was able to step into the church and worship the relic of the true cross of Jesus.

With her soul filled with gratitude, she set out to live in the desert. Bringing only 3 loaves of bread that she bought from her earnings, she became an ascetic for the next 50 years of her life.

Saint Mary is invoked by those who are battling temptations of the flesh, penitent sinners and prostitutes, the demon-possessed, and those sick with fever, or skin diseases.

Today April 1st is her feast day. Saint Mary of Egypt, pray for us!

2 APRIL

SAINT FRANCIS OF PAOLA
PATRON OF MARINERS

Do you want to get to know someone who is able to read your mind, prophesy about future events and have these come true, and stop plagues from coming to your town through his prayers? Saint Francis of Paola has done all of these and has even been able to raise someone from the dead!

One time, he met some poor men along the road and asked them for food. They said they had none. Francis told them to check their bags and there they found freshly baked bread! Instead of being consumed when they ate it, it seemed to multiply!

Being a hermit with no money, Francis was denied passage on a boat so he used his cloak and traveled over the water to Sicily! This is probably why sailors and mariners called upon him before setting out on a journey.

Francis' holiness reached far and wide and many joined the Franciscan Minim Friars, the order he founded in 1492. Due to their humility, they called themselves Minim meaning "the least".

He is the patron saint of mariners, boatmen, sailors, naval officers, and travelers. One can also ask his prayers in case of fire, plagues, and sterility. Today April 2nd is his feast day. Saint Francis of Paola, pray for us!

SAINT LUIGI SCROSOPPI OF UDINE
PATRON OF SOCCER PLAYERS

Wherever the most abandoned, poorest, and neediest were, there you would find Saint Luigi working for their betterment. He instituted a home for rescued and deaf-mute girls, and unemployed former students, and served in a hospital for the seriously ill and destitute.

"The poor and the sick are our owners and they represent the very person of Jesus Christ." - Saint Luigi Scrosoppi

Due to his love and care for young people, the popularity of the sport among students, as well as the values he represents such as fairness, perseverance, determination, and diligence, he was chosen to be the patron saint of football.

After Saint Luigi's death in 1884, a miracle of healing occurred for Peter Chungu Shitima. He was diagnosed with terminal AIDS so his community asked Saint Luigi for his intercession. After having a dream about the holy priest, Peter was completely cured. This led to the canonization of Saint Luigi.

Today April 3rd is his feast day. Saint Luigi Scrosoppi, pray for us!

SAINT ISIDORE OF SEVILLE
PATRON OF THE INTERNET

This bishop and doctor of the Catholic Church was held in high esteem for his piety and sanctity. Crowds flocked to hear him preach, and many souls were drawn to God through his influence.

We also honor him on this day because his writings served as one of the earliest sources of information for the world. His early 7th-century work, "Etymologiae" taught generation upon generation of readers about mathematics, grammar, astronomy, and many other topics as well as the tenets of the faith. It is said that Isidore was so well-educated that he knew everything.

His siblings were also canonized as saints in the Church. Saint Leander of Seville was his eldest brother and the one responsible for his excellent education when their parents passed away early. His younger brother was Saint Fulgentius of Cartagena and his sister was Saint Florentina of Cartagena.

He is not only the patron saint of the internet but of computer programmers, technicians, and students.

Today, April 4th is his feast day. Saint Isidore of Seville, pray for us!

Saint Vincent Ferrer
Patron of Builders

Vincent was born in 15th-century Valencia, Spain to pious parents. At 18, he joined the Dominicans and was ordained 10 years later. He was very active in teaching, preaching, and serving the poor. He seriously studied the Word of God, reading nothing else for 3 years and memorizing its entirety.

At 48, he contracted a serious fever and received a vision of Jesus, Saint Dominic de Guzman, and Saint Francis of Assisi. Upon his recovery, he was supernaturally empowered with missionary zeal and was able to convert as many as 25,000 Jews, thousands of Muslims and atheists. He traveled from town to town on foot across many countries in Europe and throngs of people always accompanied him on his journey.

Having the gift of tongues, he spoke only in Spanish but listeners of different nationalities understood him. His intercession was able to raise the dead, make the lame walk and cure illnesses. Even praying in front of a hospital brought healings throughout the place!

Because of his contribution to building up the Church, his prayers are sought by construction workers and builders. Today April 5th is his feast day. Saint Vincent Ferrer, pray for us!

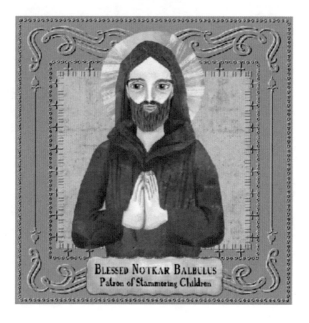

BLESSED NOTKAR BALBULUS
Patron of Stammering Children

Notkar was born in 840 at Elgg, Switzerland.

He was a man who stammered. Though he lived with this embarrassing trait, he had many talents and gave all he had to build up the Church. He was a Benedictine monk who wrote poetry and played music. He was also a writer, teacher, historian, hagiographer and wrote about the life of the saints.

He is the patron saint of stammering children and musicians.

Today, April 6, is his feast day. Blessed Notkar Balbulus, pray for us!

7
APRIL

SAINT JOHN BAPTIST
DE LA SALLE
Patron of School Principals

Saint John Baptist de la Salle is known as the "Father of Modern Education", his influence in our schools is still seen today. He is responsible for organizing students into grade levels and instituted the first school for teachers.

John was born on April 30th, 1651, in Rheims, France. From early on he desired to be a priest so he began his studies in Paris but upon the death of his parents, decided to care for his siblings instead. Seeing them flourish on their own independently, John was able to return to seminary and was ordained in his late 20's. Soon after he attained his doctorate in Theology.

He is the founder of the Brothers of the Christian Schools or La Salle Brothers. He also established highschools and trade schools.

During a severe famine in 1683, he gave away most of what he owned amounting to $400,00 and gave this to the hungry. He kept a little amount to sustain himself and not be a burden to his brothers.

He is the patron saint of school principals, teachers and the Brothers of Christian Schools. Today April 7th is his feast day. Saint John Baptist de la Salle, pray for us!

Saint Julia Billiart
Patron of Sick People

"Do what you can and don't waste time lamenting over what you can't do." - Saint Julie Billiart

The 7-year-old Julia knew her Catechism so well that she taught the other children. She loved to share her faith with others and instituted a group that provided Christian education to young girls.

One day, an accident resulted in her being paralyzed for the next 22 years. The bedridden Julia continued to teach catechism from her bed and was a source of encouragement and wisdom to all who came to visit her.

While she was sick, her friends continued the work she began. At the time of the French Revolution, they transferred Saint Julia on a haycart from house to house due to her support of priests.

On the 1st of June 1804, she was miraculously healed and she immediately resumed her charitable activities. More and more women joined and 15 convents were formed. This became known as the Congregation of the Sisters of Notre Dame (Institute of Notre Dame; Sisters of Notre Dame).

Saint Julia passed away on 8 April 1816 while she was praying. She is the patron of the sick and of the poor. Today, April 8th is her feast day. Saint Julia Billiart, pray for us!

SAINT DEMETRIUS OF SERMIUM
PATRON AGAINST EVIL SPIRITS

In the 3rd century was a man born to a noble, wealthy family in Thessalonica, Greece. He was smart, articulate, well-respected, and a strong believer in God. Many came to faith through his explanation of Church doctrine.

He chose to serve his country by enlisting as a soldier and also sought to use his gifts as a deacon. In the year 190, he became Duke of Thessaly under the reign of Emperor Maximian.

Since Christianity was against the law during that period, Saint Demetrius was arrested. He chose to die a brutal death knowing that eternal life awaited him. He was killed with the thrust of many spears in 306 at Sirmium (modern-day Serbia).

Centuries after his death, he was seen in battle fighting to defend Thessalonica. In the Balkans, over 200 churches are dedicated in his honor. His relics were reported to have exuded holy oil.

He is invoked against evil spirits and is the patron of the Crusaders, Thessalonica, Greece and Belgrade, Serbia.

Today April 9th is his feast day. Saint Demetrius of Sermium, pray for us!

SAINT MIGUEL DE SANCTIS
PATRON OF CANCER PATIENTS

Spanish-born Miguel, at the age of twelve, traveled to Barcelona, knocked on the door of the Trinitarian monks, and asked to be admitted. Prior to this, he told his parents he wanted to become a monk when he was only 6 years old.

He was known to all as a prayerful, kind, and charitable soul who led a simple life. He had a special devotion to the Holy Eucharist and was known to experience extreme joy during Holy Mass in which his soul seemed to be transported to heaven itself.

He is described in the Roman martyrology as "remarkable for innocence of life, wonderful penitence, and love for God."

When he passed away, many miracles occurred with his intercession. He is the patron saint for people afflicted with cancer.

Today, April 10th is his feast day. Saint Miguel de Sanctis, pray for us!

SAINT GEMMA GALGANI
PATRON OF PHARMACISTS

Gemma was born in 1878, in Tuscany, Italy. Despite having spinal meningitis, she set aside her education to care for her seven siblings and served them even when her true desire was to become a nun.

With great faith and devotion to the Sacred Heart of Jesus, she loved to pray and meditate. She often asked the saints for assistance, especially Saint Gabriel of Our Lady of Sorrows and Saint Marguerite Marie Alacoque. Through their intercession, she was miraculously healed of her longtime disease!

She desired to be so close to Jesus and accompany Him on the road to Calvary that she joined the Passionist Tertiaries. Then in 1899, she received the stigmata. This happened every Thursday night to Friday afternoon every week for a span of two years. She developed heavenly vision as she was able to see her guardian angel every day. She also received visions of Jesus, Saint Gabriel, and Saint Marguerite Marie Alacoque.

Because she was the daughter of a poor pharmacist, she is the patron saint of pharmacists, apothecaries, and druggists. She is also invoked against temptations and tuberculosis, and the intercessor of paratroopers, school children, and students. Today April 11th is her feast day. Saint Gemma Galgani, pray for us!

SAINT JOSEPH MOSCATI
PATRON OF PHYSICIANS

Early on, one could see Joseph's heroic virtue in the service of his fellow man. Once he got his medical degree, he served in a hospital for the "incurables" but never stopped researching for breakthrough cures.

He volunteered to help victims of the Mount Vesuvius' eruption without any public recognition. He spearheaded the efforts to halt the outbreak of cholera in Naples. He was also one of the pioneer doctors who experimented with insulin for diabetics. In World War I he enlisted but was rejected so he put up a hospital for the wounded, treating 3,000 soldiers.

He was known to sometimes bring miraculous cures to his patients and correctly diagnose their illnesses even when he had not seen them. He cured poor patients for free and treated them with kindness and generosity.

When he passed away, he appeared in a dream to a woman whose son had leukemia. She identified him in a photograph and soon her son was cured.

He is the patron of physicians, bachelors and those who were rejected by religious orders.

Today April 12th is his feast day. Saint Joseph Moscati, pray for us!

SAINT SABAS REYES SALAZAR
Protector of Children and Youth of Mexico

Saint Jose Sabas Reyes Salazar was a kind, humble and courageous priest who served the Mexican people. It was during the Cristero War that the government cracked down on Catholic believers and his parish was no exception. The statues and images were burnt or destroyed, and to desecrate the building, they used it as a stable.

Father Sabas' parishioners begged him to escape from there but he said that, "My superiors sent me here and my parish priest entrusted me with the care of the parish. If it is God's will, I will gladly accept martyrdom."

On Easter 1927 his captors caught up with him while he was praying the Holy Rosary and treated him with the utmost cruelty, tying him up and burning his hands. They wanted him to reveal where other priests were hiding but he never betrayed them.

During the torture, he prayed, "Lord of Heaven, my Mother of Guadalupe, grant me strength." He was shot several times and before he breathed his last he said, "Viva Cristo Rey!"

Today April 13th is his feast day. Saint Jose Sabas Reyes Salazar, pray for us!

SAINT PEDRO GONZALES TELMO
Patron of Fishermen

This worldly young man was quite literally thrown off his high horse when he strode into the city. His grand entrance led to embarrassment as he picked himself up from the dung heap. This humiliating episode in his life led him to God and this led him on the road to sanctity.

His pursuits turned heavenward and soon his holy wisdom was sought by many including King Saint Ferdinand III of Castile. When recognition came all too easily, he chose to withdraw to a simpler lifestyle among the fisherfolk and shepherds.

The story goes that when people went hungry, Saint Pedro would kneel and pray beside the water and the fish would leap up onto the river banks.

He is invoked by sailors for protection against bad weather.

Today April 14th is his feast day. Saint Pedro Gonzales Telmo, pray for us!

SAINT HUNNA OF ALSACE
Patron of Laundrywomen

She is known as the "Holy Washerwoman" of 7th-century France. Without a washing machine, this was a grueling task reserved only for peasants but this woman was different.

Being the daughter of a wealthy duke and wife of a nobleman, she could have lived in luxury without a care in the world but instead chose to serve others.

Hunna sought out her needy neighbors and helped them by performing menial acts of service. She would wash their clothes, mend them and if there were in too poor a state to be worn, she would replace them.

She helped the poor with cooking, cleaning, and caring for their children. She bathed those who were sick and also gave them religious instruction and encouragement.

Today April 15th is her feast day. Saint Hunna of Alsace, pray for us!

SAINT BERNADETTE SOUBIROUS
PATRON OF THE SICK

To date, millions of pilgrims have visited the charming town of Lourdes, France, and countless miracles have been documented there.

In 1858, Bernadette, during the time of her first Communion, went to collect firewood and saw a beautiful lady illuminated by a golden light. The woman smiled at Bernadette and summoned her to come closer. Bernadette saw that she was holding a rosary so she knelt before her and took out her rosary as well. This became the first of several encounters.

One time she told Bernadette, "I am the Immaculate Conception," which Bernadette did not really understand. The local bishop affirmed that it was indeed the Blessed Virgin Mary who appeared to Bernadette after miraculous signs occurred such as the blooming of wild roses during winter.

When Saint Bernadette turned twenty-two, she joined the Sisters of Nevers and remained there until her death on 16 April 1879. Her body has remained incorrupt.

Saint Bernadette is the patron of the sick, poor, people ridiculed for their piety, shepherds and Lourdes, France.

Today April 16th is her feast day. Saint Bernadette Soubirous, pray for us!

SAINT KATERI TETAKWITHA
PATRON OF ENVIRONMENTALISTS

In 17th century Osserneon (modern-day New York City) was born a native Indian girl named Tetakwitha (which means, "she who bumps into things"). When a smallpox epidemic hit, she and her parents contracted the disease but only Tetakwitha survived. The illness affected her sight and left her with a scar all her life.

When she was 20 years old, she met Father Jacques de Lamberville and he taught her the Catholic faith. She accepted this and was baptized. She was then given the Christian name Kateri in honor of Saint Catherine of Siena. Her newfound faith brought ridicule and displeasure amongst her tribe so she fled to the Christian Native American village of Sault-Sainte-Marie. She had to traverse 200 miles of wilderness to get there.

Saint Kateri wished to live only for God so she took a perpetual vow of chastity. This is why she is also known as the "Lily of the Mohawks".

When she passed away at the age of 24, the scar on her face vanished and her face beamed with radiant beauty. Many miracles are attributed to her prayers.

Today, April 17th is her feast day. Saint Kateri Tetakwitha, pray for us!

SAINT AGIA ℈ HAINALT
Patron of Lawsuits

Saint Agia is also known as Saint Aye. She was a Belgian woman during the 8th century.

She was born the daughter of a count and a relative of Saint Waldetrudis.

She was married to Saint Hidult of Hainalt until they both decided to live consecrated lives. After that, they parted ways and entered religious life.

This saint's story is quite unusual because she settled a lawsuit to have a just resolution by speaking from her grave. Thus she became the patron of lawsuits.

Today April 18 is her feast day. Saint Agia of Hainalt, pray for us!

SAINT EXPEDITUS OF MELITENE
PATRON AGAINST PROCRASTINATION

Expeditus was a Roman Centurion in the 4th century.

The story goes that the devil transformed himself into a crow and tempted Expeditus to put off his conversion to Christianity until the next day. Expeditus stomped on the bird, killing it, and said, "I'll be a Christian today!"

This is why he is known as the "Saint of Time" and invoked in the event of urgent causes.

Since believing in Jesus Christ was a death sentence at the time, he was beheaded for his faith.

His name Expeditus means "a soldier without marching pack" (he carried less equipment around). Being light on his feet reminds us not to be bogged down in doing good.

Today April 19th is his feast day. Saint Expeditus of Melitene, pray for us!

SAINT AGNES
OF MONTEPULCIANO
MIRACLE WORKER

Agnes lived in 13th-century Tuscany, Italy and desired to live the consecrated life since childhood. At 15 on the day of her installation as abbess, small white crosses were said to have rained softly down upon the congregation.

Miracles were commonplace for this saint. Even before she was born, mysterious lights in the sky were seen as if to announce her coming. During prayer, she was often seen 2 feet above the ground. Once she had a vision that it was an angel who gave Holy Communion to her. She had frequent visits from the Virgin Mary. Another time, she experienced cradling the child Jesus in her arms, and when she regained consciousness she was holding the golden crucifix that He was wearing.

Wherever she would stop to pray, violets, lilies, and roses would bloom. When they were short on rations, Saint Agnes would take a handful of bread, pray over it and it would multiply and feed the whole congregation. Many healings took place from the saint's intercession. She reportedly brought a drowned child back to life.

Even unto death, miraculous cures happened at her tomb. Her body remains incorrupt to this day. Today April 20th is her feast day. Saint Agnes of Montepulciano, pray for us!

SAINT BEUNO GASULSYCH
Patron of Sick Children

It is truly amazing how God shows His mighty power through His saints through the years. In 6th century Wales, there lived a saint who was able to do such wondrous works to glorify God.

Beuno Gasulsych was born the grandson of a Welsh prince. Some say he was also the grand-nephew of King Arthur. He answered God's calling for him to be a monk and later in life, he received many visions.

He served as the spiritual teacher and guide of his niece Saint Winifred. He also rescued her from death. Winifred had a suitor whom she did not want to marry. The man cut off Winifred's head in retaliation but Saint Beuno placed her head back in place and it reattached itself! He is also said to have brought 6 other people back from the grave!

He and his followers established many of the monasteries in North Wales. To this day, people let their sick children sit on his tomb so as to ask Saint Beuno for their healing. Many miracles have been known to have occurred through his prayers.

He is the patron of sick children, sick cattle, and sick animals.

Today April 21st is his feast day. Saint Beuno Gasulsych, pray for us!

St Theodore of Sykeon
PATRON FOR RAIN

In the 6th century there lived a Byzantine monk called Theodore. As time passed, he became more and more drawn to a life of prayer.

Wanting to forsake all comforts and draw strength from God alone, Theodore dug a pit and lived in a cave for 2 years. No one but the deacon who brought him bread and water knew where he hid. For a time he also lived in an iron cage so tiny that he could hardly stand upright. These sufferings granted him amazing gifts. Leprosy was healed and demons were exorcised through his intervention. Wild animals such as bears and wolves ate food from his hands.

A plague of locusts threatened the village of Magatia so the people turned to Saint Theodore for help. He told them to come to church. After the Divine Liturgy, the villagers discovered that all the insects had died.

In his youth, God heard his prayers when a whole region suffered a drought. Saint Theodore interceded on bended knee and instantly the rain came. This is why he is called upon when in need of rain or to stop the rain.

Today, April 22nd is his feast day. Saint Theodore of Sykeon, pray for us!

SAINT GEORGE
PATRON OF CHIVALRY

In 4th-century Middle East lived a soldier named George. He was full of Christian zeal and courage. During the 10th century, there was the Golden Legend. We do not know if this is true. In a lake in Silena, Libya lived a terrible dragon. Armies tried to vanquish it yet failed. To prevent it from attacking all the people, they offered it 2 sheep every day until there were scarcely any left. Afterwards they cast lots and a maiden would pitifully end up being its daily meal.

One day, it was a princess that was the unfortunate choice but lucky for her, George arrived on the scene. Just before the dragon reached her, he made the sign of the cross and with a single blow of this spear killed it.

He exhorted the people to turn their lives over to God and many converted to the Christian faith. The king was so grateful that he rewarded George with a vast amount of the kingdom's treasure. George then gave this to the poor and left the land in awe of his goodness.

Saint George is known to be one of the Fourteen Holy Helpers. He is the patron saint for chivalry and for the healing of many ailments.

Today April 23rd is his feast day. Saint George, pray for us!

SAINT WILLIAM FIRMATUS
PATRON AGAINST HEADACHES

By divine inspiration, William desired to live free from avarice, he gave away all he had to the poor and lived the rest of his life as a hermit on pilgrimage. He is often depicted with a raven because the bird served as his guide on his way to Jerusalem.

He lived such a holy life that when there was a drought in Dardenay, he struck his staff into the ground, then water sprung forth from it.

As a monk, he was known for his affinity with wild animals. They were perfectly at ease with him. Birds would come and eat from his hand and hide under his cloak when they felt cold. Fish would rush to his feet in the water and allow themselves to be scooped up by him and afterward gently placed back into the river.

One time a wild boar rampaged through a vegetable patch and ruined almost all of the produce. With a soft touch, Saint William took it by the ear and led it to his cell where he spent the night peacefully. The boar was as meek as a lamb with the saint and did not complain despite being made to fast throughout its time in the cell.

He is the patron of headache sufferers. Today April 24th is his feast day. Saint William Firmatus, pray for us!

LOVE THE LORD YOUR GOD WITH ALL YOUR HEART AND WITH ALL YOUR SOUL AND WITH ALL YOUR MIND AND WITH ALL YOUR STRENGTH.

-JESUS

GOSPEL OF MARK
12:30

SAINT MARK THE EVANGELIST
PATRON AGAINST IMPENITENCE

Because of Saint Mark, we know today what Jesus actually said and did during His life on earth. His writings show us what it was like in 1st-century Jerusalem. His mother's home in Jerusalem was where Christians often gathered for fellowship and worship.

Saint Mark accompanied Saint Paul and Saint Barnabas on their trip to Antioch (modern-day Turkey) and Cyprus to establish Christian communities. He traveled to Alexandria, Egypt, and became their first bishop. There he established the first famous Christian school. In paintings, Saint Mark is often depicted with a lion to symbolize Jesus Christ's resurrection. It is said that lions sleep with their eyes open so this reminds us that when our mortal bodies experience the sleep of death, we are actually born into eternal life through Jesus' rising.

Call on Saint Mark to intercede for a contrite heart pleasing to God. His prayers are also efficacious in case of scrofulous illnesses, struma, or insect bites.

Today April 25th is his feast day. Saint Mark the Evangelist, pray for us!

Saint Rafael Arnáiz Barón
Patron of Diabetics

On April 9th 1911, in Burgos, Spain, Rafael Arnáiz Barón was born. From an early age he would often get a fever and stay home from school. When he was around 10 years old, he contracted a bacterial infection and needed to recuperate for a month. When he got stronger, his father took him to a church to consecrate him to the Blessed Mother's care.

Growing up, his artistic and spiritual gifts became apparent. His disposition was always one of good humor and respect for others. After he finished high school, Rafael desired to give more of his heart to God and spent more and more time with the Trappists of San Isidro de Duenas in Palencia. There he found solace in the quiet and was enraptured with the Gregorian chants such as the Salve Regine.

In his early 20's, he developed type 1 diabetes. The illness afflicted him again and again and he would be forced to recuperate at home. Three times he returned to the convent in his desire to serve God despite his ill health.

He is the patron of those with diabetes and World Youth Day.

Today April 26th is his feast day. Saint Rafael Arnáiz Barón, pray for us!

SAINT ZITA OF LUCCA
PATRON OF LOST KEYS

In 1218 in the region of Tuscany, Italy, Zita was born to a family rich in virtue but poor in earthly riches. At age 12, Zita helped her family by working as a servant for a wealthy family. She performed household tasks as best as she could as a way to honor God.

At times, poor people would come begging for food and Zita's kind heart could not resist giving them what was meant to be her portion. Sometimes she would even give food meant for her employer. This habit irked her masters as well as the other household servants.

Saint Zita loved God and placed Him above all things. She attended Holy Mass daily before her work began. Since her duties were done with great care, she was given the role of managing the homestead and entrusted with the keys.

This is why she is the patron of lost keys. She is also the intercessor to call on for butlers, domestic servants, homemakers, people ridiculed for their piety, rape victims, single laywomen, waiters and waitresses and Lucca, Italy.

She died on 27 April 1272 and when her tomb was re-opened her body was found to be incorrupt. Today, April 27th is her feast day. Saint Zita of Lucca, pray for us!

SAINT GIANNA BERETTA MOLLA
PATRON OF PREGNANT WOMEN

"The secret of happiness is to live moment by moment and to thank God for all that He, in His goodness, sends to us day after day."- Saint Gianna Beretta Molla

Since she was a child, Gianna was kind and loving. Her parents raised her in the faith well and taught her how to be a good Christian. Her sister became a nun and 2 brothers became priests.

Before she finished her studies to be a doctor, Gianna volunteered for the Saint Vincent de Paul Society, serving the poor and elderly. In 1955 she married Pietro Molla and together they had 3 children. On her fourth pregnancy, she was found to have a large ovarian cyst that would endanger her life if she continued with the pregnancy. She chose to save the life of her child instead of her own and she died 1 week after she gave birth.

Her baby grew up to be a doctor like her mother and honored her mother by participating in activities that defend unborn babies.

"One earns Paradise with one's daily task." - Saint Gianna Beretta Molla

Saint Gianna is the patron of all pregnant women. She is also the saint invoked for unborn children. Today April 28th is her feast day. Saint Gianna Beretta Molla, pray for us!

SAINT CATHERINE OF SIENA
DOCTOR OF THE CHURCH

Catherine was born on **25 March 1347** in Tuscany, Italy. Since childhood, she was happiest when in prayer and attending to the needs of the poor and needy. At the age of 7, Catherine dedicated her whole life to God and lived as a Dominican tertiary after she received her parents' permission.

She spent most of her days alone in her room, praying and listening to God. Upon God's instruction, she shared her divine knowledge by entering into public life and even politics. Her influence was so strong that even the Pope listened to her and took her advice in her quest to bring unity and reform within the Church.

Many of her writings are still available for us to learn from today.

"You are rewarded not according to your work or your time but according to the measure of your love."

"Love transforms one into what one loves."

She is the patron saint against fire, miscarriages, temptations of the flesh, and bodily ills. She is also invoked by firefighters, nurses, people who are ridiculed for being good, and the patron saint of Siena and Varazze in Italy, the whole of Italy, and Europe as well as other places.

Today April 29th is her feast day. Saint Catherine of Siena, pray for us!

SAINT ERCONWALD OF LONDON
PATRON OF GOUT

This 7th-century Benedictine monk founded two abbeys, one for men and one for women.

In 675 he became the bishop of London. He had a significant role in drafting just laws at the time.

Despite experiencing severe gout during his lifetime, Saint Erconwald took good care of his diocese and went where he was needed the most. For this reason, he is invoked by people suffering from this same illness. The city of London also looks to him as its patron saint.

When he passed away, many people got miraculously healed just by touching the chair he used while he traveled.

Today April 30th is his feast day. Saint Erconwald, pray for us!

MAY

SAINT PEREGRINE LAZIOSI
PATRON OF CANCER PATIENTS

In 13th-century Italy, Peregrine Laziosi was a rich, young man who enjoyed worldly pursuits until he encountered Saint Philip Benizi. Peregrine hated Catholics so he struck Saint Philip in the face. The saint followed Christ's instruction to turn the other cheek and prayed for Peregrine. Afterward, Peregrine had a total change of heart and converted. The Blessed Virgin Mary appeared to him in a vision instructing him to go to Siena and join the Servite order which he did.

To atone for the times when he fought against the Church, Peregrine worked and served without sitting down and he grew in holiness. He was a powerful preacher, as well as a kind and gentle confessor.

He then suffered from a rapidly spreading cancer in his foot and the doctor recommended amputation. After a night spent in prayer, the next morning, his foot was totally healed! He lived to be 80 years old.

A long time after he passed away in 1345, people found that his body remained as it was, incorrupt. Many healings and miracles happened when Saint Peregrine was invoked so he is well known to many until this day.

Today, May 1st is his feast day. Saint Peregrine Laziosi, pray for us!

SAINT ANTONIUS OF FLORENCE
PATRON AGAINST FEVER

If poor health prevents you from pursuing your dreams, Saint Antonius knows how you feel. He wanted to join the Dominicans but was rejected as he was always sick. Because he wouldn't give up, the prior said he would be admitted only if he was able to recite the whole canon law from memory. He came back after a year of study and was able to fulfill the requirement.

In 1446, he became the archbishop of Florence and was known for his charitable works especially when a plaque hit the city in 1448 and an earthquake in 1453.

He was a theologian, healer, and diplomat. His writings include a biography of Blessed John Dominic, a history of the world, and a reference on moral theology.

He is the patron of those suffering from fever.

Today May 2nd is his feast day. Saint Antonius of Florence, pray for us!

SAINT JAMES THE LESSER
PATRON OF THE DYING

Saint James was not only one of the twelve apostles of Jesus, but he was also a cousin of our Lord. He was the brother of Saint Jude Thaddeus.

He had a strong faith in Jesus' words as he believed in the resurrection before he witnessed it for himself. He resolved not to eat until Christ came back from the dead and indeed He did, preparing a meal for James himself!

Saint James was the first bishop of Jerusalem. He was known to be a just and kind man who served the poor. He is called a "pillar of the Church". He is the author of the first Catholic epistle.

He seems to have been called the "Lesser" to distinguish him from Saint James the Great who was called to be an apostle before him or was older.

In the year 62, attackers pushed him from a cliff and then stoned and beat him with clubs. All the while, he prayed for his murderers' salvation.

He is the patron of the dying, apothecaries, druggists, pharmacists, fullers, hat makers, Uruguay, and some cities in Italy.

Today May 3rd is his feast day. Saint James the Lesser, pray for us!

4
MAY

SAINT FLORIAN OF LORCH
PATRON AGAINST FIRE

In 3rd-century Austria, there lived a Roman soldier named Florian. He was secretly a believer in Jesus Christ. One could not openly profess their faith at the time since this was punishable by death.

One day a whole town caught fire but Florian prayed and threw a single bucket of water over the blaze. This instantly quenched the fire!

When he was ordered to execute a group of Christians, he refused so he became a martyr for Christ.

He is the patron saint of firefighters. He is also invoked in case of battle, drowning, and floods.

Today May 4th is his feast day. Saint Florian of Lorch, pray for us!

BLESSED NUNTIUS SURPRIZIO
PATRON OF WORKERS

Nuntius' father passed away when he was only three years old, and his little sister died two years later. His stepfather treated him with contempt.

Instead of rebelling, he never retaliated. He grew up to be a kind and virtuous young lad. He attended Holy Mass as often as possible and patterned his life after the saints.

As soon as he could, his uncle made him work as an apprentice blacksmith. He abused and overworked Nuntius and even beat him. One winter's morning in 1831, he was tasked to carry supplies and collapsed with a terrible fever. They also saw that his leg had wounds that were not attended to so these became gangrenous. Eventually, his injuries ended his days. Until the very last, he was a witness of holiness to those around him.

When he died, his relic was placed beside a man who was in a coma from a motorcycle accident. The doctors told his family that he would remain in a vegetative state. With the family's prayers, that man soon awakened and made a full recovery.

Today May 5th is his feast day. He is the patron of workers.

Blessed Nuntius Sulprizio, pray for us!

SAINT FRANCIS DE
MONTMORENCY LAVAL
PATRON OF THE BISHOPS OF CANADA

You can get to know a man by getting to know who his friends are as well as his enemies. In the case of Saint Francis de Montmorency Laval, he counted the native Indian tribes as his friends who were in need of protection from those who wished to profit from them, namely the liquor traders. He was able to have alcohol banned from their territory and this greatly improved the lives of the people. He was someone the poor were always able to call upon in their time of need.

In 1623, Francis was born into one of the greatest families in France. He answered the call to religious life early on and was ordained a Jesuit priest at 24 years old. When he was 30, he joined the Paris Foreign Mission Society.

He zealously supported evangelistic work and provided for Jesuit and Franciscan recollect missionaries. He became Canada's first Roman Catholic bishop. He built the Immaculate Conception Cathedral, established a seminary in Quebec, and began the Catholic school system in Canada.

Today, May 6th is his feast day. Saint Francis de Montmorency Laval, pray for us!

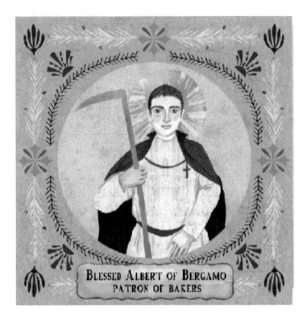

BLESSED ALBERT OF BERGAMO
PATRON OF BAKERS

In the 13th century lived a man in Cremona, Italy who had a big heart for the poor. From the age of seven, Albert wouldn't eat for half a week so as to give his food to the needy. He lived this kind of sacrificial life until he got married. His wife did not mind at first but when Albert's father passed away, she started nagging him to stop being so generous. In time, she was converted to live as Albert did and also gave up her food to those in need.

Albert honored God by going on pilgrimages. He traveled great distances throughout his life making his way to Jerusalem, 9 times to Rome, and 8 trips to Santiago de Compostela. These travels were fraught with danger during the time. In Rome, he visited the sick and gave them consolation, exhorting them to confess their sins to a priest.

He was a very hardworking farmer and he recited the psalms as he walked. When he got sick and asked a neighbor to fetch a priest, a long time passed before a priest could come so they say that a dove brought him the Holy Eucharist.

He is the patron of bakers and day laborers.

Today, May 7th is his feast day. Blessed Albert of Bergamo, pray for us!

SAINT IDA OF NIVELLES
PATRON AGAINST TOOTHACHES

Sanctity was infectious in the family of Saint Ida. Her husband and daughters are celebrated as saints in the Catholic Church.

She was married to Saint Pepin of Landen. She had two saintly daughters - Saint Gertrude of Nivelles and Saint Begga of Ardenne. She also had a son Grimoald who became mayor of the palace. She was the sister of Saint Modoald of Trier and Saint Severa.

She made a living as a writer and illustrator. She was widely known for her generosity to the poor.

When she was widowed she lived as a nun in the Benedictine monastery run by her daughter Saint Gertrude. She often had heavenly visions and was a mystic.

She is the patron of those with toothaches and erysipelas (bacterial infections of the skin).

Today May 8th is her feast day. Saint Ida of Nivelles, pray for us!

9 MAY

SAINT GREGORY OF OSTIA
PATRON FOR THE PROTECTION OF CROPS

When Saint Gregory was made Cardinal-Bishop of Ostia, he was able to help the people grow closer to God through his holy preaching and celebration of religious feasts.

Then a plague of locusts threatened to wipe out all the crops in the area. Saint Gregory exhorted the townspeople to do three days of prayers and fasting and after he imparted his blessing through the sign of the cross, the locusts departed.

For hundreds of years, water has been touched to Saint Gregory's relics and sprinkled upon fields, gardens, and vineyards so as to protect these from pests.

Today, May 9th is his feast day. Saint Gregory of Ostia, pray for us!

SAINT JOHN OF AVILA
PATRON OF SPAIN

Saint John was the spiritual advisor of many saints.

He was born into a rich family and yet at the age of seventeen, John gave away most of the fortune he inherited from his parents to the poor.

"The proof of perfect love of our Lord is seen in the perfect love of our neighbour". - Saint John of Avila

He answered the call to religious life and became a traveling preacher for 40 years. He was the spiritual guide of Saint Teresa of Avila, Saint Francis Borgia, Saint John of God, Saint John of the Cross, Saint Peter of Alcantara, and Saint Louis of Granada.

He is a Doctor of the Catholic Church and Patron of Spain.

Today May 10th is his feast day. Saint John of Avila, pray for us!

SAINT GENGULPHUS OF BURGUNDY
PATRON OF SEPARATED SPOUSES

In the 8th century lived a knight and courtier who came from a rich noble family. He married a noblewoman who for the life of her could not remain faithful to him.

Because he was ashamed of his wife but did not wish to do her harm, he hid away in his castle in Avallon, France, and lived the life of a hermit. He left his wife in the care of his servants.

His life met a bitter end when his wife's lover stealthily murdered him in his bed.

He is the patron of separated spouses, difficult marriages, knights, and victims of adultery and unfaithfulness.

Today May 11th is his feast day. Saint Gengulphus of Burgundy, pray for us!

BLESSED IMELDA
LAMBERTINI
PATRON OF FIRST COMMUNICANTS

In the fourteenth century in Bologna, Italy lived a little girl who loved God so much that she prepared a little place in their home dedicated for prayer. She was always found there spending time in prayer. She wanted to serve the Lord as a nun from an early age.

She had a devotion to the Holy Eucharist, the Blessed Mother, Queen of the Angels, and Saint Agnes of Rome and may have had visions of her.

She miraculously received her first communion and after this most momentous and joyful event, she was so enraptured that her soul flew up to heaven and passed from this life.

Today May 12th is her feast day. Blessed Imelda Lambertini, pray for us!

SAINT CRISTANZIANO OF PICENO
PATRON OF HAIL

He was the very first soul who was converted to Christianity in his area of Ascoli Piceno, Italy. He was baptized by Saint Emidius and given the name fitting for his stature as a believer - Cristanziano. He was thereby taught the tenets of the faith and was given the role of a deacon.

Since believing in Jesus was illegal in 3rd century Italy, Saint Emidius gave his life for Christ. Throughout that time, Saint Cristanziano stood by him as his assistant. Eventually, holy Cristanzaino joined him in martyrdom as well during the reign of Maxentius.

On the day he was sentenced to die, a hail storm occurred halting the execution. This had serious implications for the people's harvest so Cristanziano waved his hand and said a prayer and this stopped the storm immediately. The crops were saved and the saint's beheading took place as scheduled.

Aside from being invoked during hail, he is also the patron against discord, influenza, lightning, storms, war and the places of Agnone, Casalciprano and Maltignano in Italy.

Today May 13th is his feast day. Saint Cristanziano of Piceno, pray for us!

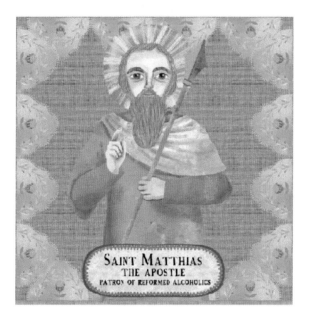

SAINT MATTHIAS
THE APOSTLE
PATRON OF REFORMED ALCOHOLICS

When Judas Iscariot fell away from the disciples, they chose Saint Matthias to replace him. He was one of the believers who could attest to the powerful resurrection of Jesus Christ.

For thirty years, he preached the Word of God to those in Judea, Cappadocia, Egypt, and Ethiopia. He frequently taught the faithful how to mortify fleshly desires so as to allow God's Spirit to flourish in the soul.

"It behooves us to combat the flesh and make use of it, without pampering it by unlawful gratifications. As to the soul, we must develop her power by faith and knowledge." - Saint Matthias

He is often depicted carrying a lance or a spear as this was how he suffered at the hands of his captors before he died of stoning in the year 80.

He is the patron of reformed alcoholics, carpenters, tailors, and invoked against smallpox. He is also the patron of hope and perseverance.

Today, May 14th is his feast day. Saint Matthias the Apostle, pray for us!

SAINT ISIDORE THE FARMER
PATRON OF AGRICULTURAL WORKERS

Saint Isidore went to Holy Mass early in the morning before his labor in the fields. His fellow servants were disgruntled that Isidore's work was neglected and told their master about it. The master upon investigation found Isidore immersed in prayer while angels worked the land in his place!

Another time, they saw Isidore plowing the fields with an angel on his right and left side so his work equaled to that of three men!

He was a credit to his master because when his daughter died, Isidore was able to bring her back to life through his prayers. He is also said to have provided fresh spring water when his master was thirsty.

Saint Isidore and his wife Saint Mary de la Cabeza lived piously and did many good works throughout their lifetime. They had a son together but he died in his youth.

When Saint Isidore passed away, the site of his grave was where many miracles occurred. In 1212, his body after torrential rains was found to be incorrupt.

He is the patron of agricultural workers, farmers, field hands, ranchers, day laborers, livestock and is invoked against the death of children. Today May 15th is his feast day. Saint Isidore the Farmer, pray for us!

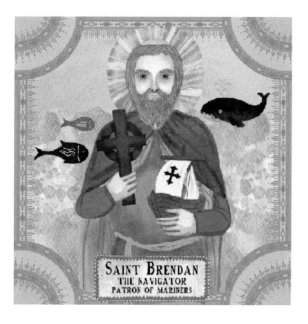

SAINT BRENDAN
THE NAVIGATOR
PATRON OF MARINERS

Ahoy there! They spotted land and gave thanks by celebrating Holy Mass on Easter Sunday. What Saint Brendan and his brother monks did not know though was that they did not reach land but were on a giant whale!

This is one of the tales of Saint Brendan as they traveled the seas of the Atlantic spreading the Word of God to all that they met. Some say that they reached the Americas in the 6th century.

Saint Brendan was ordained in 512. He belonged to an order with at least three thousand monks. Their way of life was given to them by an angel with Saint Brendan faithfully writing this down for the congregation to follow.

He is the patron of everyone who works on the sea such as mariners, cruise ship staff, sailors, and such. He is also the patron of whales and of Ardfert, Clonfert, and Kerry in Ireland.

Today May 16th is his feast day. Saint Brendan the Navigator, pray for us!

SAINT PASCAL BAYLON
PATRON OF COOKS

There was once a boy born to saintly peasant parents on the 24th of May in 1540. His name was Pascal Baylon. From a very young age, he had a special love for the Holy Eucharist.

When he was seven years old, he began to help his family by working as a shepherd. He did this until he was twenty-four. All that time, he would help the other shepherds to live as piously as they could.

He sought to serve God who was his all as a Franciscan lay brother with the friars of the Alcantarine Reform. His duties included cooking all the food or being the doorkeeper. These simple tasks he did with devotion and care as his service to God. As a friar, he was known for his great compassionate heart for the poor and needy. Even with his simple background, his wisdom was sought out by the poor and rich alike for he had the enlightenment of the Holy Spirit.

He is the patron of cooks, shepherds, Eucharistic congresses and organizations as well as the diocese of Segorbe-Castellón de la Plana, Spain and Obando, Bulacan, Philippines.

Today, May 17th is his feast day. Saint Pascal Baylon, pray for us!

BLESSED BURCHARD OF BEINWIL
PATRON OF BEINWIL SWITZERLAND

In the 12th century in Beinwil, Switzerland lived a priest who served his parish with great care and devotion. He attended to the spiritual and material needs of his flock to the best of his ability.

Burchard was known to have raised a bird since it was a chick. This was no ordinary bird as it was Burchard's feathered friend and it was able to speak and hold conversations with him. In fact, when Burchard left his home, upon his return the bird would tell him what had gone on and report any bad behavior it had seen.

One day, the servants who despised the bird killed it and threw its body in a mine shaft located near the vicarage. When Burchard arrived, the dead bird came back to life and told him what the servants did!

Another miracle occurred when a dying woman asked for the saint's presence. It seemed too late to help her when a messenger said she had already died. Despite this, Saint Burchard continued the journey. He prayed over her and the breath of life returned to the woman! He then gave her the last rites so she could pass on to the next life blessed with the Holy Sacraments. Today May 18th is his feast day. Blessed Burchard of Beinwil, pray for us!

SAINT IVO OF KERMARTIN
PATRON OF LAWYERS

When he prayed, God listened. He was a miracle worker since from a single loaf of bread, he was able to feed hundreds.

Ivo (otherwise known as Yves) was born into a rich, noble family at Kermartin in the northwestern region of France. As a young teen of fourteen, he began his studies to become a civil and canon lawyer. He also studied philosophy and theology in Paris and Orleans.

Whilst other lawyers amassed large fortunes through their work, Ivo frequently chose to defend the poor without payment. He would visit them in prison and look to their needs while they waited for their trials. He sacrificed much for others and often fasted from meals.

All this time he wished to live simply and serve God so he joined the Third Order of the Franciscans. In 1284 he was ordained and soon after resigned from his legal duties to focus solely on his parishioners.

From his earnings, he built a hospital for the poor and fed them with the harvest from his lands. He is the patron of lawyers, advocates, canonists, the abandoned, notaries, orphans and Brittany.

Today May 19 is this feast day. Saint Ivo of Kermartin, pray for us!

BLESSED COLUMBA OF RIETI
PATRON AGAINST SORCERY

Blessed Columba was so kind and good but Lucrezia Borgia disliked her so intensely for years and years. She accused Columba of practicing black magic but there was no truth to this at all. In fact, Columba from the day of her birth was a child close to heaven. It is said that when she was born, angels gathered around her home to sing.

Her holy life bore fruit it many miracles. Her prayers were able to free others from evil spirits. She prayed for the sick and they got well. Even those that died were raised back to life through her intercession!

God gave her the gift of divine visions and one time, she was transported to the Holy Land and walked where our Lord walked. Many people looked to Blessed Columba for guidance and direction. A group of kidnappers even tried to abduct her so she could work wonders on their behalf but she was able to flee from their scheme. Blessed Columba also foretold what the future held as told to her by God.

She is the patron invoked against magic and sorcery.

Today, May 20th is her feast day. Blessed Columba of Rieti, pray for us!

SAINT EUGENE DE MAZENOD
Patron of Dysfunctional Families

"Learn who you are in the eyes of God." - Saint Eugene de Mazenod

On Good Friday in 1807, at the foot of the cross, Eugene chose God and a life of goodness. By grace, he was powerfully touched by the love of Christ. He entered seminary the following year and was ordained in 1811 at the age of twenty-nine.

Saint Eugene went on to build up the Church by giving up his family's riches and served the poor, sick, prisoners, and abandoned. He almost died from typhus while working in prisons.

His mission attracted many lay people as well as clergy who served alongside him. He founded the Oblates of Mary Immaculate, founded 23 parishes, built and repaired 50 churches, and more than doubled the number of priests in his diocese.

His legacy continues to this day with the Oblates present in 68 countries with over five thousand missionaries.

Today, May 21st is his feast day. Saint Eugene de Mazenod, pray for us!

SAINT RITA OF CASCIA
Patron of Impossible Causes

Rita lived In 14th-century Umbria, Italy. She was married to Paolo, a cruel man who had a temper, and sometimes even beat her. Despite this, Rita treated him with kindness, forgiveness, and patience. Throughout the eighteen years of marriage, she constantly prayed for him. God's love through Rita won Paolo over and his ways gradually changed. Together they had two sons.

Later in life, after her sons passed away, Rita entered religious life. In the forty years of convent life, she brought harmony to the region through her holy life and prayer. She brought peace to the long-standing feud of two prominent families. Her spirituality was centered on our Lord's passion and in her desire to offer sacrifice and reparation, she received a wound on her head like she wore a crown of thorns. She offered up this pain in union with Jesus for fifteen years.

Saint Rita is the patron of impossible, forgotten, and lost causes, abuse victims, parents, and widows. She is also invoked in cases of infertility, loneliness, sickness, wounds, and difficult marriages.

Today, May 22nd is her feast day. Saint Rita of Cascia, pray for us!

SAINT WILLIAM OF ROCHESTER
PATRON OF ADOPTED CHILDREN

There was a woman known to all the townsfolk as mentally ill. One day she found a dead body lying on the wayside. In an act of kindness, she plaited honeysuckle flowers and placed this on the body. Upon doing so, her madness was instantly cured!

Little did she know it but here lay before her the body of Saint William Rochester, a saint who entered heaven. On his tomb, many miraculous healings occurred so it has become a place of pilgrimage.

The young William had a wild, rebellious nature but as he grew older, he chose to live a life of virtue. He went to Holy Mass every day and tithed religiously from his earnings as a baker. He felt drawn to caring for children who were in need and who had no one to care for them.

When someone left a baby boy on his doorstep, he named him David and adopted him as his own. He raised David and taught him all he knew. Through the years, David was shown kindness by William. It is with sadness then that David repaid him with evil. While on a journey to the Holy Land, David beat William with a club, cut his throat, stole his valuables, and ran away. Saint William is the patron of adopted children. Today, May 23rd is his feast day. Saint William of Rochester, pray for us!

· SAINT JOANNA THE MYRRHBEARER ·

"Joanna the wife of Chuza, the manager of Herod's household; Susanna; and many others. These women were helping to support them out of their own means." - Luke 8:3

Saint Joanna lived in the first century and she was one of the women who served our Lord's mission through whatever she had. She was married to Chuza, the steward of King Herod Antipas. In Eastern tradition, it is said that she gave the head of John the Baptist an honorable burial.

Saint Joanna was also one of the women who came to anoint Jesus' body in the tomb and discovered that it was empty.

"It was Mary Magdalene, Joanna, Mary the mother of James, and the others with them who told this to the apostles."- Luke 24:10

Today May 24th is her feast day. Saint Joanna, pray for us!

SAINT BEDE THE VENERABLE
PATRON OF LECTORS

"He alone loves the Creator perfectly who manifests a pure love for his neighbour." - Saint Bede the Venerable

This 7th-century Benedictine monk was known as the Father of English History and the most knowledgeable man of his time. He created our present dating system. AD or "anno domini" comes from his book "Historia Ecclesiastica" which helped to bring about spiritual and cultural unity during a time of violence and barbarism.

All that we know of England before the 8th century is because of Saint Bede's writings. He was a teacher and prolific writer of history, math, music, astronomy, poetry, grammar, philosophy, scripture study, and more.

He was declared a Doctor of the Catholic Church in 1899 by Pope Leo XIII.

Today May 25th is his feast day. Saint Bede the Venerable, pray for us!

SAINT PHILIP NERI
PATRON OF LAUGHTER & JOY

"Cheerfulness strengthens the heart and makes us persevere in a good life.- Saint Philip Neri

Philip lived in 16th-century Florence. His family was poor though they had relations with Italian nobility. Growing up, he was known to be kind and virtuous. He had the habit of stealing away to the mountains and praying at a Dominical chapel there. He often recited the psalms.

Philip found great joy in taking care of the sick as well as poor pilgrims. His work with them attracted others who joined him in the mission. Saint Ignatius of Loyola became one of his friends.

Saint Philip's love for God was infectious and he won many over to the faith by his preaching. He was always friendly, cheerful, and full of joy. In 1551, he took his priestly vows. When he heard confessions, he knew what sins were committed even before they were spoken of by the penitents!

He is called the Saint of Joy and the patron of Rome.

Today May 26th is his feast day. Saint Philip Neri, pray for us!

SAINT MELANGELL
PATRON OF RABBITS

There once was a princess in Wales who lived in the 6th century. Her father wished that she marry a nobleman but she only desired a solitary life of prayer and meditation. She traveled to Powys and lived there for fifteen years without seeing a single man.

One day, the prince of Powys, Brochwel Yscythrog, went hunting and spotted a hare. In hot pursuit, he finally found the hare hiding under the cloak of a beautiful maiden. It was Melangell in her quiet time with God. Soon his dogs stopped their howling and the trumpet stuck to the huntsmen's lips. The rabbit was saved!

The prince decided to give the land where they were standing as a peaceful sanctuary for all and where a convent would be built. Melangell became its abbess.

She is the patron of hares.

Today, May 27th is her feast day. Saint Melangell, pray for us!

BLESSED MARIA BAGNESI
PATRON OF ABUSE VICTIMS

In spite of the fact that she was often neglected by her parents, Maria was a beautiful and happy child. She was a tiny child who was often in the care of her sister who was a Dominican nun. There, she grew up so happy and content that she, along with her four other sisters chose to become nuns.

Blessed Maria then started to develop heavenly visions of saints, angels, and even evil spirits. She was able to talk with them and soon the townsfolk came to her room to learn from her holy wisdom. Her room had such a tranquil atmosphere that animals congregated there as well. Cats would sit with her, lay on her bed, surround her, and protect her songbirds. They say that one time when she was hungry, one of the cats fetched her some cheese.

She grew to love Saint Bartholomew the Apostle and even added his name to hers. Her prayer life turned all the more mystical as she meditated on the Glorious and Sorrowful Mysteries. People saw her levitate in a state of ecstasy. Many years after she died on May 28, 1577, her body was found to be incorrupt.

She is the patron of abuse victims and the sick. She is also invoked against the death of parents. Today, May 28th is her feast day. Blessed Maria Bagnesi, pray for us!

SAINT BONA OF PISA
PATRON OF FLIGHT ATTENDANTS

From a very young age, Bona could see heavenly visions and had mystical experiences. When she was 10 years of age, she joined the Augustinians in their good works as a lay member of the tertiary order.

When she was 14 years old, she courageously decided to travel to the Holy Land because she wanted to see her father. He was there fighting in the Crusades. She had a fruitful journey there but upon her return, she was wounded and captured by Muslim pirates in the Mediterranean. By God's grace, she was saved from harm. With the help of some Christians from her native Pisa, she was ransomed and was able to continue her way back home.

Saint Bona lived an active life, often guiding pilgrims to holy places. At a time when traveling was strife with danger and difficulty, this was no mean feat. She visited Rome, Italy, and also traveled 9 times to Santiago de Compostela, Spain.

She is often represented with a shell which was a symbol that showed the way to pilgrims along the Camino in Spain. When setting out on a journey, it would be good to bring Saint Bona with us in prayer. She is the patron of flight attendants, couriers, guides, pilgrims, travelers, and Pisa, Italy. Today, May 29th is her feast day. Saint Bona of Pisa, pray for us!

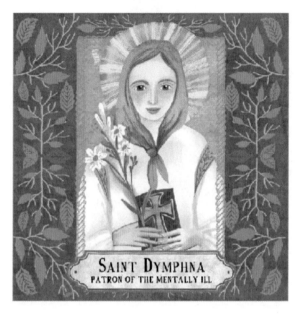

SAINT DYMPHNA
PATRON OF THE MENTALLY ILL

The town of Gheel, Belgium has a long-standing tradition of caring for the mentally ill. This was all because of Saint Dymphna.

In 7th-century Ireland lived the holy and chaste Dymphna. Sadly, when she was only a teenager, her mother passed away and her father began to go insane due to despair. Since Dymphna looked like his beautiful beloved wife, he wanted her for his bride.

To flee from her father, Dymphna, along with her priest confessor, Saint Gerebernus traveled to Gheel, Belgium. There, she used her wealth to build a hospice for the destitute and infirm. News of her acts of kindness in the region eventually allowed her father to find her. Sadly, when he found them, her father drew his sword and killed both Saint Gerebernus and Saint Dymphna.

The story does not end here though for many miraculous healings of the insane and possessed took place in the place where she died.

She is the patron of the mentally insane, sleepwakers, epileptics, possessed, victims of rape and incest, princesses, and runaways. She is also the patron of family happiness.

Today, May 30th is her feast day. Saint Dymphna, pray for us!

BLESSED VITALIS OF ASSISI
PATRON AGAINST BLADDER DISEASE

When he was younger, Vitalis spent his days in immoral activities but in time he realized the error of his ways and underwent a deep conversion. To atone for his previous life, he traveled to Europe's pilgrimage sites and then entered religious life as a Benedictine monk.

He chose to live simply, walking barefoot with only a container for water as his sole possession.

His holy life of prayer, virtue, and friendship with God allowed him to work miracles and healings throughout the region.

He is the patron of those with disorders of the bladder and genitals.

Today, May 31st is his feast day. Blessed Vitalis of Assisi, please pray for us!

JUNE

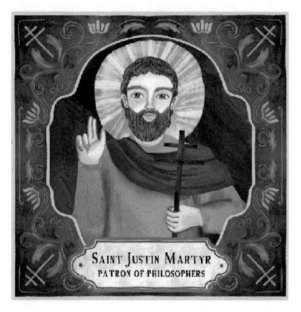

SAINT JUSTIN MARTYR
PATRON OF PHILOSOPHERS

Justin was dissatisfied with the worldviews taught to him throughout his childhood and youth. He spent much time in study and continually sought the truth. Finally, when he was 30 years old, he found what his heart was longing for in Christianity. Reading Scripture and drawing inspiration from the life and heroism of the saints gave him a fervor to defend the faith.

He dedicated his time to sharing his discoveries with pagans and established a school for debate and public discourse in Rome. Soon his fame spread throughout the region. Since being a Christian was punishable by death in 2nd century Italy, he was put on trial and executed along with some of his students.

"As by the Word of God, Jesus our Savior was made Flesh and had both Flesh and Blood for our salvation, so also the food which has been blessed by the word of the prayer instituted by Him is both the Flesh and Blood of Jesus Incarnate." - Saint Justin Martyr

He is the patron of philosophers, orators, speakers, and apologists.

Today, June 1st is his feast day. Saint Justin Martyr, pray for us!

SAINT ERASMUS
PATRON AGAINST STOMACH PAIN

Bishop Erasmus lived in 3rd-century Italy. He was often captured by Roman soldiers because Christianity was outlawed at the time and his life and teachings brought about many conversions. The first time he was imprisoned, an angel came and freed him!

One time, the cruel Western Roman Emperor Maximian ordered his arrest and forced him to visit a pagan temple. Upon entering, all the idols, fell and fire ravaged the area and idol worshippers. This so enraged the emperor that he had Erasmus put inside a barrel with sharp spikes jutting out. The barrel was made to roll down a hill severely injuring Erasmus. Again, an angel came and healed his wounds.

The emperor had him subjected to more torture. This time they planned to starve him to death but he somehow managed to get away. Once freed the holy bishop wasted no time and began to preach to unbelievers and convert many. His captors caught up with him and this time they disemboweled him, winding his intestines around a windlass.

He is the patron of those suffering from stomach pain, birth pains, appendicitis, and colic.

Today, June 2nd is his feast day. Saint Erasmus, pray for us!

SAINT CLOTILDE
Patron of Brides

There once was a princess born to the king of Burgundy, France in the 5th century. Her name was Clotilde which meant "Famous in Battle". She married young to King Clovis who did not share her Christian faith.

Being a devout believer in God, Clotilde prayed constantly for his conversion. Her desire was granted in the year 496 when Clovis turned to prayer on the eve of his battle against Germanic tribes. He made a vow to be baptized if he was given victory. When indeed they emerged triumphant, Clovis was baptized by Bishop Remigius of Reims.

Together, Clotilde and Clovis built the Church of the Holy Apostles in Paris. In the year 511, Clovis passed away. Sadly after that, Clotilde's 3 sons fought over the kingdom for many years. She instead dedicated her life to serving the poor and infirm.

Saint Clotilde's pious way of life converted many souls to Christianity. In fact, she is credited with spreading the faith in Western Europe.

She is the patron of brides, adopted children, people in exile, parents of large families, widows, and queens. She is also asked for prayers against the death of children and in cases of disappointing children.

Today, June 3rd is her feast day. Saint Clotilde, pray for us!

SAINT PETROC
PATRON OF DEVON & CORNWALL

In 6th-century England, there once was a powerful serpent that squash all the enemies of King Teudar. It took 3 saints - Saints Petroc, Wethnoc, and Samson to vanquish it.

Saint Petroc was known to be a man of humility. Though born a prince to a Welsh chieftain, and urged to rule the kingdom, he chose to serve God instead.

One story about him shows how even saints can be mistaken. After being an abbot for 30 years, Saint Petroc went on a pilgrimage to Rome. Upon his return, a downpour began and he said that the weather would clear in the morning. The next days, the opposite happened. The rain was continuous. Petroc in his hasty presumption responded by going on another pilgrimage as penance.

Saint Petroc traveled as far as India. There he was able to tame a wolf and even brought it back to England with him.

He was the founder of a monastery and a school.

This saint is the patron of many places in the United Kingdom and France. Among these are Devon, Cornwall, Exeter, and Saint-Meen.

Today, June 4th is his feast day. Saint Petroc, pray for us!

SAINT BONIFACE
PATRON OF GERMANY

A strong bishop leads many to lives of faith and upright moral convictions. In the 7th century, there lived Saint Boniface who was a good example of one. He courageously spoke and acted in defense of Christ despite the norms of his day.

There were many German tribes who worshipped and offered ritual sacrifice at an enormous old oak tree. Saint Boniface got an axe and with one swing cut a notch at its base. Surprisingly after that, an unseen force caused the giant tree to crash to the ground. The way the tree fell caused so much awe and reverence that the pagans converted. The wood from the tree was then used to build a church.

In her voyage across the ocean of this world, the Church is like a great ship being pounded by the waves of life's different stresses. Our duty is not to abandon ship but to keep her on her course. Let us stand fast in what is right and prepare our souls for trial. Let us wait upon God's strengthening aid and say to him "O Lord, You have been our refuge in all generations." - Saint Boniface

He is the patron of Germany, tailors, file cutters, and brewers.

Today June 5th is his feast day. Saint Boniface, pray for us!

JUNE

SAINT NORBERT OF XANTEN
PATRON AGAINST BIRTH COMPLICATIONS

In early 12th-century Belgium arose a disbelief in the sacraments. Saint Norbert, through his powerful and Spirit-filled preaching, was able to instruct the people, and the whole town was converted back to the faith. Once again, the truth of the real presence of Christ in the Holy Eucharist prevailed.

Saint Norbert did not start out having this exemplary missionary zeal. In fact, at one point, he shirked his duties to the church. But when he was almost killed by a thunderbolt during a storm, he began a 3-year period of reflection. Thereafter he became a changed man and seriously preached the Gospel in Germany, Belgium, and France. He founded the Norbertines or Premonstratensians.

During the schism caused by the death of Pope Honorius II, Saint Norbert, together with Saint Bernard of Clairvaux and Saint Hugh of Grenoble, brought peace to the Church.

He is the patron against birth complications, for peace, Bohemia, and the archdiocese of Magdeburg, Germany.

Today June 6th is his feast day. Saint Norbert of Xanten, pray for us!

SAINT DEOCHAR
PATRON OF THE BLIND

In the late 8th century lived a monk who served the Blessed Alcuin in the court of Charlemagne.

One day he encountered a young boy who was suffering from blindness. Wanting to help him, the monk prayed to God for his healing. Immediately, the young boy's eyes were restored to normal and he was cured! That monk was Saint Deochar.

Though he lived in solitude as a hermit in Bavaria, Germany, Saint Deochar was able to establish the first monastery in Herrieden. He also became its abbot.

He is often depicted in front of the tomb of the great Saint Boniface because in 819, he helped transfer his relics to Fulda.

He is the patron of the blind.

Today, June 7th is his feast day. Saint Deochar, pray for us!

SAINT MEDARD OF NOYON
PATRON FOR GOOD WEATHER

When Medard was a young boy, he was caught in the rain. Just then, an eagle hovered directly above him and sheltered him from getting wet. This story is why people take note of what kind of weather is observed on this saint's feast day. Traditionally, if it rained today, the next 40 days will be similarly wet. If the weather was fine, the next 40 days will be fair too.

Saint Medard was born into nobility in 5th-century France. Growing up, he was virtuous and studious. He took his religious vows when he was 33 years old.

In the year 530, he was ordained a bishop and he became one of the most renowned and beloved during this time.

Images of Saint Medard also picture him as laughing out loud. This is why he is also the patron against toothaches. He is the patron of brewers, peasants, vineyards, invoked for good harvests, and in cases of imprisonment, sterility, and mental disorders.

Today June 8th is his feast day. Saint Medard of Noyon, pray for us!

SAINT COLUMBA OF IONA
PATRON AGAINST FLOODS

Columba was born into an Irish royal family in the 6th century. He sought to serve God and became a monk and preacher.

He is said to have written poetry as well as 300 books and is known as one of the 12 Apostles of Ireland. Since he converted the Picts as well as King Brude, he is credited with spreading the faith in Ireland and Scotland.

A story handed down through generations recounts him as a man who banished a large sea creature from the Nesa (Ness) River.

At the end of his life, most of the people of Scotland were Christianized.

The day he died was June 9, 597 so today is his feast day. He is the patron of Ireland, Scotland, bookbinders, and poets. He is also invoked in case of floods.

Saint Columba of Iona, pray for us!

BLESSED EDWARD JOANNES
MARIA POPPE
PATRON OF LABORERS

Edward lived in 19th-century Belgium. He was the 3rd child in a large family that was pious and hardworking. His brother became a priest and his 5 sisters became nuns. Early on, he too felt called to the religious life. Even before he took his vows, Edward actively lived his faith. During World War I he worked as a battlefield nurse which took a toll on his health. His prayers to Saint Joseph were instrumental in freeing several prisoners of war. As a priest, he was often found in front of the Tabernacle.

Ordained in 1916 at the age of 25, he had a devotion to St. Therese of the Liseux, adopted her "Little Way, and visited her tomb in 1920. His ministry was geared towards alleviating the suffering of the poor, the dying, and to children. He served tirelessly throughout his life (even when he was sick) forming Eucharistic associations, teaching catechism, and writing about the errors of Marxism, secularism, and materialism.

He is the patron of Moerzeke, laborers, and military chaplains.

Today, June 10th is his feast day. Blessed Edward Joannes Maria Poppe pray for us!

SAINT BARNABAS THE APOSTLE
PATRON OF PEACE

"Barnabas" means "son of encouragement" or "son of consolation". He is one of the founders of the early Christian community in Antioch where believers were first called "Christians".

After becoming a Christian on Pentecost, he gave up all his property. Since he was born into a wealthy Jewish family, the proceeds from his large estate brought in a sizable amount that was then laid down in service of the Church (Acts 4:36). He proclaimed God's glory and redeeming work through the Cross wherever he went. He accompanied Saint Paul and afterward, Saint Mark doing missionary work. He was "a good man, full of the Holy Spirit and faith" - Saint Luke's description of Saint Barnabas in Acts 6:24

Saint Barnabas gave his all until his last breath. During his martyrdom, he held in his hands the Gospel of Saint Matthew which he had copied by hand.

Due in part to his death by stoning, he is the patron invoked against hailstorms. In experiencing theological conflict in his ministry, he is a patron for promoting peace.

Today, June 11th is his feast day. Saint Barnabas pray for us!

SAINT ONUPHRIUS
PATRON OF WEAVERS

Saint Onuphrius lived as a hermit for 70 years in Egypt in the 4th or 5th century. He patterned his life after Saint John the Baptist.

One day he encountered Paphnutius who wished to live as he did. The two men started talking and Onuphrius shared that he was led into the desert to experience all its discomforts and dangers by his guardian angel. Though days were filled with hunger, thirst, extreme heat, or cold, he was blessed by the weekly Sunday visit of an angel who brought him the Holy Eucharist.

After conversing until sunset, bread and water miraculously appeared outside the hermit's shelter.

It was to be Saint Onuphrius' last day on earth so he was blessed by Paphnutius. When he passed, Paphnutius covered his body with a cloak and buried him among the rocks. After which the shelter crumbled into the earth.

Saint Onuphrius' leaves covering is why he is the patron of weavers

Today, June 12th is his feast day. Saint Onuphrius, pray for us!

SAINT ANTHONY OF PADUA
PATRON OF LOST ARTICLES

Saint Anthony of Padua is one of the most famous saints of all time. He was born in 1195 in Lisbon, Portugal. Despite the chance to live comfortable as a wealthy nobleman, he chose a life of poverty, chastity, and obedience as a Franciscan friar. Every day he dwelt in a cave, only going out to attend Holy Mass and to sweep at a monastery nearby.

When a preacher did not show up, Anthony was forced by his brothers to do the day's sermon. His words were so powerful that he was thereafter appointed to be a missionary and teacher of theology, spreading the Gospel throughout Italy and France. He was so mesmerizing to hear that even the fish came to listen!

He evangelized countless souls through his preaching and miraculous signs. He is always depicted with the Child Jesus in his arms because one night, he was seen kneeling in ecstatic awe and wonder with a beautiful child embracing him. Saint Anthony's childlike simplicity and purity are also symbolized by a lily in his portraits.

Because he appeared in a vision to a novice who stole his prayer book, forcing the man to return the book, he is the patron of lost articles.

His feast day is today, June 13th. Saint Anthony of Padua, pray for us!

BLESSED FRANCISCA DE PAULA
DE JESUS ISABEL
PATRON OF THE BRAZILIAN POOR

In 1810 in São João del Rei, Gerais, Brazil, Francisca was born to a slave woman. She was an illegitimate child who never learned to read or write. When she was 10 years old, her mother died. It was then that she put herself in the care of the Blessed Virgin Mary.

Before her mother passed away, she told Francisca to dedicate her life to serving the poor. Francisca took this to heart and lived as a poor, lay celibate, refusing all the marriage proposals offered to her. Every day was a chance for her to minister to all who came to visit. She donated all she had to construct a Marian Chapel where the poor could come and find solace. She became known as the "Mother of the Poor".

When she died at the age of 85, there was a heavenly aroma that permeated her grave. 103 years later, her tomb was opened, and the smell of perfume once again filled the air. She was beatified in 1995 after the miraculous healing of a woman from pulmonary hypertension.

Today, June 14th is her feast day. Blessed Francisca de Paula de Jesus Isabel, pray for us!

SAINT GERMAINE COUSIN
PATRON OF THE UNATTRACTIVE

Born in 1579 in France to a poor family, she was always sick and was beset with scrofula (tuberculosis of the throat). Her mother died when she was still a baby. Sadly, her father and step-family cruelly maltreated her. She ate meager leftovers and was ordered to sleep in the stable or on a cupboard under the stairs. They often beat her and even threw hot water on her. At age 9, she tended the sheep and only left them to go to daily Mass. She asked the help of her guardian angel to watch over the sheep while she was at church and no harm ever befell them while she was away.

She loved to pray the Rosary with knotted string. She grew in piety, helping those even poorer than herself and teaching catechism to the children. She was always kind to all, even when mocked and called names.

One winter day her stepmother was cross with her thinking she had stolen bread in her apron. When she opened her apron, summer flowers in full bloom miraculously tumbled out! From then on, her family treated her with more respect.

When she died, more than 400 miracles were attributed to her intercession. Her body was found to be incorrupt. She is the patron of the unattractive, abandoned, abused, and sick. Today, June 15th is her feast day. Saint Germaine Cousin, pray for us!

SAINT LUTGARDIS
PATRON OF THE BLIND

Lutgardis was a normal teenage girl who was pretty and loved dressing up in different outfits. She was not particularly close to God but her life took a sudden turn when she turned 12. Her dowry was lost in a business deal so there was no chance for her to win a husband so she was sent to the Black Benedictine convent to become a nun.

No one expected her to take her vocation seriously but after a few years in the monastery, she had a vision of Jesus showing her His wounds. This inflamed a great love for God and became the first of many mystical experiences. Her meditations of Christ's passion were so deep that sometimes she was seen levitating and at other times, blood dripped from her forehead.

She had the first known vision of the Sacred Heart of Jesus that we celebrate today. After this, Saint Lutgardis overflowed with the supernatural gifts of healing, prophecy, and teaching scripture. In her later years, she grew blind and yet the saint counted this as a gift. More than ever, her blindness enabled her to focus on God alone and spend her days in silence and contemplation. She was so attuned with God that she knew the day she was to die.

Today, June 16th is her feast day. Saint Lutgardis, pray for us!

SAINT BOTULPH OF IKANHOE
PATRON OF TRAVELERS

There was once a barren land, so remote and reportedly haunted that people avoided it altogether. This place was in Ikanhoe, England. Despite another royal estate offered to them, it was at Ikanhoe that Saint Botulph, together with other saintly brothers, chose to build a Benedictine monastery.

It required much work and many helping hands but in 654 they were able to gather all the support needed. Soon the wild marshlands turned into farmlands and sheltering structures were raised.

Through these humble efforts, the order flourished through the centuries. Dozens of churches at city gates were named after the saint. These became places of refuge for travelers as journeys were fraught with all sorts of dangers during that time.

The Historia Abbatum, written in 654 describes him to be "a man of distinguished achievement, and learning, dedicated to the spiritual life".

He is the patron of travelers, farmers, sailors, and 7 cities.

Today, June 17th is his feast day. Saint Botulph of Ikanhoe, pray for us!

BLESSED OSANNA ANDREASI
PATRON OF SCHOOL GIRLS

From the tender age of 6, Blessed Osanna saw a vision of heaven. She saw angels and Jesus wearing a crown of thorns and carrying the cross. This set the tone for her whole life. She loved the Lord so much that she desired to share in His sufferings for humanity.

She endured many discomforts and even pains with great joy. Though she always tried to hide this, God granted her the grace to bear the stigmata. Her head, side, and feet would hurt so much that sometimes she couldn't walk. She was so far detached from earthly pleasures and enraptured by God that she hardly ever ate. God allowed her to have many mystical apparitions and experiences.

Blessed Osanna knew that all they had came from God. She gave away much of the family's wealth (which was considerable) to the poor and sick.

Today, June 18th is her feast day. She is the patron of school girls. Blessed Osanna Andreasi, pray for us!

BLESSED MICHELINA OF PESARO
PATRON FOR IN-LAW PROBLEMS

When Michelina's husband, Duke Malatesta died, only a brief period of time passed before her only son passed away too. Stricken with grief, she turned to God. Her chambermaid, Blessed Soriana, was a holy woman and her dear friend. She advised Michelina to pray and see things in a heavenly light. Michelina was thus consoled and she gave away all that she had (which was a large fortune) to widows and orphans. She also joined the Franciscan Third Order. She was granted mystical visions of Jesus speaking to her from the cross.

These actions prompted her family to think her insane. Eventually, she was released and she returned to doing good work. With Blessed Francis Zanferdini of Pesaro, she established the Confraternita dell'Annunziata (Confraternity of the Annunciation) which was dedicated to the care of the poor and sick.

She can pray for us when we have problems with our in-laws. She is also the patron saint for widows, mentally ill people, Pesaro in Italy, the Confraternita dell'Annunziata, and against the death of children.

Today, June 19th is her feast day. Blessed Michelina of Pesaro, pray for us!

BLESSED DERMOT O'HURLEY
IRISH MARTYR

Once in a while, there are men and women of great courage who are imbued with the grace to stand up for the truth. One such man was the Archbishop of Cashel in 16th-century Ireland.

During that time in history, the monarch Queen Elizabeth I wished to be honored as the head of the Catholic Church, and whosoever believed otherwise was punished for the crime of treason.

Knowing all the dangers he was exposed to, Blessed Dermot traveled to Ireland whilst hiding from the authorities. In order to prevent any trouble coming to those who gave him refuge, he eventually surrendered.

Despite pressure even from his sister to recant, the saint endured torture and death by hanging so as to be faithful. Before his execution, he forgave his torturers "with all his heart".

His tomb has become a pilgrimage site where many miracles are said to have occurred. Some have even seen visions of the bishop saying the Tridentine Mass there.

More than 260 Irish martyrs who died in the years 1537 to 1714. Today, June 20th is their feast day. Blessed Dermot O'Hurley and all Irish martyrs, pray for us!

SAINT ALOYSIUS GONZAGA
PATRON OF TEENAGERS

Born into a rich, noble life and growing up in a castle did not give the young Aloysius a predilection for luxury or wealth. Instead, at age 7 he experienced a profound conversion that led him to true spiritual riches.

His father wished for him to become a great military hero but his desire to serve in God's army was greater.

As a young boy, he prayed often, reciting the Psalms, the Office of Mary, and other devotions. He fasted 3 days a week and taught the Catholic faith to poor boys. He was untouched by 16th-century Florence's worldly society.

He developed kidney disease but was grateful for it because he was able to devote more time to prayer. When he turned 18, he gave away all of his inheritance to his brother and entered religious life as a Jesuit novice.

In 1591 a severe plague hit Rome and he chose to nurse the victims back to health. At the age of 23, he himself contracted the disease and joyfully died. He is the patron of teenagers, AIDS patients and caregivers, Catholic youth, Jesuit students, and invoked in case of sore eyes, pestilence, and to grow in the virtue of chastity.

Today, June 21st is his feast day. Saint Aloysius Gonzaga, pray for us!

SAINT THOMAS MORE
PATRON OF POLITICIANS

"What does it avail to know that there is a God, which you not only believe by faith, but also know by reason: what does it avail that you know Him if you think little of Him?" - Saint Thomas More

Saint Thomas More was someone who attained great influence, power and success in his career. He was an English judge, lawyer, philosopher and served as Lord High Chancellor of England to King Henry VIII.

He was a devoted family man who loved to make others laugh and be in good spirits.

He had it all but out of his love for God and the desire to uphold what was true and good, he made the ultimate sacrifice. As a consequence of his inability to declare the king as supreme head of the church in England and bow to the king's views on his royal divorce, he was imprisoned and eventually executed. Before his beheading, he said, "I die the King's good servant, and God's first".

He is the patron of politicians, civil servants, court clerks, lawyers, difficult marriages, large families, adopted children, widowers, step-parents and several schools and societies.

Today, June 22nd is his feast day. Saint Thomas More, pray for us!

SAINT JOSEPH CAFASSO
PATRON OF PRISONS

On the 15th of January, 1811 in Castelnuovo d'Asti, Italy was born a boy with spinal damage. He grew to be short and crippled and yet he was destined for sainthood.

He felt the call to the priesthood and took his vows when he was 22 years old. He taught moral theology at Turin, gave retreats, and served as a pastor at Saint Francis Church. Many came to him for confession. He oftentimes encouraged others to honor the Blessed Sacrament.

He wrote about the life of his namesake Saint Joseph saying, "A single word from him - a look, a smile, his very presence - sufficed to dispel melancholy, drive away temptation and produce holy resolution in the soul."

Saint Joseph devoted much of his ministry to those in prison. He instituted reforms so as to make their lives better and brought them the sacraments to bring them closer to God. At one time, he accompanied 60 new converts to the gallows after hearing their confessions and giving them absolution. He called them the "hanged saints".

He is the patron saint of prisons, prisoners, and prison chaplains.

Today, June 23rd is his feast day. Saint Joseph Cafasso, pray for us!

SAINT JOHN THE BAPTIST
PATRON OF BAPTISM

"Truly I tell you, among those born of women there has not risen anyone greater than John the Baptist.." - Jesus

John's whole life was dedicated to preparing the world for the coming of the Messiah. In fact, with the inspiration of the Holy Spirit, he "recognized" Jesus in the womb of the Virgin Mary even before he was born and "leaped" for joy! This holy man spoke the truth in love for all to hear. To save souls, he preached against wrongdoing and encouraged the people to turn to God. This got into trouble with Herod who had relations with his brother's wife.

Saint John the Baptist is revered not only by Christians but by Muslims alike. Like the Blessed Virgin Mary, he is also mentioned in the Quran.

He is the patron saint for baptism as well as monks, converts, convulsive children, farriers, cutters, bird dealers, epileptics, lambs, tailors, printers, motorways, and innkeepers.

Today, June 24 is his birthday and memorial. Saint John the Baptist, pray for us!

BLESSED DOROTHY OF MONTAU
PATRON OF DIFFICULT MARRIAGES

This holy woman is often depicted holding 5 arrows because of the many travails that she went through in life.

Dorothy was born in 14th-century Poland to a family of wealthy peasants. When she was 7 years old, a pot of boiling water fell on her burning off most of her body. She did not scream out or complain despite the torturous pain this caused. When asked she replied that when it happened she heard a loving voice say to her, "I will make a new person out of you."

This is when her spiritual awakening began and as she matured, she also grew in sanctity. At 17, she was married off to an abusive man in his 40s. He mocked her and sometimes even beat her and yet the more he did this, the more Dorothy offered up her misery and joined these to Jesus' sufferings. She ceaselessly cared for and loved her husband despite his cruelty to her. Through God's grace, he was eventually converted to the faith. When asked about this, Dorothy confided that her strength came from God as he told her that she was a "martyr for the indissolubility of marriage."

When her husband died, she became a Benedictine nun. Today, June 25th is her feast day. Blessed Dorothy of Montau, pray for us!

SAINT JOSEMARIA ESCRIVA
PATRON OF OPUS DEI

"I want you to be happy always, for cheerfulness is an essential part of your way. Pray that the same supernatural joy may be granted to us all." - Saint Josemaria Escriva

God can use anything to enkindle in us a desire for Him. For Saint Josemaria Escriva, it was the sight of bare footprints on snow by a monk. This moved him deeply and set him on his path to the priesthood.

Before his ordination, his father passed away so he supported his family while he studied. A year after he made his final vows, his powerful encounter with the Lord at a retreat inspired him to establish Opus Dei on October 2, 1928.

This organization composed mostly of laypeople grew rapidly and by the time of his death had a membership of 80,000 in over 5 continents.

Today, June 26th is his feast day. Saint Josemaria Escriva, pray for us!

St. Cyril of Alexandria
Pillar of Faith

We oftentimes wish to avoid trouble but as a defender of truth, trouble can find us. This was characteristic of the life of the bishop of Alexandria in 5th-century Alexandria, Egypt.

Cyril is one of the doctors of the Church, being one of the key figures during the Council of Ephesus. He stood up to defend orthodox truth against the heresy of the time, Nestorianism. Constantinople's bishop Nestoria proclaimed that Jesus had 2 separate natures: one divine and one human. Saint Cyril upheld Church teaching that Jesus' nature is a unity of being true God and true man.

For his steadfast pursuit to uphold truth, he is counted as among the Church Fathers and also a Doctor of the Church. He is also known as the Seal of all the Fathers.

Saint Cyril is the patron saint of Alexandria, Egypt.

Today, June 27th is his feast day. Saint Cyril, pray for us!

· SAINT IRENAEUS OF LYON ·

"The glory of God gives life; those who see God receive life." - Saint Irenaeus of Lyons

We owe much to the Church Fathers who have been able to preserve God's Word through their writings. Saint Irenaeus, who is known as the first great Western ecclesiastical writer and theologian, was able to preserve the deposit of faith by his defense of doctrine against Gnosticism. His work highlighted how the Old and New Testaments were united.

Born in 2nd-century Asia Minor (in modern-day Turkey), he was a disciple of Saint Polycarp of Smyrna. He was ordained in 177 and became the bishop of Lugdunum, Gaul, France.

"One should not seek among others the truth that can be easily gotten from the Church. For in her, as in a rich treasury, the apostles have placed all that pertains to truth, so that everyone can drink this beverage of life. She is the door of life." - Saint Irenaeus

Today, June 28th is his feast day. - Saint Irenaeus, pray for us!

SAINTS PETER AND PAUL
PILLARS OF THE CHURCH

Today's saints were men of great zeal, passion and love for God.

Saint Peter was an "ordinary" man, a fisherman who left all when he was called by Jesus. He was chosen by God to lead the Church as its first Pope and was renamed the "rock" so as to establish its foundation.

By the grace given by the Holy Spirit, he powerfully led souls to Christ by preaching the Gospel. He was able to work miraculous wonders. Even if only his shadow passed by the sick, they would be healed!

Saint Paul was a studious follower of the Jewish Talmud, he thought he was doing the right thing when he was arresting and persecuting Christians. Then, he experienced a dramatic conversion on the way to Damascus.

Realizing that he was fighting against God, he changed his course and became one of Christianity's greatest evangelists. Much of the Bible's New Testament is composed of his letters.

Both these saints gave their whole life in service to God until their martyrs' deaths. They are powerful intercessors for us!

Today, June 29 is their feast day. Saints Peter and Paul the Apostles, pray for us!

ST. DONATUS OF MÜNSTEREIFEL
PATRON AGAINST STORMS

One miracle leads to another. When the non-believer Faustus became severely ill, he was cured by the miraculous intervention of Saint Gervasius. This healing had a profound effect on his son Donatus so much so that he was converted to the faith. He adopted the beliefs of his Christian mother Flaminia.

When he turned 17 he joined the army and in a few years, he was promoted to captain of the 12th Imperial Roman legion.

During the battle of 166 with Germanic tribes, his troops found themselves in dire straights. Surrounded and unable to access water for days, the soldiers cried out to their Roman gods to no avail. Donatus secretly gathered his fellow believers to pray. God answered their prayers by sending a storm that quenched their thirst. Lightning attacked the German camp and brought triumph to Donatus' army.

Since Christianity was against Roman law, Donatus' faith led him to be executed.

He is invoked against storms, lightning, fire and the patron of bakers, wine makers, Buda, Hungary and Saint Donatus, Iowa.

Today, June 30 is his feast day. Saint Donatus, pray for us!

JULY

SAINT JUNIPERA SERA
PATRON OF VOCATIONS

Saint Serra lived in the 18th century and was a Franciscan friar. His mission was to serve God and to bring souls to baptism and live holy lives.

Every step Saint Serra took was marked with pain. This was due to his asthma and complications from a mosquito bite while on a mission trip. Despite his many struggles, he was able to convert thousands of Native Americans, founded 21 missions and promoted vocations.

Saint Serra is also called the "Father of California Wine" because the first vineyard of grapes from Spain was planted through his leadership. Aside from agriculture, he also taught the natives animal husbandry and crafts.

When abuses from Spanish soldiers became rampant, Saint Serra did all he could to protect the native Americans. He went against politicians as well as the military despite threats to his life and safety. He traveled to Mexico to plead with the viceroy, documented the cases and drafted the Representacion document which protected their rights.

Today, July 1st is his feast day. He is the patron of vocations. Saint Junipera Serra, pray for us!

ST. BERNADINE REALINO
PATRON OF LECCE

Bernardine Realino was born into a noble Italian family in the 16th century. He first became a lawyer, then a judge, then the chief tax collector. Afterward, he became the mayor of Cassine and then Superintendent of Naples.

After he came from a retreat he entered religious life as a Jesuit. He was then assigned to establish a college in the southern city of Lecce. There he soon became the most loved man because of his kind-hearted concern for the poor and the galley slaves.

A popular story about this saint is how his small wine pitcher would never run out until everyone has had their fill.

Today, July 2nd is his feast day. He is the patron of Lecce, Italy. Saint Bernardine Realino, pray for us!

SAINT THOMAS THE APOSTLE
PATRON OF THE DOUBTFUL

"In a marvelous way, God's mercy arranged that the disbelieving disciple, in touching the wounds of his master's body, should heal our wounds of disbelief." - from a homily by Pope Saint Gregory the Great

"Doubting Thomas" could not believe that Jesus had risen from the dead but when Jesus appeared again to the disciples, this time, he was there. Seeing Christ before him with his wounded flesh he exclaimed, "My Lord and my God!" - John 20:24-29

Saint Thomas fulfilled the Great Commission. He traveled as far as southern India to preach the Gospel, winning countless souls and building many churches along the way.

At one time he offered to build a palace for a king. The king gave him all the money he needed to do so but the saint gave all of this away to the poor. To explain his actions, he said that the palace he was to build was in heaven and not on earth.

Saint Thomas was a man of courage who was ready to die with Jesus when he went to Jerusalem. He was later killed by a spear while he was praying on a hill in Mylapur, India. Today, July 3rd is his feast day. Saint Thomas, pray for us!

SAINT ELIZABETH OF PORTUGAL
PATRON OF DIFFICULT MARRIAGES

Elizabeth was a beautiful, rich princess who became a queen at the age of 12. She was kind-hearted and pious, attending Holy Mass every day in thanksgiving to God. She spent her days doing works of mercy for the poor and the sick despite the ridicule of the other ladies of the court.

Sadly, her husband, King Diniz was unfaithful. For many years, Saint Elizabeth suffered through his infidelities by praying for his conversion. They had 2 children, Prince Constantia and Prince Affonso.

King Diniz's adultery resulted in illegitimate children and this caused Prince Affonso to rebel against him. War was waged between the armies of the king and prince and just when the clash was about to start, Saint Elizabeth rode onto the battlefield and persuaded both sides to make peace. Thus she was known as a peacemaker.

Before his passing, King Diniz turned to God, and Elizabeth's fervent prayer was answered. She then gave away all she had to the poor and joined the Franciscans as a tertiary.

Saint Elizabeth lived in 13th-century Spain and is the patron against jealousy and invoked by those with difficult marriages.

Today, July 4th is her feast day. Saint Elizabeth, pray for us!

SAINT DOMÈCE
PATRON OF HIP PROBLEMS

In 4th-century Turkey lived a physician named Domèce. He served the Roman Emperor Valens and was a non-believer and abuser of Christians.

One day, an angel appeared before him, reprimanding him for his behavior. Domèce realized the error of his ways and in response, hid himself in a cave on Mount Qouros in Armenia for 30 years.

As a hermit, he lived alone but still served those who came to him for healing. He received all including animals and cured many of them. Through his prayers, different illnesses were healed such as sciatica.

He is the patron invoked in case of hip problems.

Today, July 5th is his feast day. Saint Domèce, pray for us!

SAINT MARIA GORETTI
PATRON OF CHILDREN

Maria was born on October 16, 1890, in Ancona, Italy to a poor farm family. When she was 9 years old, her father passed away and Maria religiously prayed for his eternal repose by reciting a daily Rosary.

To earn a living, they had to move to the Serenelli farm. There, her mother worked the fields while Maria took on household chores and cared for her younger siblings. At the age of 11, the unthinkable happened. 20-year-old farmhand Alessandro Serenelli who often made advances on the young Maria attacked her and tried to rape her.

Maria shouted, "No! It is a sin! God does not want it!" and in a fit of rage, Alessandro choked and stabbed her 14 times. Maria was taken to the hospital and in agony, underwent surgery without anesthesia. She suffered for 2 days before passing away but before her last breath she said, "Yes, for the love of Jesus I forgive him..and I want him to be with me in Paradise."

While Alessandro was in prison, Maria appeared to him in a vision and he was converted to the faith. He asked forgiveness from Maria's mother.

Saint Maria Goretti is the patron of children, girls, martyrs, poor people, rape victims, and for the virtue of purity.

Today, July 6th is her feast day. Saint Maria Goretti, pray for us!

Blessed Maria Romero Meneses
SOCIAL APOSTLE OF COSTA RICA

A teacher with a kind heart is a powerful messenger of God's love and mercy to the world. Today's saint was born into a rich family in Granada, Nicaragua in 1902. Her father was a government minister.

At age 12, she was afflicted by rheumatic fever. She got so sick that she couldn't move for 6 months and her heart was permanently damaged. Thankfully, Our Lady, Help of Christians appeared to her in a vision and she was healed! This led her to enter religious life as a Salesian sister.

After her final profession in 1929, she served as a teacher of music, drawing, and typing to rich school girls while she taught catechism and trade to the poor. Her students were influenced by her way of life and many of them joined her to help the needy.

In time they were able to raise funds and improved the lives of the poor. Through Maria's initiative, recreational and food distribution centers in Costa Rica were instituted. Afterward, she established a school for poor girls and a clinic where volunteer doctors served. This was not enough. She also started up the Centro San Jose village by housing impoverished families.

Her fruitful efforts earned her the title of "Social Apostle of Costa Rica". Today, July 7th is her feast day. Blessed Maria Romero Meneses, pray for us!

SAINT KILLIAN
PATRON AGAINST RHEUMATISM

In the county of Cavan near the town of Mullagh, Ireland stands the holy well of Saint Killian. Every 8th of July, on his feast day, people come to the well to pray and remember his life.

Killian was born into Irish nobility and yet chose the religious life. He lived as an Irish monk and bishop in the 7th century traveling around Ireland and converting souls to the faith. He and his companions reached Wurzburg, Germany, and most of the pagan people were baptized into Christianity including Duke Gozbert.

Since Saint Killian secured the promise of the duke to leave his unlawful marriage to Geilana, she was infuriated and had the saint killed along with Saints Colman and Totnan.

Many cures have since occurred through his intercession. He is invoked by those who are sick with rheumatism, gout, and whitewashers. He is also the patron of places such as Bavaria, Germany, the archdiocese of Paderborn, Germany, the diocese of Wurzburg and Tuosist, County Kerry in Ireland.

Today, July 8th is his feast day. Saint Killian, pray for us!

SAINT PAULINA DO CORAÇÃO
AGONIZANTE DE JESUS
PATRON OF DIABETICS

Wherever she went, she did a world of good. Amabile Lucia Visintainer was born in 1855 to a poor yet God-fearing family in Trent, Italy. At the age of 10, her family, along with 100 other townspeople immigrated to Brazil in the hopes of a better life.

As a young teenager, she shared her Catholic faith with other children, cleaned the church, and visited the sick.

As a young woman in her 20's she and a friend cared for a woman with cancer and this became the start of the Congregation of the Little Sisters of the Immaculate Conception. By age 25 she was ready to make her final vows and she took on her new life with the new name of Sister Pauline of the Agonizing Heart of Jesus.

Many women were attracted by their way of life and joined Sister Pauline's order. In 1903, she journeyed to Sao Paulo to serve orphans, children of slaves, and elderly slaves who could no longer work. Her holy life was marked by prayer and service.

In 1938 she contracted diabetes and passed away from this disease. This is why she is the patron of diabetics. She is the first Brazilian saint. Today, July 9th is her feast day. Saint Paulina, pray for us!

SAINT AMALBULGA OF MAUBERGE
PATRON AGAINST ARM PAIN

This mother fulfilled her vocation well as she raised 5 saints: Saint Emebert, Saint Reineldis, Saint Pharaildis, Saint Ermelindis, and Saint Gudula.

Saint Amalburga lived in 7th-century Belgium. Her father was Saint Geremarus and a relative of Saint Pippin of Landen. She married the Duke of Lorraine, Count Witger.

When all her children were grown, she and her husband retired with the Benedictines. Count Witger lived as a monk at Lobbes, Belgium while she devoted the rest of her life to prayer and asceticism at the Mauberge Abbey.

She received the veil from Saint Willibrord of Echternach.

One story about this holy woman was when she needed to cross a lake, she did so with God's help by riding on a giant sturgeon.

She is the patron of those suffering from arm pain, bruises, and fever. She is also the favorite intercessor of farmers and the patron of Ghent, Belgium. Today, July 10th is her feast day. Saint Amalburga of Mauberge, pray for us!

SAINT BENEDICT OF NURSIA
PATRON AGAINST SORCERY

Saint Benedict was born into a noble Roman family and his twin sister was Saint Scholastica. He studied in Rome but was disheartened by his fellow student's waywardness. He longed for a holy life and journeyed to the mountains near Subiaco, Italy, and lived as a hermit instead. In solitude for 3 years, his food was supplied by a raven.

His saintly life drew the attention of an abbey and they asked him to lead them. Thus the Monte Cassino monastery was established where he wrote the Rule. This was the first of 12 he eventually founded.

He was so close to God that he could read consciences, knew what the future held, walked on water, and could save someone from the devil's attacks. His prayers even raised a monk from the dead. He put an end to many diabolic rituals and practices by destroying statues and altars.

One day, some monks in rebellion, put poison in Saint Benedict's cup. After blessing it, no harm came to him.

He is known as the founder of Western Christian monasticism.

He is the saint to call in cases of sorcery, witchcraft, poison, and kidney disease. Today, July 11th is his feast day. Saint Benedict, pray for us!

SAINT VERONICA
PATRON AGAINST HEMORRHAGING

Saint Veronica was one of the people who gave comfort to Jesus during His Passion. She braved the Roman guards to give Jesus her veil to wipe the blood and sweat off his face. During that time, the image of our Lord was miraculously imprinted on the cloth.

Her veil has been preserved through the ages and is known to have healed many, even curing the blind and raising the dead.

Saint Veronica is the patron to call in cases of bleeding and hemorrhages. She is also invoked by photographers, domestic workers, laundry workers, linen weavers, maids, housekeepers, seamstresses, and dying people.

Today, July 12th is her feast day. Saint Veronica, pray for us!

SAINT HENRY II
PATRON OF THE CHILDLESS

There once lived Good King Henry (as he was called) in the 10th century. He desired to live as a monk but was bound by his duty to reign as king. He was crowned as King of Pavia, Italy in 1004 and married Cunegunda whose holy life led her to be proclaimed as a saint by the Church.

King Henry II was intent on establishing peace in Europe. He was able to subdue rebellious factions and protect his people. He founded schools and started the construction of the cathedral in Basel, Switzerland (which took almost 400 years to build). He established Bamberg, Germany as an area for missionaries to bring the faith to Slavic countries.

He and his wife, Saint Cunegunda were active in bettering the lives of the poor and were extremely generous. They were also very prayerful. They did not have any children. Later in life, he was cured of an illness through the prayers of Saint Benedictine of Nursia. Upon the death of his wife, he considered entering religious life yet again but was influenced by an abbot to continue doing good works as king.

Saint Henry II is the patron of the childless, and against sterility.

Today, July 13th is his feast day. Saint Henry II, pray for us!

SAINT CAMILLUS DE LELLIS
PATRON OF THE SICK

On the 25th of May 1550 in Naples, Italy, Camillus was born. His father was a military officer and his mother died when he was still very young. Despite having painful abscesses on his feet, he spent his young life fighting the Turks and defending Naples as a soldier.

He enjoyed gambling so much that his debts piled up. Being a large man of 6'6", he took on work as a construction worker for the Capuchins. Being in their company led to his conversion.

Camillus felt a calling to the religious life but this was delayed due to a persistent leg injury. Seeking treatment, he was admitted to the San Giacomo Hospital for the terminally ill. In time, Camillus became its administrator.

Saint Camillus was known to tend to the sick even when he himself was suffering. He saw Jesus in everyone, especially in the infirm. God endowed him with the gifts of healing and prophesy. During his last days, he left his bed to tend to other patients.

He is the patron of the sick, nurses, and hospitals.

Today, July 14th is his feast day. Saint Camillus, pray for us!

SAINT BONAVENTURE OF BAGNOREGIO
PATRON FOR HEALING INTESTINAL SICKNESS

John of Fidanza was born in 1218 in Tuscany Italy. When he was young, he had a serious illness so his mother brought him to Saint Francis of Assisi for prayers. Thankfully, God heard their prayers and he was cured. At this Saint Francis exclaimed, "O BUONO VENTURA!" which means "O good fortune!" Since that time, John was called Bonaventure.

This miracle had a great impact on young Bonaventure's life and he professed his final vows as a Franciscan friar at the age of 22. He then became a bishop and later on, earned the title of Seraphic (Angelic) Doctor of the Church.

He wrote several books and is regarded as one of the greatest philosophers of the Middle Ages. His words teach us how to gain wisdom and joy in life.

He is invoked in cases of intestinal issues. He is also the patron of Bagnoregio in Italy, Cochiti Indian Pueblo, and Saint Bonaventure University in New York.

Today, July 15th is his feast day. Saint Bonaventure, pray for us!

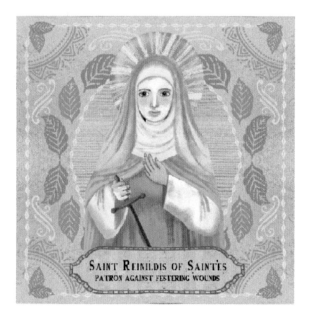

SAINT REINILDIS OF SAINTES
PATRON AGAINST FESTERING WOUNDS

Saint Reinildis came from a family of saints. Her mother was Saint Amalburga of Mauberge and her siblings lived holy lives. Among them were Saint Gudula of Brussels and Saint Emebert of Cambrai.

Her mother taught her the tenets of the faith and she lived virtuously, giving her whole self to Christ. She gave all her worldly goods to the abbey of Lobbes and stayed there for 2 years. She traveled to the Holy Land as a pilgrim and when she returned home, she brought back many relics.

She lived the rest of her days as a hermitess at Saintes, Belgium. When the Huns invaded the lands, she was given a martyr's death. This is why she is often depicted with a sword.

In the place of her death now stands the parish church of Sainte-Reinildis. Beside this is a well where many miraculous healings of the eyes have taken place.

She is the patron of those suffering from festering wounds and those with eye diseases. She is also the intercessor of Saintes, Belgium.

Today, July 16th is her feast day. Saint Reinildis, pray for us!

SAINT JUSTINA & SAINT RUFINA
PATRON OF POTTERS

In 3rd-century Seville, Spain, it was customary for people to offer worship to Roman gods by burning incense. The sisters Justina and Rufina did not do this for they were Christians. They sold earthenware pottery and they helped many of the poor people in the city with their earnings.

One day when there was a pagan festival, the locals wished to buy a large part of their wares as part of the ceremonies. Justina and Rufina refused to sell these as they would be used in rituals that would dishonor God. The people began to break all their pottery. Justina and Rufina then destroyed a statue of Venus. The people were enraged and the siblings were immediately arrested.

They were brutally tortured while given the chance to renounce their faith but they never gave in until their heroic death for God.

They are the patron of potters and of Seville, Spain. They are traditionally the protectors of the Giralda (which they are always depicted with on paintings) and the Cathedral of Spain. It is said that their prayers prevented damage to these structures during the 1755 earthquake in Lisbon.

Today, July 17th is their feast day. Saint Justina and Saint Rufina, pray for us!

SAINT GONÉRI OF TRÉGUIER
PATRON OF THE ANXIOUS

Born in the British Isles in the 6th century, Gonéri was the son of Saint Elibouban. When the Anglo-Saxons invaded his homeland, he escaped to the northwestern region of Brittany, France. There he lived as an exile among the Bretons, who were a Celtic people.

Wishing to be totally committed to God, he lived as a hermit in Tréguier. Sought out for his holy wisdom, he aided in the conversion of Prince Alwand to Christianity.

He is the saint to ask for prayers in case you are anxious or have a fever. He is the patron of Saint-Gonnery, Morbihan, Brittany, France.

Today, July 18th is his feast day. Saint Gonéri, pray for us!

SAINT PETER CRISCI OF FOLIGNO
FOOL FOR CHRIST

When he was young, Peter only lived for himself. He thought nothing of the afterlife and did not think much of what consequences his actions would bring upon himself or others.

Peter was in his 30s when his parents died. He was struck with thoughts of his own mortality and contemplated the emptiness of his life. He underwent a deep conversion of spirit. He gave away all his large inheritance to the poor. He then sold himself into slavery, thinking of giving more money to the needy but his buyer gave him his freedom back.

At this point, Peter stationed himself at the cathedral in Foligno, Italy, and spent his days cleaning it. As a penance for his former life, he wore sackcloth and begged for his daily meal. He would stay at the bell tower and sleep on the church steps. He regularly spoke to the people about God and they listened to him with intent. At times he would make a barefoot pilgrimage to Rome and Assisi.

His eccentric behavior in earned him the reputation of being a "fool for Christ".

Today, July 19th is his feast day. Saint Peter Crisci of Foligno, pray for us!

SAINT MARGARET OF ANTIOCH
PATRON OF NURSING MOTHERS

In the ancient city of Antioch (modern-day Turkey) lived a beautiful maiden named Margaret. She grew up as a devout Christian. One day, a Roman prefect saw her and was instantly enamored. Margaret made a personal vow to live a consecrated life, and never marry so the official exposed her as a Christian and she was arrested.

She was given the chance to escape harm if she would offer sacrifice to pagan gods but Margaret refused. Her torturers tried to burn her and then boil her but nothing worked. Each time, her prayers shielded her from any pain. Finally, she was executed by beheading.

Many call upon Saint Margaret's prayers in their time of need. Saint Joan of Arc once recounted that the saint appeared to her and gave her consolation. She is known to be one of the Fourteen Holy Helpers.

It is said that Margaret was once attacked by the devil in the form of a dragon. She was swallowed up within its belly but thankfully, she did not perish. At the time, she was carrying a cross and this caused the creature pain and it released her. From then on, she was associated with childbirth.

She is the patron of nursing mothers, against sterility and pregnant women. Today, July 20th is her feast day. Saint Margaret, pray for us!

JULY

SAINT PRAXEDES OF ROME
PATRON OF SINGLE WOMEN

In 2nd-century Rome lived a young woman named Praxedes. She was the daughter of Senator Pudens and Saint Claudia. She was the sister of Saint Prudentiana.

All her life, she treated others with kindness and loving care. She lived her life wholly for God as a consecrated virgin. Whatever wealth she had, she gave in service to the Church.

When Emperor Marcus Antoninus started arresting Christians, Praxedes rushed to their aid by hiding them in her home and providing for all their needs. She encouraged the persecuted to stand firm in faith and supported those in prison. She also ensured that those who were martyred were given proper burials.

All of her brethren's sufferings burdened her poor heart so much so that this led her to pray to God that He take her to Himself. God soon heard her prayer and she was taken up to heaven.

She is the patron of single women.

Today, July 21st is her feast day. Saint Praxedes of Rome, pray for us!

SAINT MARY MAGDALENE
PATRON OF PENITENT SINNERS

Mary was tormented day and night not by 1 or 2 but by 7 evil spirits. And yet Jesus came and freed her and exorcised the demons from her life. She became a new creation and received new life in Christ! She went through a radical conversion and started to dedicate her whole life to God. She, along with other women gave whatever means of support she had so Jesus and his disciples could preach the Gospel.

Her faithful devotion to Christ was undeniable as she was there at the foot of the cross His crucifixion and was also the first to announce His resurrection! She is often depicted holding an alabaster jar for many believe that she is the unnamed woman mentioned in the Bible who anointed the feet of Jesus with costly perfume using her long hair.

Down through the ages, many penitent sinners and all who desired to change their lives for the good have called on Saint Mary Magdalene as a strong intercessor. She is the patron of pharmacists, contemplatives, glove makers, hairdressers, perfumers, reformed prostitutes, tanners, and people ridiculed for their piety. She is also someone to ask prayers for in times of sexual temptation.

Today, July 22nd is her feast day. Saint Mary Magdalene, pray for us!

SAINT BRIDGET OF SWEDEN
PATRON OF EUROPE

Saint Bridget was beautiful, rich, powerful and married to a prince but she her heart wished to live for God and for heaven. The young Bridget was raised in the Catholic faith and she started receiving visions of Christ's passion at the age of 7. She wrote these down and a record of this survives to this day. Her writings inspired many of the faithful during the Middle Ages.

When she turned 13, she dutifully consented to an arranged marriage with Prince Ulfo of Nercia. Together they raised 8 children, one of whom was Saint Catherine of Sweden.

Saint Bridget's holy life led many people of influence to seek her counsel. She was a trusted advisor to King Magnus II and Queen Blanche of Namur. Her friends were priests and theologians.

When Prince Ulfo died, Saint Bridget renounced her title as a princess. She pursued the consecrated life as a Franciscan tertiary despite the ridicule of members of the court. She founded the Order of the Most Holy Savior in Vadstena, Sweden.

She is the patron of Europe, Sweden, and widows.

Today, July 23rd is her feast day. Saint Bridget, pray for us!

SAINT CHRISTINA THE ASTONISHING
PATRON OF MENTAL ILLNESS

The life of Saint Christina s nothing short of astonishing. When she was 21, she had what appeared to be an epileptic seizure and died. At the funeral Mass, she suddenly came back to life and to the amazement of all, levitated to the ceiling of the church! The priest told her to come back down and she instantly obeyed. She told everyone that day that she experienced going to hell, purgatory, and heaven. God then brought her back so as to pray for the souls in purgatory.

Christina seemed to acquire supernatural powers. When in the presence of someone who had done much evil, she was able to smell a foul odor emanating from that person. She could not stand the stench and hide by climbing a tree or literally flying away. She was unharmed by fire even when she would touch it or roll around in it. She could withstand being in freezing water during the dead of winter or being dragged by a mill wheel without injury.

She was a mystic in that she would experience ecstasies where in she would lead the souls of the dead to purgatory. Those who were in purgatory, she would lead to heaven.

She is the patron of those suffering from mental illness. Today, July 24th is her feast day. Saint Christina, pray for us!

SAINT JAMES THE GREATER
PATRON OF PILGRIMS

Since the 9th century, pilgrims have flocked to the Cathedral of Santiago de Compostela in Spain, led by scallop shells along the path. Through stars (compostela) that led the way, the saint's remains were discovered.

Saint James was a fisherman who was a follower of Saint John the Baptist. He was the son of Zebedee and Salome and the brother of Saint John the Apostle. He is the apostle called "the Greater" to differentiate him from the other Saint James who joined the apostles at a later time.

One interesting story about the saint was that he helped a boy come back to life after being dead for 5 weeks. The boy's father was notified of the miracle but he would not believe it. He was eating dinner at the time and exclaimed that his son was as dead as the roasted fowl on his table. At that instant, the cooked bird sprang to life, grew feathers, and flew away!

Saint James traveled to Samaria, Judea, and Spain preaching the Good News, and was the first of the apostles to be martyred.

He is the patron of pilgrim

Today, July 25th is his feast day. Saint James, pray for us!

SAINT ANNE
PATRON OF GRANDMOTHERS

"_While leading a devout and holy life in your human nature, you gave birth to a daughter nobler than the angels, whose queen she now is." - from a sermon by Bishop Saint John Damascene

Saint Anne is the mother of the Blessed Virgin Mary and the wife of Saint Joachim. She and her husband were well advanced in years when she conceived Mary. She was their only child. They took care of her and raised her in piety and love until she was 3 years old. After this, Mary was dedicated to God and served at the temple.

She is the patron of grandmothers, grandparents, homemakers, pregnant women, carpenters, broom makers, mothers, cabinetmakers, equestrians, seamstresses, stablemen, lacemakers, lost articles, miners, turners, the poor, the childless, Canada and France and many other places.

Today, July 26th is her feast day. Saint Anne, pray for us!

SAINT PANTELEON
PATRON OF BACHELORS

Panteleon was a 4th-century physician to Emperor Maximian. He was a Christian who at one point turned his back on God. He followed the ways of the world and fell into idolatrous practices. This way of life depressed him so with the help of the priest Hermolaus, Panteleon came back to the Church and became a devoted Christian.

As a single doctor, he gave away all his wealth to the poor and when they were sick, he treated them without ever being paid. Sometimes, he cured patients only by prayer.

During the persecutions of Emperor Diocletian, the other doctors notified the authorities that he was a believer. When he was brought to trial, Saint Panteleon challenged the court to see whose methods would bring healing to incurable patients - those of the pagan physicians or his. The palsied paralytic in their midst could not be helped by the other doctors but he was instantly cured by God through Saint Panteleon's prayers. Thus, many who witnessed this were converted.

The saint was given many chances to renounce his faith to avoid torture and death but he chose his eternal reward in heaven and he is known as one of the 14 Holy Helpers. He is the patron of bachelors.

Today, July 27th is his feast day. Saint Panteleon, pray for us!

SAINT ALPHONSA OF INDIA
PATRON OF THE SICK

Anna was born in 1910 in Kerala, India. Her ailments began when she was only 3 years old. For over a year, she was afflicted with infected eczema. Then, an accident occurred when she fell into burning chaff and her feet were badly injured. This left her partially disabled all her life.

By the age of 18, she responded to the call of religious life as a poor Clare nun and took on the name of Sister Alphonsa. Her duty was to teach primary school children who loved her gentle and cheerful demeanor.

Many times she could not come to class due to her being sick. In all the hardships she went through, Saint Alphonsa was long-suffering, patient, and silent, offering up her pains to God.

In 1945 she passed away from a stomach disease. After her death, the people asked the intercession of Saint Alphonsa and many miraculous healings took place. Many of them involved the children from the convent school and the straightening of clubbed feet.

She is the patron of the sick and against the death of parents.

Today, July 28th is her feast day. Saint Alphonsa, pray for us!

SAINT MARTHA OF BETHANY
PATRON OF HOMEMAKERS

"Know that even when you are in the kitchen, our Lord moves amidst the pots and pans." - St. Teresa of Avila

When we find ourselves often busy in the service of others, we can find a friend in Saint Martha. She who was preparing a meal for the most important guest of all - Jesus, was anxious and upset about many things. The Lord gently showed her what was most essential and that she need not be troubled.

God indeed accompanies us and can teach us profound truths even while we are doing the simplest of tasks. It is doing all things with love that matters the most.

In another biblical passage, Saint Martha shows us how to be full of faith at the time of our greatest need. Her brother Lazarus died and despite her grief, she proclaimed God's greatness.

She is the patron of homemakers, cooks, servants, innkeepers, butlers, lay single women, and the people of Villajoyosa, Spain.

Today, July 29th is her feast day. Saint Martha, pray for us!

SAINT PETER CHRYSOLOGUS
PATRON AGAINST FEVER

"Keep burning continually the sweet-smelling incense of prayer. Take up the sword of the Spirit. Let your heart be an altar." from a sermon by Saint Peter Chrysologus

In 5th-century Imola, Italy, Peter was converted to Christianity when he was an adult. Fully embracing his newfound faith, he entered into religious life as a deacon, then a priest, and eventually became the bishop of Ravenna in 433.

Many pagan beliefs pervaded the culture at the time and Bishop Peter upheld the deposit of faith staunchly. He built many churches and beautiful altars and preached the Truth with great eloquence. His skill was such that he was given the name "Chrysologus" which means "Golden Word".

To this day 176 of his sermons can still be read. In these one can learn with more clarity about Incarnation, the saints, salvation, and more. His wisdom led Pope Benedict XIII to proclaim him as a Doctor of the Church in 1729.

He is the patron against fever and in cases of mad dogs as well as Imola, Italy.

Today, July 30th is his feast day. Saint Peter Chrysologus, pray for us!

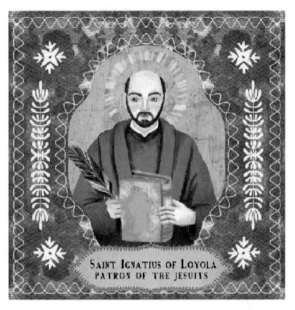

SAINT IGNATIUS OF LOYOLA
PATRON OF THE JESUITS

"It is not hard to obey when we love the one whom we obey." - Saint Ignatius of Loyola

Inigo Lopez de Loyola was born into Spanish aristocracy and dreamt of becoming a great leader one day. After fighting many battles, his leg was hit by a cannonball, and was forced to recuperate at home. The only reading material was The Golden Legend, a book about the lives of the saints, and The Life of Christ by Ludolph the Carthusian. When he read these, his life was forever changed.

He made a promise to God to live as a celibate and surrendered his sword to the Virgin of Montserrat. He lived an ascetic life in a cave and made pilgrimages to Rome and the Holy Land. In 1534, God led him to establish the Constitutions of the Society of Jesus. The Jesuits, as they are called these days, run over 500 universities and 30,000 members.

Saint Ignatius wrote the Spiritual Exercises which is still often read today. It is a good guide for discernment.

He is the patron of the Jesuits, and soldiers. as well as the military ordinariate of the Philippines.

Today, July 31st is his feast day. Saint Ignatius of Loyola, pray for us!

AUGUST

SAINT ALPHONSUS MARIA DE LIGUORI
PATRON OF CONFESSORS

Saint Alphonsus Maria de Liguori was born in 1696 to a pious, noble Italian family. He was a highly intelligent youth who completed his degree in both canon and civil law at 16 years old and by age 21, had his own legal practice, becoming one of the top lawyers at the time.

One day, he visited a hospital for the terminally ill and consequently received a vision that led him to lead a consecrated life. He entered the priesthood, studied theology, and was ordained at the age of 23.

For 30 years, he cared for the poor, taught the faith, instituted reforms in the seminary, and wrote many books. His preaching was simple and he was one of the kindest and most understanding of confessors.

He established the Redemptoristines women's order in 1730 and the Congregation of the Most Holy Redeemer in 1732. He did as many good works as he could despite having to endure daily pains from rheumatism. He fulfilled his vocation well and lived for over 90 years. He was proclaimed Doctor of the Church by Pope Pius IX in 1871. He is the patron of confessors.

Today, August 1 is his feast day. Saint Alphonsus Maria de Liguori, pray for us!

BLESSED CEFERINO JIMENEZ MALLA
PATRON OF THE ROMANI PEOPLE

There once lived a simple Spanish man who had little schooling but was known by everyone to be kind and good. He was a gypsy, a "Gitano" in Spanish, and he worked to improve relations between his people, the Romanis, and non-gypsies.

He was Ceferino Jimenez Malla, oftentimes known as "El Pele". He was baptized as an adult and was married to Teresa at the age of 51. He adopted his niece Pepita and raised her as his own.

One day, a man suffering from tuberculosis collapsed on the street. Ceferino unhesitatingly hoisted him onto his shoulders and carried him home. In gratitude, the man that he gave Ceferino a large sum of money. With this amount, he started a mule-trading business and became a successful businessman in the town of Barbastro.

When his wife passed away, he decided to serve as a city councilman. He generously served the church as Catechist, choir director, Rosary leader, and Eucharistic minister. He was a wise man whom the bishop sought out for advice. He also treated the poor and needy with dignity, giving what he could to better their lives. His desire to be close to God led him to become a Franciscan tertiary.

SAINT WALTHEOF OF MELROSE
CISTERCIAN MONK AND MIRACLE WORKER

Waltheof came from an English noble family and was descended from William the Conqueror, who was the grand-uncle of his mother Maud. His father was Simon, the second son of the Earl of Huntingdon. Saint Waldef of Northumbria was his grandfather. When his father passed away, they moved to Scotland and there, his mother married King David I.

In Scotland, he came under the tutelage of Saint Aelred of Rielvaulx who served the Royal household. His true calling was the religious life so he traveled to Yorkshire, England, and became an Augustinian canon and consequently the abbot of Kirkham. Afterward, he lived as a Cistercian monk.

Saint Waltheof was known to all as someone who loved God and His people, especially those in need. He was always gentle with those he was called to lead. His prayers were so powerful that miracles such as the multiplication of food, and healing of the sick (such as the blind receiving their sight) have been reported. He was also a mystic who had visions of Christ, heaven, and hell.

Today, August 3rd is his feast day. Saint Waltheof of Melrose, please pray for us.

SAINT JOHN MARY VIANNEY
PATRON OF PRIESTS AND CONFESSORS

"This is the glorious duty of man: to pray and to love. If you pray and love, that is where a man's happiness lies."- Saint John Mary Vianney

This wise and outstanding man of God came from simple beginnings. He was born in 1786 to a farm family and wasn't well educated. He was terrible at Latin and but what he knew of prayers and of the Catholic faith, he shared with other children.

When he was around 29 he was ordained and served in a small parish in France. There were only a few churchgoers. He started to get to know his parishioners by visiting their homes, giving priority to the poor and sick. He was so prayerful that he would spend days before the Blessed Sacrament, always offering penance for his flock.

In time, more and more people came to attend Holy Mass and go to confession. By 1855, 20,000 pilgrims came each year to Ars.

God endowed him with many spiritual gifts and he was also a miracle worker. He faithfully worked to bring people closer to God for 40 years.

He is the patron of priests and confessors. Today, August 4th is his feast day. Saint John Mary Vianney, pray for us!

SAINT OSWALD OF NORTHUMBRIA
PATRON OF ZUG, SWITZERLAND

Oswald was born into a royal family. He was a soldier who, upon winning a battle was proclaimed king. He then invited Saint Aidan of Lindisfarne to serve as the bishop of his kingdom. To encourage his people to live pious lives, he built many Churches and monasteries.

This saintly king saw what wealth he had as God's property and used it as such. One Easter day, when he was about to feast with Saint Aidan, some people arrived begging for food. Saint Oswald in all generosity of heart, gave all their food and whatever money he was carrying to the poor instead. Even the silverware was broken up and distributed to the needy.

Saint Aidan upon seeing this was moved to grasp the king's right hand and say, "May this hand never perish!"

Indeed, the hand has survived the test of time as a relic at Bamburgh Church. When he was attacked and killed by invaders, St. Oswald's pet raven of many years, carried his severed hand to an ash tree. When the arm fell on the grown, water sprang up and it became known as a holy well. Miraculous healings happened at the sites where he died.

Saint Oswald is the saint of Zug, Switzerland.

Today, August 5th is his feast day. Saint Oswald, pray for us.

BLESSED GEZELIN OF SCHLEBUSCH
PATRON AGAINST HEADACHES

In the 12th century, there lived a man called Gezelin. He devoted his life to God as a single layman and as a hermit. He spent his days tending the sheep as a Cistercian brother in Gut Alkenrath, Schlebusch, Germany.

In time, the people knew him as a miracle worker because when a drought swept over the land, Gezelin struck the earth with his shepherd's crook. Water sprung up from the spot where he hit and the people were saved! Since then, many people came to visit the spring and have reported miraculous cures.

He is invoked in cases of headaches, epilepsy in children, and eye disorders. He is also the patron of children.

Today, August 6th is his feast day. Blessed Gezelin, pray for us.

SAINT CAJETAN
PATRON OF JOB SEEKERS

As an infant, Cajetan's pious parents dedicated him to the Blessed Virgin Mary. As a young child, he was known to all as "The Saint". He excelled in his schooling and studied law in Padua, Italy. Though he was pressured to serve in government, his true calling was in the priesthood.

Cajetan, who came from a noble family was ordained at 36 and gave up his considerable wealth to build hospitals. Those inflicted with the plague often found him nursing them back to health. To help the poor improve their living conditions, and avoid loan sharks, he setup a bank that was later called the Bank of Naples.

He brought his flock closer to God in a playful manner by having them say prayers in exchange for his help.

All his life, he asked the Blessed Mother to intercede for him and one Christmas Eve, she appeared before Saint Cajetan and placed the Infant Jesus in his arms. In his last days, she came to him again and with a host of angels escorted him to heaven.He is otherwise known as "The Hunter of Souls". He is the patron of job seekers and the unemployed.

Today, August 7th is his feast day. Saint Cajetan, pray for us!

SAINT DOMINIC DE GUZMAN
PATRON OF ASTRONOMERS

Saint Dominic's mother, prayed fervently to God for a child and asked Saint Dominic of Silos' intercession. Soon she became pregnant and had a vision that the babe in her womb would be like a dog with a torch in its mouth setting all the world on fire. When the baby was born, she named him Dominic in honor of the saint of Silos. As the child grew, one day, she saw a star shining from his chest. This is why Saint Dominic is often depicted with a star.

Upon maturity, he became an Augustinian friar. His wisdom and knowledge of the faith enabled him to combat the heresy of Albigensianism.

During a time of discouragement, Saint Dominic saw the Blessed Mother in a vision. She told him to pray the Holy Rosary daily as well as encourage others to do so. The saint was greatly empowered to return to his mission and true to her word, the heresy ceased.

Along with Blessed Peter of Castelnau, they founded the Order of Friars Preachers (Dominicans) in 1215. Their rule was marked by living simply and prayerfully. He is the patron of astronomers and scientists.

Today, August 8th is his feast day. Saint Dominic, pray for us!

SAINT TERESA BENEDICTA
OF THE CROSS
PATRON OF EUROPE

"Anyone who seeks truth seeks God, whether or not he realizes it." - Saint Teresa Benedicta of the Cross

Edith Stein was born to a Jewish family on the 12th of October 1891 in Breslaw, Dolnoslaskie, Germany (now Wroclaw, Poland). She was the youngest of 7 children. Once she came into her teenage years, Edith lost all interest in Judaism. She had a brilliant mind and excelled in her studies. By the age of 25, she earned her doctorate in Philosophy.

Impressed by the faith of her Catholic friends, she read the catechism and fell in love with God. She was baptized in 1922. After 12 years, she joined the Carmelites and took on the name Teresa Benedicta of the Cross. She fulfilled her vocation as a writer, teacher, and lecturer.

World War II hit and both Catholics and Jews' lives were in danger. Her friends helped her hide, whisking her away to the Netherlands in 1938. The Nazis eventually caught up with her and she was arrested alongside her sister Rose. They both died in a gas chamber at Auschwitz. Saint Teresa Benedicta died on August 9, 1942.

She is the patron of Europe. Today August 9th is her feast day. Saint Teresa Benedicta of the Cross, pray for us!

SAINT LAWRENCE OF ROME
PATRON OF COOKS

Saint Lawrence did not lose his cheerfulness and sense of humor even in the midst of extreme pain. He is always pictured with a gridiron because that is what his torturers used. When he had been suffering on the hot metal for a long while, he said, "I'm well done on this side. Turn me over."

Known as the "keeper of the treasures of the Church", 3rd-century Roman Emperor Valerian commanded the saint to hand over all the wealth of the Church to him. Saint Lawrence came back with the poor, crippled, blind, and sick as he said that they were the church's true treasures.

He is the patron of cooks, butchers, brewers, comedians, confectioners, deacons, restauranteurs, cutlers, glaziers, laundry workers, librarians, schoolchildren, tanners, wine makers, seminarians, and stained glass workers. He is also invoked in cases of fire and lumbago.

Today, August 10th is his feast day. Saint Lawrence, pray for us!

SAINT CLARE OF ASSISI
PATRON OF TELEVISION

One day, a rich, young girl by the name of Clare heard the sermon of Saint Francis as he preached on the streets of Assisi. She later confided in him that she wanted to devote her life to God and this began their lifelong friendship. When she turned 18, she and her cousin stole away in the middle of the night to enter religious life. She took her vows from Saint Francis at the Church of Our Lady of the Angels.

Renouncing all her wealth, she and a growing band of women lived solely on alms and became totally dependent on God for her sustenance. They became known as the Poor Clares. In time, her mother and sisters joined them.

On one occasion, their convent was in danger from attackers. Saint Clare brought the Blessed Sacrament in a monstrance to the gates and prayed before it. This repelled the attackers and their convent was saved.

In time, she was too ill to leave her bed so an image of the Holy Mass was placed before her on the wall. This is why she became the patron of television.

Today, August 11th is her feast day. Saint Clare of Assisi, pray for us!

SAINT JEANNE DE CHANTAL
PATRON FOR IN-LAWS

"Hold your eyes on God and leave the doing to him. That is all the doing you have to worry about." - Saint Jeanne de Chantal

In 1592, the beautiful, young Jeanne was wed to Baron de Chantal. The pair lived in a castle and was blessed with 4 children. After just 8 years of marriage, tragedy struck. Her husband was accidentally killed during hunting and he died in her arms.

After this event, Jeanne submitted fully to God's holy will and wished to live celibately. Thereupon she had no choice but to live with her father-in-law which was not to her liking. She lived a life of prayer and grew closer to God. One day, she had a vision of a holy man who was to be her spiritual director. Later in life, the vision was fulfilled. That man was Saint Frances de Sales who became her mentor and close friend. They exchanged letters for many years.

In 1610, Saint Jeanne established the Order of the Visitation of Holy Mary and oversaw 69 convents. Through the order, women who were sickly or elderly were still able to enter consecrated life.

Saint Jeanne is the patron for in-laws and the forgotten. Today, August 12th is her feast day. Saint Jeanne de Chantal, pray for us.

SAINT RADEGUNDE
PATRON FOR DIFFICULT MARRIAGES

Born into a royal family in the year 518, Saxony, Ragunde was destined to be queen. She was the princess of Thuringia in Eastern Germany. When her father was killed by the Franks, she became the hostage of King Clotaire I. While in captivity, she was converted to Christianity.

Her faith became her refuge. After some time, Clotaire forced her to be his bride. Being a queen was no consolation. Her husband had many wives and treated her badly. He beat her and blamed her for not giving him any children.

In 550, Clotaire killed Radegunde's brother. This tragedy led her to escape the castle. With Saint Medard's help, she took on religious vows.

Saint Radegunde was then able to live a peaceful life of prayer and great acts of charity. She lived an extremely simple life, living only on vegetables and water. She was found to have the gift of healing. She founded the Abbey of the Holy Cross which in an age of violence and war, was a beacon of beauty, piety, grace, and nobility. In their chapel was a piece of the True Cross of Christ.

She is the patron for difficult marriages. Today, August 13th is her feast day. Saint Radegunde, please pray for us.

SAINT MAXIMILIAN KOLBE
PATRON OF DRUG ADDICTS

One day, the mother of a mischievous boy asked him in exasperation, "What will become of you?" The child felt remorse. That night, the Blessed Virgin Mary appeared to him holding two crowns - one white, the other red. She asked the boy if he was willing to accept either of these crowns.

"The white one meant that I should persevere in purity and the red that I should become a martyr. I said that I would accept them both." - Saint Maximilian Kolbe, After this vision, his life dramatically changed.

He grew to be a pious man and joined the priesthood in 1914. He and his brothers formed the Immaculata Movement that sought to win souls for the faith. God called him to bring the Gospel to Japan in 1930 and they founded a monastery in Nagasaki and since its location was on the other side of the mountain, it was shielded from the atomic bomb. The brothers were then able to care for the sick and injured survivors.

Due to poor health, he returned to Poland but then the Nazis invaded the country and Saint Max was arrested. In Auschwitz, he volunteered to take the place of a man who was to be executed and served his fellow prisoners until his last breath.

Today, August 14th is his feast day. Saint Maximilian Kolbe, pray for us!

SAINT STANISLAUS KOSTKA
PATRON OF LAST SACRAMENTS

Stanislaus became seriously ill to the point of death. Being a devout Catholic, he longed to receive Jesus in the most Holy Eucharist. But alas, there was no one there who was willing to call a priest for him.

Stanislaus prayed to God and asked Saint Barbara's intercession as she was his personal patron saint. Saint Barbara appeared to him in a vision with two angels. Then, he was able to partake Communion.

Soon after this, he was miraculously cured! He attributed this to the intercession of the Blessed Virgin Mary. She also guided Stanislaus to enter religious life as a Jesuit. His family was opposed to this idea but Stanislaus was determined to serve God.

He traveled to Rome for further studies and was a Jesuit novice by 1567. He became the friend of Saint Peter Canisius and was a student of Saint Francis Borgia. The next year on the feast of the Assumption of Our Lady, he contracted a high fever and passed away to receive his heavenly reward.

He is the patron of last sacraments, Poland, against broken bones, and aspirants to the Oblates of Saint Joseph.

Today, August 15th is his feast day. Saint Stanislaus Kostka, pray for us!

SAINT STEPHEN OF HUNGARY
PATRON OF HUNGARY

This king was born in Esztergom, Hungary in the year 969. He was named Vajk at birth. His family did not know the faith and it was only when he was 10 years old that he became a Christian. He was baptized together with his father and took on the name of Stephen.

Born to rule, he became the King of the Magyars and was married to Blessed Gisella of Ungarn who was the sister of Emperor Saint Henry II. Both kings desired that all of their people worship God and turn away from their pagan idols so they spread the Good News throughout their lands.

King Stephen united the Magyar clans and finally, while he reigned, there was peace. He established monasteries and organized dioceses to care for his people. Merchants and pilgrims had safe passage in his kingdom, compared to other dangerous routes.

He brought up a godly son, Saint Emeric whose tutor was Saint Gerard Sagredo.

He is the patron of Hungary, kings, bricklayers, masons, stonecutters, and against the death of children.

Today, August 16th is his feast day. Saint Stephen, pray for us.

SAINT HYACINTH
PATRON OF POLAND

Saint Hyacinth was a priest and Doctor of Law and Sacred Studies in 12th-century Poland.

While he was working with his uncle, Bishop Ivo Konski, in Rome, he saw a miracle take place through the prayers of Saint Dominic de Guzman. They soon became friends and Saint Hyacinth became one of the first Dominicans.

He generously shared the Dominican way of life with his native countrymen and many were converted. He then traveled to Lithuania, Sweden, Scotland, Russia, Turkey, Greece, and many other places in Europe spreading the faith.

One time, a monastery became under siege and Saint Hyacinth surprised all when he was able to carry a heavy statue of the Blessed Mother and a crucifix out of harm's way. He normally would not be able to lift this weight by himself so this was quite miraculous.

He is the patron of Poland, against drowning, Lithuania, Camalaniugan, and Ermita de Piedra de San Jacinto, Tuguegarao in the Philippines.

Today, August 17th is his feast day. Saint Hyacinth, pray for us!

ST. HELENA OF CONSTANTINOPLE
PATRON OF DIVORCED PEOPLE

Helena was born in the year 248 in Bithynia, Asia Minor. She converted to the faith as an adult and was married to a powerful official in the Roman Empire. She gave birth to a son - now known as Constantine the Great.

Sadly, her husband mistreated, divorced and sent her away. After his death, her son Constantine stepped into power and sent for her return.

Saint Helena used all her wealth and influence to share the truth and beauty of the Catholic faith with all the people. She had many churches built throughout the region.

At 80 years old, she went on a pilgrimage to find the True Cross of Christ. They discovered 3 crosses. Unable to determine which one was Jesus', they brought it to a woman who was seriously ill. When she touched one of them, she was immediately healed proving its authenticity.

She had the Church of the Holy Sepulchre built on the site where the cross was found and brought back pieces of the Cross for veneration to Rome and Constantinople.

She is the patron of divorced people and those with difficult marriages.

Today, August 18th is her feast day. Saint Helena, pray for us!

SAINT SEBALDUS
PATRON AGAINST COLD WEATHER

Saint Sebaldus lived in 8th-century Germany and was able to bring many souls to God.

A time came when food grew scarce for the missionaries. Saint Sebaldus took some stones and blessed them. These turned into bread and wine!

One day a heretical man spewed blasphemies at him. In response, the saint prayed and suddenly the earth shook and opened up where the man was standing. Through the earth's cracked surface, the remorseful man asked for forgiveness. When he did this, the ground swelled so much that the man was able to resurface.

The saint's prayers were so powerful that when a cruel master blinded his servant, he prayed over the peasant, and his sight was restored!

Another story goes that during a severe winter, Saint Sebaldus had compassion for the poor who were experiencing great discomfort. He took some icicles and used these in place of firewood to warm them. This is why he is the patron against cold weather. He is also the intercessor of Bavaria and Nuremberg in Germany.

Today, August 19th is his feast day. Saint Sebaldus, pray for us!

SAINT BERNARD
OF CLAIRVAUX
PATRON OF BEEKEEPERS

On August 20, we remember the "Honey-Sweet Doctor of the Church" or "Doctor Mellifluus". His articulation of the truths of the faith ignited a deep love for God in the hearts of his hearers. This is why he is the patron saint of beekeepers.

This holy monk was Saint Bernard of Clairvaux. To start his day, he would ask himself, "Why have I come here?" The answer was always, "to lead a holy life." This indeed, he did.

As a Benedictine priest, he established the Monastery of Clairvaux and 160 houses for nuns. His ministry flourished and the number of monks increased to 700. His life's work included the reform of the Cistercian order, the defense of the Church from Albigensianism, and bringing peace to the schism led by anti-Pope Anacletus II. He was counsel to King Louis the Fat and King Louis the Young.

So as to save Christians from being killed or sold into slavery in Mesopotamia, Saint Bernard helped organize the Second Crusade.

August 20 is also the National Honey Bee Day in the United States. Today is his feast day. Saint Bernard of Clairvaux, please pray for us!

POPE SAINT PIUS X
PATRON OF FIRST
COMMUNICANTS

Early on, Giuseppe Melchiorre Sarto knew he had a calling to live the consecrated life. Since he was young, he would go to Mass, eat breakfast and walk 6 kilometers to school. Because they were poor, he carried his shoes so as not to wear them out.

He was ordained in 1858. He was an active priest in the life of the community and since his reputation for piety grew, he earned the nickname "Don Santo".

Despite being busy restoring the church, expanding the hospital, working to help indigent students get a proper education, and many other good works, he often accompanied young children to prepare for their First Communion.

In 1903 he was chosen as Pope and took on the name of Pius X. He promoted reading the Bible and did what he could to support missionaries. He brought back the use of Gregorian Chants at Mass. He encouraged the frequent reception of Holy Communion and made it possible for children to receive their First Communion by the age of 7 instead of 12 or 14. Hence, he is the patron of first communicants, pilgrims, and 7 dioceses.

Today, August 21st is his feast day. Pope Saint Pius X, please pray for us.

SAINT PHILIP BENIZI
MIRACLE WORKER AND HEALER

Saint Philip was born into an Italian noble family in the 13th century. He had a brilliant mind and was an excellent student. By the age of 19, he had already received his doctorates in both medicine and philosophy.

After about a year of medical practice, he received a vision of the Blessed Virgin Mary and his life took a dramatic turn. He put aside everything he was doing to join the Servite Order as a lay brother. In 1258 he took his final vows and used all his intelligence and abilities to heal wounded souls instead.

While preaching in Forli, Italy, a man screamed at him and violently hit him. Instead of retaliating, Saint Philip turned the other cheek as it is commanded in the Holy Bible. The man was taken aback and converted into a believer. We now know that man as Saint Peregrine Laziosi.

Saint Philip was known for his love of prayer. He would often hide himself away in a cave in order to meditate. When 2 Dominicans visited him, they were so awestruck by the man's goodness that after their meeting, they zealously pursued the priesthood.

Today, August 22nd is his feast day. Saint Philip Benizi, pray for us!

SAINT ROSE OF LIMA
PATRON OF LATIN AMERICA

This lady was so beautiful that she attracted so many admirers. Since she made a vow to live solely for God, she put pepper and lye on her face so as to ruin her complexion and dissuade all her suitors.

Rose was born in 1586 to a couple who immigrated to the New World from Spain. She was known to all as a kind and obedient daughter who lived simply. She loved praying in the garden, tending to her crop of vegetables, and sewing embroidery to help her family earn a living. Whatever she had, she also shared with the needy.

She often experienced heavenly visions and was able to immerse herself totally in meditation. At times God allowed her to be afflicted with illnesses and yet she offered these up for the salvation of souls. She is the first saint born in the Americas. She is the founder of social work in Peru.

Aside from being the patron of Latin America, she is also the intercessor for the Philippines, India, Peru, West Indies, and many other places. She is invoked by embroiderers, florists, gardeners, needleworkers, and people ridiculed for their piety. She is the patron against vanity.

Today, August 23rd is her feast day. Saint Rose of Lima, please pray for us!

SAINT BARTHOLOMEW
THE APOSTLE
PATRON FOR NEUROLOGICAL DISEASES

Good friends are great blessings in our lives especially when they share the Good News with us. Saint Bartholomew was introduced to Jesus, the Truth, the Way, and the Life by Saint Philip, his close friend.

Saint Bartholomew is also known as Nathaniel by modern-day scholars. He was one of the 12 apostles who lived and traveled with Jesus as He walked the earth. After Jesus rose from the dead, traditional records mention that he went on a mission to India, Mesopotamia, Parthia, Lycaonia, and Ethiopia.

Together with Saint Jude "Thaddeus", he is credited to have formed the first Armenian Christian community in the 1st century and thus he is the patron saint of the Armenian Apostolic Church.

Saint Bartholomew was a martyr for the faith. Since he was able to convert Armenian King Polymius to Christianity, this was considered a grave offense against the Roman Empire. The king's brother ordered the saint's torture and execution. He is often represented with a knife because he was flayed alive.

He is the patron of those with neurological diseases.

Today, August 24th is his feast day. Saint Bartholomew, pray for us!

SAINT JOSEPH CALASANZ
PATRON OF CATHOLIC SCHOOLS

Many of us have noble dreams to help better society. Saint Joseph Calasanz worked hard and became the founder of the first free public school in modern Europe. At a time when the poor had no access to education, he was able to provide them with a much brighter future.

Joseph was born in a castle in 16th-century Spain. He had an excellent education and finished degrees in canon law and theology. He then had a powerful vision that led him to give away all his wealth and inheritance. He discerned that he was for the religious life and was ordained at age 27.

When a plague hit the region in 1595, Fr. Joseph worked tirelessly to tend to the sick. At the time, there were many poor and homeless children who roamed the streets. Fr. Joseph routinely brougthm them to school but due to their meager earnings, teachers did not want to take them in.

Papal support enabled his group to do good work and this has continued to this day. St. Joseph Calasanz is the patron of Catholic schools, students, and schoolchildren.

Today, August 25th is his feast day. St. Joseph Calasanz, pray for us!

SAINT TERESA DE GESU JORNET Y IBARS
PATRON FOR THOSE REJECTED BY RELIGIOUS ORDERS

In Lerida, Spain, in the year 1843, lived a girl who loved God so much that she wished to give her all to Him.

Little Teresa was raised on a farm. She was a kind and compassionate child who always took care of the poor. She would bring them to her aunt for food and care.

Later on in life, earned her living as a teacher. Her true longing was to live as a nun so she tried to join the Poor Clares monastery. Due to the anti-clerical laws at the time, she could not be accepted by the monastery. Instead, she joined the Secular Carmelites.

On the advice of her spiritual director, she gathered together other women who wished to live consecrated life. They became the Little Sisters of the Poor at Barbastra in 1872 and was able to make her final vows the following year. The congregation grew to 58 houses with Saint Teresa as their superioress.

She is the patron of people rejected by religious orders.

Today, August 26th is her feast day. Saint Teresa de Gesu, please pray for us!

SAINT MONICA
PATRON OF MOTHERS

When she was a child, Saint Monica learned about God through her family. When she was of age, she consented to an arranged marriage with Patricius who was not a good husband to her. He was an unbeliever, unfaithful, and had a bad temper. Saint Monica prayed for him until he converted to Catholicism on his deathbed.

Saint Monica was grateful to God for saving her from the vice of alcoholism. She had a pagan son who lived an immoral life. She prayed for him fervently and asked for the guidance of Saint Ambrose of Milan. Most of her life was spent praying for him but she never gave up. Her prayers were finally answered when Augustine was overwhelmed by God's mercy and converted to the faith. He became one of the most important church fathers, Saint Augustine of Hippo.

She is the patron of mothers, alcoholics, difficult marriages, disappointing children, and homemakers.

Today, August 27th is her feast day. Saint Monica, please pray for us!

SAINT AUGUSTINE OF HIPPO
PATRON OF THEOLOGIANS

"Our hearts were made for You, O Lord, and they are restless until they rest in You."- Saint Augustine of Hippo

4th-century Numidia, North Africa was home to one of the most influential saints in all of history and Western civilization.

He was raised a Christian but was ambitious and chose to live solely for himself. He sought whatever would give him pleasure and lived in a wild, pagan way. He lived with a woman outside of marriage and had a son with her. This caused deep sadness for his mother, Saint Monica who never ceased to pray for the salvation of his soul.

It was in Milan when he was 30 years old that finally God was able to shine His truth into Augustine's troubled heart. He was baptized by Saint Ambrose. Upon his conversion, he gave up all his wealth, donated this to the poor, and founded a monastery. He became the bishop of Hippo and many of his writings survive to this day

He is the patron of theologians, printers, brewers, 7 dioceses, and 7 cities.

Today, August 28th is his feast day. Saint Augustine, please pray for us.

SAINT JEANNE JUGAN
LITTLE SISTERS OF THE POOR FOUNDRESS

"Little Sisters, take good care for the aged, for in them you are caring for Christ Himself." - Saint Jeanne Jugan

Jeanne grew up in 18th-century France during the French Revolution. It was a time of persecution for Christians but despite this, her mother taught her about the Catholic faith.

At 16, Jeanne went to work for a very generous Christian woman. They would often serve the poor and needy by giving them food and care. It was during this time that Jeanne's desire for a consecrated life grew. She chose to decline marriage proposals and live singly for God.

At 25, Jeanne gave away most of what little she had to the poor. She continued serving them in a hospital. She focused all her energies on helping the needy and even went door to door begging for support for poor widows. Other women followed Saint Jeanne. Their group became known as the Little Sisters of the Poor with Saint Jeanne as their superioress. She dedicated her life to charitable service until her last breath.

Today, August 29th is her feast day. Saint Jeanne Jugan, please pray for us.

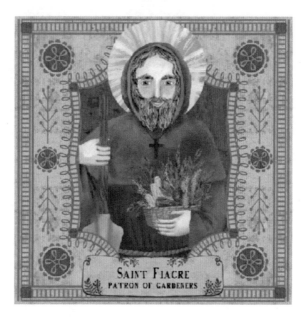

SAINT FIACRE
PATRON OF GARDENERS

Educated in an Irish monastery, Saint Fiacre learned all about healing herbs. Because he wanted a garden to cultivate food, he asked the bishop for land. The bishop said that he could have whatever area he could entrench in a day. He proceeded to walk, dragging a spade behind him, around the place he wanted to secure. Wherever his spade touched, the ground miraculously sunk, trees fell, and bushes were uprooted. The garden became a place of pilgrimage for centuries.

Saint Fiacre prayed over the blind and touched their eyes and they would be able to see! Other recorded healings were of fever, hemorrhoids, and polypus. A certain type of fistula or tumor was named after him because of the effectiveness of his methods. It is now known as "le fic de S. Fiacre".

In times past, the Hotel de Saint Fiacre in Paris rented carriages out and these were eventually replaced by taxis. People started calling these cabs as fiacres without them knowing the saint. So he became the patron saint of taxicab drivers.

He is the patron of gardeners. Today, August 30th is his feast day. Saint Fiacre, pray for us!

SEPTEMBER

SAINT GILES
PATRON OF THE HANDICAPPED

Saint Giles was born into a rich family in Athens Greece. When his parents died, he gave all his wealth away to the poor.

Wherever he went, there were miracles. He lived as a hermit in a cave and dedicated his whole life to God in ascetic living and prayer. His only sustenance was milk that came from a deer.

One day, a hind rushed into his cave. A royal hunting party was hot on its pursuit and an arrow was shot into the cave but instead of hitting the hind, it hit Saint Giles' leg. Crippling him, the king sent for a doctor despite the saint's protests and wanting to be left alone. From then on, the king often visited the saint.

The story became known and people flocked to the cave to seek his wisdom. One time, when the saint was explaining about the Blessed Mother's perpetual virginity, 3 lilies suddenly appeared on the sandy ground.

The king built the monastery of Saint Gilles du Gard with Saint Giles as its first abbot. A small town eventually grew around the monastery and became a place of pilgrimage.

He is the patron of the handicapped, abandoned and beggars. Today, September 1st is his feast day. Saint Giles, please pray for us!

SAINT NONNOSUS
OF MONTE SORATTE
PATRON AGAINST WEAKNESS

In the 6th century, on Monte Soratte, north of Rome, lived Saint Nonnosus, a Benedictine monk. In his writings, Pope Saint Gregory the Great described him as a kind and good-natured man. He was close to God and lived the faith devoutly.

One day, Saint Nonnosus wanted to plant cabbage in the monastery garden. Before this was possible, a huge rock had to be moved. 50 pairs of oxen could not make it budge. Saint Nonnosus prayed over the rock and it moved by itself!

Another time, the people grew troubled since the olive harvest that year was very meager and they would starve. Saint Nonnosus prayed over the empty jars and olive oil appeared in them saving the town from poverty.

The holy saint's prayers were also known to have restored a broken oil lamp!

He is the one to ask for prayers if you are suffering from weakness, infirmity, or kidney ailments. He is also the patron of the Diocese of Nepi-Sutri and Castel Sant'Elia in Italy and Freising, Germany.

Today, September 2nd is his feast day. Saint Nonnosus, pray for us!

POPE SAINT GREGORY THE GREAT
PATRON OF MUSICIANS

Today's saint compiled melodies and chants to be used in Holy Mass. These are now known as Gregorian Chants.

Also known as the "Father of Fathers", Pope Saint Gregory the Great lived in 6th-century Rome. His aunts Emiliana and Tarsilla, as well as his great-grandfather Pope Felix III, are also proclaimed saints in the Catholic Church.

He received an excellent education and afterward became the prefect of Rome for a year. He could have spent his wealth on a life of leisure but he chose to enter religious life, sell everything he owned, and used the money to build 6 monasteries in Sicily and Rome. His own home was turned into a Benedictine monastery.

In the year 590, he was unanimously elected to be the 64th Pope of the Catholic Church. He then did what he could to bring liberation to souls across Europe, sending missionaries to England, France, Spain, and even Africa.

He is one of the 4 great Doctors of the Latin Church and the patron of musicians, singers, and choir boys. Today, September 3rd is his feast day. Pope Saint Gregory, please pray for us!

SAINT IDA OF HERZFELD
PATRON OF BRIDES

In Hofstadt, Westphalia in the northwestern region of Germany stands the beautiful church of Saint Ida of Herzfeld. Every year in September, the people gather to celebrate "Ida Week" and the saint's relics are marched through the city in memory of her life and be blessed.

Ida's holy life is an example to all as she was kind and generous of heart. She lived in the years 770 to 825.

She was born into royalty, being the granddaughter of Charlemagne, the King of the Francs, and grew up in his court. Her father was a count and she was given in marriage to Lord Egbert, a Saxon Duke. Their marriage was a happy one.

Inspired by a dream, Ida and her husband constructed the church and monastery of Herzfeld. It became the first Catholic community in the area.

Sadly, her husband died while still young. Even then, Saint Ida continued to serve God and the poor. She knew that her true home lay beyond this life and to remind her of eternity, she had a daily habit of filling up a stone coffin with food. All the food was then given to the needy.

She is the patron of brides and widows. Today, September 4th is her feast day. Saint Ida of Herzfeld, please pray for us!

MOTHER TERESA OF CALCUTTA
SAINT OF THE GUTTERS

"I am a little pencil in the hand of a writing God who is sending a love letter to the world." - Mother Teresa.

Agnes Gonxha Bojaxhiu was born on August 26, 1910, in Skopje, Albania. When she was only 9 years old, her father passed away. At the age of 12, she wanted to become a missionary in India. As she matured, she felt a calling to religious life, and by 1926, her dream of working as a missionary teacher in Calcutta, India was fulfilled.

At 38 years old, she responded to God's proddings in her heart to serve the poorest of the poor who were dying in the streets. She said, "Each one of them is Jesus in disguise."

For a time she did this all on her own but afterward, some of her students, who were well-to-do, helped her. She also lived simply like those she served, starting each day with prayer at 4 in the morning. Her only possessions in life were a bucket and 2 saris.

In 1950, she established the Congregation of the Missionaries of Charity. By 1997, the group was operating in 123 countries.

Today, September 5th is her feast day. Saint Teresa of Calcutta, please pray for us!

SAINT MAGNUS OF FÜSSEN
PATRON AGAINST VERMIN

One day, Saint Magnus was walking around the monastery and a great big bear approached him. The bear motioned to him, allowing him to see that the area was rich with iron ore.

To reward the bear, the saint gave it some cake. Knowing this could help the town, the saint went back to the abbey and collected some tools (with the bear following closely behind him). He also called other monks to accompany him. When they were ready, the bear led them to all the sources of iron ore in the mountains. This is how the townspeople made a living and this eventually became the region's main industry.

Another time, a place called Kempten was treacherously full of snakes. Saint Magnus came and shooed all the snakes away from that area.

Saint Magnus was a Benedictine priest who lived in the 7th century in Fussen, Bavaria (modern-day Germany). He was mentored by Saint Columban and Saint Gall at Arbon. He established the monastery at Fussen.

He is the patron against vermin, snakes, caterpillars, hailstorms, and lightning. He is also known to pray for the protection of crops.

Today, September 6th is his feast day. Saint Magnus, pray for us!

SAINT CLOUD
PATRON OF NAIL MAKERS

Saint Cloud was born a prince in Gaul in the year 522. His father was King Clodomir and his mother was Clotilde. He was the grandson of King Clovis and Saint Clotilda.

Though he was in line for the throne, he renounced the throne as he desired only to serve God as a hermit.

In Provence, he lived a life of simplicity and quiet prayer in a hermitage. There he grew in holiness and wisdom under the guidance of Saint Severin. Because the people soon found out that he had the gift of healing, they flocked to him and the area became a place of pilgrimage.

Avoiding the crowds, Saint Cloud returned to Paris where the people rejoiced at his return. With the wealth his uncle bequeathed to him, he built a monastery there in honor of Saint Martin of Tours. By divine revelation, he knew the day he was to die and after his passing, many miracles occurred near his grave.

He is the patron of nail makers.

Today, September 7th is his feast day. Saint Cloud, please pray for us!

BLESSED
ANTOINE-FRÉDÉRIC
OZANAM

While still young, Antoine-Frederic experienced doubts about his Catholic faith. With the help of his teacher Fr. Abbe Noirot, he was enlightened. He soon wrote Réflexions sur la Doctrine de Saint-Simon in defense of the Church.

Antoine-Frederic studied law in Paris and then later married Amelie Soulacroix. They had a daughter, Marie. He worked in the judicial service in Lyons and then became a teacher.

He used his literary talents to inspire charitable service for those in need. With opposing voices challenging him and his friends, they would hold lively debates. One time, someone said, "What is your church doing now? What is she doing for the poor of Paris? Show us your works and we will believe you!"

It was then that Blessed Antoine-Frederic with the help of his students, established the Society of Saint Vincent de Paul in 1833. By the time he passed away, the membership had grown to 2,000. The international organization of volunteers continues its mission of uplifting the poor to this day.

Today, September 8th, is his feast day. Blessed Antoine-Frederic Ozanam, please pray for us!

SAINT PETER CLAVER
SLAVE OF THE SLAVES

Pedro Claver Corbero grew up in 6th-century Catalonia, Spain, He responded to God's calling in his life to enter into religious life and was ordained a Jesuit priest at the age of 20. He was greatly encouraged by Saint Alphonsus Rodriguez to serve as a missionary in America.

Seeing the pitiful plight of African slaves as they arrived from ships into Cartegena, he ministered to the sick and cared for their physical as well as spiritual needs. He tirelessly lobbied for humane treatment and worked to improve their lives on the plantations for 40 years. His friendship with them converted 300,000 to the faith.

The joy in their eyes as they looked at us was something to see. This was how we spoke to them, not with words but with our hands and our actions." - from a letter by Saint Peter Claver

He is the patron of African missions, African Americans, slaves, foreign missionaries, inter-racial justice, the Missionary Sisters of Saint Peter Claver as well as many places such as Columbia.

Today, September 9th is his feast day. Saint Peter Claver, please pray for us!

SAINT NICHOLAS OF TOLENTINO
PATRON OF THE SOULS IN PURGATORY

Saint Nicholas was an Augustinian friar who served the city of Tolentino in 1274. He brought peace to that war-torn place. Every day, he radiated Christ's love whether by enlightening souls with his preaching, visiting prisoners, or blessing the sick and curing them. His fasts were rigorous and his prayers lasted all night, especially for those recently deceased.

One time a tragedy struck. A hundred children died from drowning. Saint Nicholas came and prayed over them and they came back to life! Another story goes that he was once served a roasted fowl. Since he was a vegetarian, he made the sign of the cross over the bird and it resurrected and flew out the window!

When he himself contracted a serious illness, he saw a vision of the Blessed Mother, Saint Augustine of Hippo, and his mother Saint Monica. They instructed him to eat bread dipped in water. Once he obeyed, he was instantly healed. From then, Saint Nicholas would pray over moistened bread to cure others of various ailments. Today Saint Nicholas Bread is still present at his shrine.

He is the patron of the holy souls in purgatory, babies, animals, dying people, boatmen, and sailors. Today, September 10th is his feast day. Saint Nicholas of Tolentino, please pray for us!

SAINT JEAN-GABRIEL PERBOYRE

Jean-Gabriel was born in 1802 in the south of France. He was a model of piety to other youth. He entered the Congregation of the Mission of Saint Vincent on Christmas day and was ordained in 1825.

Due to his sanctity and wisdom in teaching dogmatic theology, he was appointed as superior at the Saint Flour seminary. After some time, a fervent desire grew in his heart to be a missionary to China. He prayed and pleaded with his superiors to allow him to preach, suffer and die there.

At age 33, he finally reached Macao and began studying the language. His dedication to sharing the Word of God won many souls for the Kingdom.

After 4 years, persecution against Christians began in China. One of his newly baptized converts betrayed him for 30 ounces of silver. The authorities clothed him with rags, bound him, and lashed him with bamboo rods.

Not unlike our Lord, the saint was executed on a cross atop a hill named "Red Mountain". He suffered much to proclaim Jesus Christ as Lord.

Today, September 11th is his feast day. Saint Jean-Gabriel Perboyre, please pray for us!

SAINT GUY OF ANDERLECHT
·PATRON OF BACHELORS·

Saint Guy was raised in the fear of the Lord. Despite not having much himself, Guy habitually served the needy as well as the sick. He was a hard worker in the fields but his desired more to commune with God.

Sometimes an angel would do the plowing so Saint Guy could spend more time in prayer. As much as he could, he would stay at the church so the priest assigned him to be the parish sacristan. At this point, he decided to live in the church and would often spend the whole night praying.

On one point in his life, he set off as a barefoot pilgrim to Rome and then to Jerusalem. He worked for a time as a guide at these holy places. Though he was never ordained, he lived chastely and piously.

When Saint Guy passed away, many healings and miracles were attributed to him. An annual festival was celebrated around his grave. After some time, his grave could not be found but it was a horse who uncovered it. This is why he is the patron of workhorses.

He is also the patron of bachelors, sacristans, and farmers. He is invoked to pray for the protection of sheds and stables and in cases of epilepsy, and rabies. Today, September 12th is his feast day. Saint Guy, please pray for us!

SAINT JOHN CHRYSOSTOM
PATRON OF SPEAKERS

"God asks little, but He gives much." - Saint John Chrysostom

He is called the greatest Greek Church Father and his sermons won him the acclaim of being "golden-mouthed" from which the name "Chrysostom" is coined.

He spoke with clarity and courage the truths of the faith knowing some of his hearers would not take his words with ease. His preaching challenged the rich to share their wealth with the poor and the clergy to be reformed. He also sought to strengthen marriages and uphold justice in his sermons (some of which lasted for 2 hours).

The reluctant bishop of Constantinople's words angered many of the nobles and he was exiled for this.

He is the patron of speakers, orators, lecturers, preachers, and those afflicted with epilepsy.

Today, September 13th is his feast day. Saint John Chrysostom, please pray for us!

SAINT NOTBURGA ·
PATRON OF WAITRESSES

Though she loved to work and serve others, Saint Notburga loved God more than these. She was a simple peasant whose priority was to attend Holy Mass before doing her daily duties.

One day, her master demanded that she not go to mass but work instead. She replied, "Let my sickle be judge between me and you." She threw her sickle into the air and lo and behold, it did not come down but remained hoisted up in the air. Everyone was dumbfounded by the miracle. Saint Notburga was then able to go to church.

Sometimes, her mistress would catch her in the act of giving away food to the destitute. Once, she stopped the saint in her tracks and demanded she show her apron. The food in her apron miraculously turned into wood shavings and vinegar!

In her last days, she asked her employer the Count to let 2 oxen carry her body on a wagon and bury her where the oxen would stop. The oxen drew the wagon to Saint Rupert's Chapel so that is where she was buried. It is widely reported that many miracles occurred at her grave.

She is the patron of waitresses, peasants, servants, and farm workers.

Today, September 14th is her feast day. Saint Notburga, pray for us!

SAINT CATHERINE OF GENOA
PATRON OF WIVES

Catherine grew up to be prayerful and kind. She desired to be a nun only to be turned away by the convent. Three years later, her parents arranged for her to marry the nobleman Giuliano Adorno. It was a sad union for her husband turned out to be violent, cruel, and unfaithful. He wasted away all their money. They were also childless.

Feeling hopeless, Catherine went to confession and encountered the Lord. He revealed to her in a vision of her all-encompassing love for her and she was convicted of her sins. This event strengthened her all her life.

She went home filled with the Holy Spirit and began to love and serve her husband despite his waywardness. In time, he converted. Together, they put God at the center of their home and served the poor and sick.

Upon her husband's passing, Catherine became a Franciscan tertiary and started writing down the divine revelations she received during her visions. The Holy Office, during her canonization process, declared that her writings alone were proof of her sanctity.

She is the patron of wives. Today, September 15th is her feast day. Saint Catherine of Genoa, please pray for us!

SAINT ANDREW KIM TAEGON
PATRON OF THE KOREAN CLERGY

"It is for Him that I die. My immortal life is on the point of beginning." - Saint Andrew Kim Taegon's last words

On August 21, 1821, Andrew Kim was born into a Korean noble family. He grew up during a time when Christianity was strictly prohibited and his father was executed for his faith.

When he was 15, Andrew Kim, like his parents, converted to the faith and was baptized. He not only believed but responded to God's call to the priesthood. He traveled 1,300 miles to Macao, China to study in seminary. He also continued his formation at Bocaue, Bulacan, Philippines

After 9 years he was ordained and subsequently returned to Korea. He was able to bring many to the church to experience fullness life in Christ.

He was the first priest to die a martyr's death in Korea. He is the patron of all Korean clergy.

Today, September 16th is his feast day. Saint Andrew Kim Taegon, please pray for us!

ST. EMMANUEL NGUYEN VAN TRIEU

This man was a soldier defending his people but more than that, he was a faithful soldier to his king and Lord Jesus Christ.

Emmanuel Nguyen Van Trieu was born in 1756 in Phu Xuan (modern-day Hue), Vietnam. He was raised in the Catholic faith by his parents. His father was in the military and died in battle. At age 15, Emmanuel joined the army.

When he retired from being a soldier, he entered into the seminary with the Paris Foreign Mission Society under Bishop Emmanuel Obelar - Kham. He then served the Church as a parish priest in the apostolic vicariate of Cochinchina.

In 1798, the authorities outlawed Christianity. Many believers were asked to step on the Holy Cross as a sign of recanting their faith but those who were courageous did not and were tortured and executed.

Saint Emmanuel stood firm and was one of those who were arrested and martyred for the love of Christ. His head bone is still preserved at the Duong Son Parish Church in the Archdiocese of Hue.

Today, September 17th is his feast day. Saint Emmanuel Nguyen Van Trieu, please pray for us!

SAINT JOSEPH OF CUPERTINO
PATRON OF AIR TRAVELERS

Joseph was born in a stable to a poor couple so he grew up with hardly any education, unable to read or write. He couldn't explain a single verse of the Bible except for Luke 11:27.

Desiring to be a priest, he needed to pass an oral exam. The bishop randomly opened the Bible and pointed at a verse for Joseph to explain. Lo and behold, the verse was Luke 11:27! He passed the text easily!

Since he was 8 years old, he received heavenly visions and this continued into his adulthood. The mere mention of God, the Blessed Mother, the saints, or upon hearing the church bells ring would render him motionless and in a state of divine ecstasy. He was so entranced by the beautiful revelations as well as angelic music that he was often seen floating!

Because of his joyful disposition and piety, despite his lack of education, he was ordained as a Franciscan priest at the age of 25. He had an unshakeable faith and observed 7 seasons of Lent every year to honor Christ's Passion.

He is the patron of air travelers. Today, September 18th is his feast day. Saint Joseph of Cupertino, please pray for us!

SAINT JANUARIUS OF NAPLES
PATRON OF BLOOD BANKS

To this day, miracles are witnessed 3 times a year in Naples.

There, dried blood collected from Saint Januarius who died in the year 305, would liquefy on the days designated in his honor. Thousands would gather every year to see this supernatural phenomenon.

There have been rare occasions in recent times when the blood did not liquefy. This is considered an ominous sign.

Saint Januarius was born in 3rd-century Naples to a rich noble family. He became a priest early on in life at the age of 15 and was declared a bishop by the time he was 20.

Christianity was banned and was punishable by death so Saint Januarius was arrested and thrown into the arena with wild, hungry bears. The animals refused to attack him so they were executed by beheading.

When Mount Vesuvius erupted, Naples was in grave danger and the people asked Saint Januarius to pray for their safety. Thankfully, Naples was spared and on December 16th, he was honored as their patron.

He is the patron of blood banks, volcanic eruptions, and Naples, Italy.

Today, September 19th is his feast day. Saint Januarius, pray for us!

SAINT EUSTACHIUS
PATRON OF DIFFICULT SITUATIONS

One day a Roman general while on a hunting trip, saw a stag with a glowing cross between its antlers. The sight instantly converted him to Christianity. He was then convicted that he would suffer for Christ. Together with his wife and 2 sons, they were all baptized and he was given the Christian name, Eustachius.

Becoming a Christian cost him much. The government confiscated his property and took his wife and children away.

When barbarians attacked Rome, he was called back to fight and they won the battle. Afterward it was a custom to sacrifice to pagan gods after every victory, Saint Eustachius and his family refused to deny God.

This resulted in a sentence of death. They were thrown to hungry lions but the animals only acted like large kittens around the family and did not harm them. They were eventually martyred by fire when they were put in a large bronze bull.

Saint Eustachius is one of the Fourteen Holy Helpers. He is the patron of difficult situations, fire prevention, firefighters, hunters, torture victims, and places in Spain and Italy.

Today, September 20th is his feast day. Saint Eustachius, pray for us!

SAINT MATTHEW
THE APOSTLE
PATRON OF ACCOUNTANTS

Saint Matthew was a tax collector, despised by most of the people. He would sit at the tax office, counting and collecting money every day. In the midst of his routine, God entered into his life, and he was saved by grace.

Saint Matthew's life from that moment was changed. He lived, ate, talked, and walked with the Lord Jesus throughout His public ministry.

At around 41 and 50 AD, many years after Jesus' crucifixion, Saint Matthew began writing what we know today as the Gospel of Matthew. He wrote it in Aramaic so that the Jewish people would know that the Messiah had come and that their waiting was over. He preached to the Jews for 15 years. It is also said that he went to other places where Jews congregated such as Ethiopia.

He is the patron of accountants, bankers, customs officers, financial managers, guards, security forces, stock brokers, tax collectors, the diocese of Trier, Germany, the diocese of Washington, D.C., and 5 other cities.

Today, September 21st is his feast day. Saint Matthew the Apostle, please pray for us!

SAINT IGNATIUS OF SANTHIA
PATRON OF CHAPLAINS

Every day, thousands of people came from near and far to receive this simple Capuchin friar's blessing.

Lawrence Belvisotti was born in 1686. His devotion to God prompted him to join religious life and he took on the name Ignatius after Saint Ignatius of Loyola. His first role was to be the parish priest in Vercelli and after 6 years he was offered a diocesan role but out of his great humility, he declined. He opted instead to be a novice at the Capuchins of Turin. It was there that he served as a sacristan and then served as the novice master. When he developed an eye disorder, he stepped down for around 2 years.

Upon recovery, he took on the role of head chaplain for the King of Piedmont's armies. He took special care of the injured. When the war ended, he returned to Capuchin Hill and worked as the religious instructor for lay brothers as well as a confessor.

During the latter years of his life, he lived in Turin and ministered constantly to the poor and ill.

He is the patron of chaplains.

Today, September 22nd is his feast day. Saint Ignatius of Santhia, please pray for us!

SAINT PADRE PIO

"Pray, hope, and don't worry. - Saint Padre Pio

On May 25, 1887, Saint Padre Pio was born in the south of Italy to a farm family. From a young age, he knew that he had a special calling to the priesthood and he entered the Capuchin friars novitiate in Morcone, Italy. He was ordained at the age of 22.

His whole life was immersed in prayer. On September 20, 1918, while he was meditating on the Lord and looking at the cross, he received the stigmata. He is the first priest to be blessed with this mystical gift. In World War II, he was seen flying in the skies in order to protect the town from being bombed. The people also saw Padre Pio levitate, cure the sick just by touching them, and even bilocate.

Word soon spread of the miracles surrounding the saint and people started coming in droves. They lined up for confession and Saint Pio would be in the confessional for hours. He was so close to his guardian angel and to God that he had supernatural knowledge of people's sins before they even confessed them.

Today, September 23rd is his feast day. Saint Padre Pio, please pray for us!

BLESSED ANTON MARTIN SLOMŠEK
PATRON OF EDUCATORS

Today, a whole region is almost 100% literate because of this one man.

Anton Martin Slomsek was born to a peasant family in the year 1800. He grew up in the Austro-Hungarian empire of Savinjska, Slovenia.

When he was 24 years old, he made his final vows to the priesthood and served as a parish priest for 5 years. Afterward, he took on the role of spiritual director for the Klagenfurt seminary.

During that period, when the Germans ruled the land, the native language was fast disappearing so he taught this to the seminarians.

As the bishop of Lavant (modern-day Maribor), he shared his love for the Slovenian culture and language by establishing new schools, writing, and editing books. He propagated devotion to God by distributing a weekly newspaper with his sermons and episcopal statements.

He is the patron of educators, students, writers, poets, winemakers and the diocese of Lavant. He is the first Slovene to be beatified.

Today, September 24th is his feast day. Blessed Anton Martin Slomsek, please pray for us!

SAINT SERGIUS OF MOSCOW
PATRON OF RUSSIA

In 14th-century Russia lived a holy man called Sergius. He and his brother Stephen were born into a noble family. When they were young, their city of Rostov was attacked, so they fled to Radonezh. In moving to another place, they lost all their earthly possessions and had to live as peasants.

When their parents died, both he and his brother retreated to Makovka to live separately as hermits. There, Sergius earned a reputation for his piety and people started asking for him to be their spiritual mentor.

As there were so many souls craving for his guidance, he founded the Holy Trinity monastery. After he was ordained, he became its first abbot.

He was sought out as an advisor by the Prince of Moscow. Through his influence, the Mongol domination of Russia ended. Thereafter, he established 40 more monasteries.

He is the patron saint of Russia.

Today, September 25th is his feast day. Saint Sergius, please pray for us!

BLESSED LOUIS TEZZA
PATRON OF THE DAUGHTERS
OF SAINT CAMILLUS

Born in 19th-century Conegliano, Italy, Louis (or Luigi) was the only son of Augustine and Catherine Tezza. His father, who was a physician, died when Louis was 9 years old. His mother then brought him to Padova.

At the age of 17, he entered the Ministers of the Sick of Saint Camillus de Lellis. Afterward, his mother entered into the nunnery.

Ordained in 1864, he was assigned as a formator of priests. When he became the Provincial of the Order in France, he provided the sick with health facilities.

In 1880, Catholicism was suppressed and he was forced to leave the country. He then returned covertly to strengthen the scattered faithful, uniting them.

During a retreat in Rome, he met Blessed Josephine Vannini and they each felt God's call to have a women's congregation in the spirit of Saint Camillus de Lellis. After prayer and discernment, they established the group and it continues to grow until today. Blessed Louis Tezza is their patron saint.

Today, September 26th is his feast day. Blessed Louis Tezza, pray for us!

27 SEPTEMBER

SAINT VINCENT DE PAUL
PATRON OF CHARITIES

Upon hearing the confession of a peasant upon his deathbed, this simple 16th-century priest in France was moved to attend to the spiritual as well as material needs of the poor. His temperamental spirit was replaced with compassion, kindness and affection.

With the support of Countess de Gondi and her husband, their group of priests and missionaries dedicated their lives to serving country folk and tenant farmers in smaller towns and villages.

Saint Vincent mobilized efforts in every parish to care for the sick and needy. He was able to collect funds from the wealthy to establish several hospitals and even ransom over 1,200 galley slaves from North Africa. He reinvigorated the life of the Church by founding seminaries and conducting retreats for priests - many of whom were growing complacent in the faith.

He is the patron of charities, volunteers, hospitals, lepers, lost articles, prisoners, and horses. Among other institutions, he is also the intercessor for the Vincentian Service Corps, Saint Vincent de Paul societies, and Sisters of Charity.

Today, September 27th is his feast day. Saint Vincent de Paul, please pray for us!

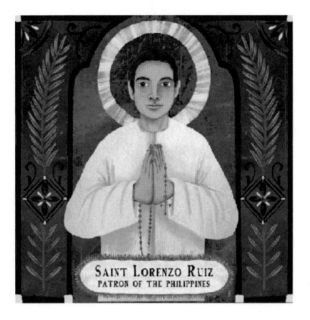

SAINT LORENZO RUIZ
PATRON OF THE PHILIPPINES

"I am a Catholic and wholeheartedly do accept death for God; Had I a thousand lives, all these to Him shall I offer." - Saint Lorenzo's last words

Lorenzo was born in 1594. As a youth, he served as an altar boy at the Binondo church and was taught by Dominican friars. He joined the Confraternity of the Most Holy Rosary.

He had his own family with his wife Rosario and 3 children. They led a quiet and contented life together until trouble came in 1636.

At the time, Lorenzo was working as a clerk at the Binondo church. A Spaniard was murdered and Lorenzo was wrongfully accused of committing the crime. Along with 3 Dominican priests, a Japanese priest, and a lay leper, Lorenzo sought asylum and sailed away to Okinawa.

Upon reaching Japan, the Tokugawa Shogun had declared Christianity illegal akin to treason. They were arrested and imprisoned and soon transferred to Nagasaki to face trial by torture. Despite the terrible suffering he endured, Saint Lorenzo never recanted his faith.

He is the patron of the Philippines. Today, September 28th is his feast day. Saint Lorenzo Ruiz, please pray for us!

SAINT RENE GOUPIL
PATRON OF ANESTHESIOLOGISTS

Renatus "Rene" Goupil lived in 17th-century Anjou, France. He studied medicine but what he really wanted to be was a priest.

He joined the Jesuits as a novice but because he was hard of hearing, he could not be ordained. At the age of 33, he jumped at the chance to be a medic for the Jesuit missionaries in America. He himself did missionary work with the Hurons and he attended to the poor and sick without any pay. He assisted the missionary priest Saint Isaac Jogues.

On one of these missionary trips, their group was captured by the Iroquois tribe who were enemies of the Hurons. When Saint Rene made the sign of the cross over a child, they mistakenly thought this was a curse so they subjected him and his companions to torture and martyr's deaths.

Shortly before his death, Father Isaac received him into the order as a religious brother. Saint Rene Goupil was the first martyr in North America.

Because his death was caused by a tomahawk blow to the head, he became the patron of anesthesiologists.

Today, September 29th is his feast day. Saint Rene Goupil, please pray for us!

SAINT JEROME
PATRON OF TRANSLATORS

"Ignorance of the Scriptures is ignorance of Christ." - Saint Jerome

Saint Jerome spent 30 years of his life translating the Hebrew Bible text into Latin (called the Vulgate) which is still the standard used today.

Jerome was born into a rich family of unbelievers in 4th-century Strido, Dalmatia (in modern-day Slovenia). He finished studying to be a lawyer in Rome. There, he led a self-indulgent life but yet felt remorse after committing sins. To assuage his troubled heart, he would visit the sepulchers of the holy Apostles and martyrs in the catacombs. Eventually, he surrendered his life to God and was baptized.

He chose to live in the Syrian desert as an ascetic monk and studied Scripture daily.

One day, he saw a lion who was in agony for a thorn was stuck within its paws. Saint Jerome fearlessly removed it and the lion became his friend, staying at his side in the years of his isolation.

He is a Doctor of the Church and one of its Church Fathers.

He is the patron of translators and Bible scholars. Today, September 30th is his feast day. Saint Jerome, please pray for us!

OCTOBER

SAINT THERESE OF LISEUX
PATRON OF MISSIONARIES

Saint Therese of the Child Jesus and the Holy Face is also known as the Little Flower of Jesus. Pope Pius X called her the "greatest saint of modern times". She was born in France, 1873 to Blessed Louis Martin and Blessed Marie-Azelie Guerin Martin who were later canonized together as saints .

She grew up in a pious Catholic home with her 8 siblings (4 of whom became nuns). At age 4, her mother passed away and this affected her deeply. At the age of 13, she was given a heavenly sign - she saw the Child Jesus and by divine revelation realized how much God loved her and how much He had sacrificed for her. When she was 15, she made her final vows as a Carmelite nun. Her book, "History of a Soul" is highly recommended reading since it helps one on the path to heaven using the "Little Way" in which one develops a child-like love and trust in God.

"As I grew older I loved the good God more and more, and very frequently did I offer Him my heart, ... most watchful never to offend Him."

She is the patron of missionaries, pilots, florists and flower growers.

Today, October 1st is her feast day. Saint Therese of Liseux, please pray for us!

BLESSED ANTOINE CHEVRIER
PATRON OF THE PRIESTS & SISTERS OF PRADO

When Blessed Antoine Chevrier passed away, 10,000 people came to his funeral. Many of them were personally helped by this holy priest.

He was first assigned to a parish located among the poorest of the poor in Lyon, Rhone. He made it his life's work to uplift the lives of his flock while recruiting others to assist in the mission. He stirred the conscience of the greedy by encouraging them to be generous.

One Christmas, the sight of Christ's humble birth inspired him to establish a religious congregation committed to the care of the needy. With the wise counsel of Saint John Marie Vianney, he proceeded to shelter, feed, clothe, the city's abandoned children. He also attended to the children working in factories and those that were released from prisons.

In 1859 he converted an old ballroom into a chapel that provided a home and school for the children. Soon, some young men and boys in his care also wished to become priests so he founded a seminary for them. This became known as the Institute of the Priests of Prado. Afterward, the Sisters of Prado was also formed.

Today, October 2nd is his feast day. Blessed Antoine Chevrier, please pray for us!

SAINT THEODORE GUERIN
PATRON OF THE DIOCESE OF INDIANA,
LAFAYETTE

Born in 1798, in France, the young Anne-Therese had a desire to live her whole life for God. Despite encountering many struggles, her faith remained steadfast. She delayed her desire to enter the nunnery in order to care for her mother and sister. At age 25, she finally pursued her true calling to consecrated life and she took on the name of Sister Saint Theodore.

In 1840, Catholics who immigrated to the New World were in need of spiritual support. Saint Theodore traveled the seas for almost 3 months on a difficult voyage only to arrive in Saint Mary-of-the-Woods, Indiana, a remote wilderness without a single house standing.

"Love the children first, and then teach them." - Saint Theodore Guerin

Despite the tremendous challenge, Saint Theodore and her companions were able to establish the Academy of Saint Mary-of-the-Woods in less than a year's time. This was the first Catholic women's liberal arts college in the United States. They kept moving forward and were able to open 2 orphanages in Vincennes as well as a pharmacy providing free medicine.

Her life and journal writings have touched countless lives. She is the patron of the Diocese of Indiana, Lafayette.

Today, October 3rd is her feast day. Saint Theodore Guerin, pray for us!

SAINT FRANCIS
Patron of Animals

"Sanctify yourself and you will sanctify society." - Saint Francis of Assisi

He is easily one of the most famous saints of all time. He lived in 12th-century Assisi, Italy, and was born into a wealthy family who led a wasteful life of partying and street brawls. When he was 20 years old, he was converted and gave up all his wealth and strove to live a different life.

One day while deep in meditation, he heard the Lord say, "Go, Francis, and repair my house, which as you see is falling into ruin."

He immediately went to work, thinking he was to repair an old stone church in the village. Little did he know that God would use him to build up the whole Church through his life. In 1209, he founded the Franciscan order and led a life of austere simplicity and charity. With his brother friars, they visited hospitals, cared for the sick, preached to passersby, and served the poor. He was also known to be a miracle worker.

He is best known for his love of animals and nature. He would preach to the birds who had no fear of him and they would be quiet during his sermons, listening intently.

He is the patron of animals. Today, October 4th is his feast day. Saint Francis of Assisi, please pray for us!

SAINT FAUSTINA KOWALSKA
PATRON OF MERCY

This holy Polish nun was born to a poor family so she only had 3 years of education. She was a kind and prayerful child. At age 7, she had a strong desire to be a nun. She sensed God invite her to a "more perfect life".

Her family needed her to work so she obeyed them and set aside her dream. At age 18, compelled by a vision of Christ, she traveled 75 miles to Warsaw, empty-handed, to find a congregation who would accept her. When she was accepted by the Sisters of Our Lady of Mercy, she said "it seemed to me that I had stepped into the life of Paradise."

Amidst her simple duties as a nun, she received many messages and private revelations from Jesus. Upon the counsel of her superiors, she wrote all about these in a diary. These heavenly visions sparked the devotion of Divine Mercy which allowed more souls to benefit from God's infinite love and mercy. Many have since spread these messages and the Church has instituted the Feast of Divine Mercy.

Saint Faustina is the patron of souls in need of God's mercy.

Today October 5th is her feast day. Saint Faustina Kowalska, please pray for us!

SAINT FAITH
PATRON OF PILGRIMS

The story of Saint Faith has given inspiration in the face of adversity to many beleaguered souls. Her beautiful countenance reflected the purity and brilliance of her heart for God.

She lived in Agen, Aquitaine (modern-day France) during a time of great tribulation for the believers. Since Christianity was strictly prohibited, she was brought to trial.

Though the emperor gave her many chances to escape death if she renounced her faith, she steadfastly held on and was eager to give her life for God. She was full of courage and despite her bitter end spurred many of our countrymen to embrace Christianity with great zeal and fervor. They also refused to sacrifice to pagan gods and chose to be beheaded with Saint Faith.

She is the patron of pilgrims, soldiers, and prisoners.

Today, October 6th is her feast day. Saint Faith, please pray for us!

SAINT LIBAIRE THE GREAT
PATRON OF SAINTE-LIVIÈRE

In 1793, a precious comb was enshrined in Grand, Vosges, France. This belonged to Saint Libaire.

She was born in mid-4th century Gaul (modern-day France) to a patrician Imperial Royal family. She lived a most joyful life by tending a flock of sheep. She was often found singing hymns in the fields while praying all the while.

One fateful day, the emperor Julian while traveling saw Libaire and thought to talk with her. As they conversed about religion, the emperor tried to influence her to worship the Roman gods. He showed her a golden statue of Apollo.

Libaire, who was strong in her faith, struck the statue with her staff and it broke apart. Incensed, the emperor beheaded her on the spot.

The story goes that Saint Libaire's body was seen to carry her head to town. It even combed her hair so as to prepare it for burial. A spring appeared where she was killed and many healing miracles occurred there.

She is the patron of Sainte-Livière, Haute-Marne, France.

Today, October 7th is her feast day. Saint Libaire, please pray for us!

SAINT PELAGIA THE PENITENT
PATRON OF ACTRESSES

In the 5th century, there lived a famous woman, Pelagia, whose life led men on the road to perdition. She was an actress and professional dancer. She was a scandalously "loose" woman who always wore clothes that showed off her figure. One day, she walked around town. She was bedecked in jewelry and her clothes left nothing to the imagination.

A holy bishop, Saint Nonnus of Edessa saw her and with great sadness prayed to God on his knees for her. He knew that just by looking at her, many souls would be lost and his life's work of bringing them to sanctity would all be for nothing.

That night the good bishop dreamt that Pelagia would be converted.

The bishop's dream came true because Pelagia came to Holy Mass and listened to the sermon attentively. In it, he spoke of a temptress, a stripper, whose only aim in life was to be beautiful but did nothing for God.

She was baptized and **afterward** gave away all her riches and wealth to the poor. She sometimes wore men's clothing so as not to attract attention.

She is the patron of actresses.

Today, October 8th is her feast day. Saint Pelagia, please pray for us!

OCTOBER

SAINT JOHN HENRY NEWMAN
PATRON OF POETS

"I shall do good, I shall do His work; I shall be an angel of peace, a preacher of truth in my own place, while not intending it, if I do but keep His commandments and serve Him in my calling. Therefore I will trust Him." - Saint John Henry Newman

Born in 1801 in London, England, John Henry was ordained as an Anglican minister. Further studies led him deeper into the truth, history, and depth of riches in the Catholic faith. By 1845, he converted and was subsequently ordained in Rome after a year.

He was a prolific writer whose influence brought hundreds of souls into the Church. In 1879, he was appointed to be a cardinal by Pope Leo XIII.

He is the patron of poets and of the Personal Ordinariate of Our Lady of Walsingham.

Today, October 9th is his feast day. Saint John Henry Newman, please pray for us!

SAINT DANIEL COMBONI
PATRON OF AID WORKERS

Daniel was born on 15 March 1831 at Limone sul Garda, Italy. His parents were poor gardeners but were rich in virtue and faith.

At the age of 12, he traveled to Verona for his education and there he felt a calling for the priesthood. He particularly dreamed of being a missionary in Africa after reading about the lives of Japanese martyrs.

In 1854, he was ordained and 3 years later, he was working in Sudan to liberate slave children. He encountered numerous challenges such as the heat, illness, and deaths of his fellow missionaries.

When he himself grew ill and was forced to go back home, he used the time to collect aid and solidify his plan for the "Save Africa Through Africa" project. He established the Istituto delle Missioni per la Nigrizia.

Upon his return, he ministered to the material and spiritual needs of the people. The slave trade was significantly decreased in the region and lives were enriched through the schools, missions, and orphanages. What he established continues to uplift lives to this day.

He is the patron of aid workers and missionaries. Today, October 10th is his feast day. Saint Daniel Comboni, please pray for us!

SAINT GUMMARUS
PATRON OF SEPARATED
SPOUSES

In the outskirts of Antwerp, Belgium lies the town of Lier where Saint Gummarus lived. He was a servant of the king.

The king arranged a marriage for him to a noblewoman named Guinmarie. While Gummarus was kind-hearted and virtuous, his wife was mean-spirited, extravagant and cruel. All the while, Gummarus tried to bring his wife to a godly life. They did not have any children.

When he was tasked to serve in the army, he was gone for 8 years. Upon his return, he discovered how his wife abused the servants, withheld payment, and caused much disorder. Saint Gummarus made reparations to each one and this made his wife somewhat ashamed of her deeds.

Sadly, his wife was thoroughly unrepentant and caused misery wherever she was. In time, they mutually agreed to live apart. Saint Gummarus retired as a hermit and founded an abbey where people started to gather and live. This area is now known as Lier.

When he died in 774, many miracles occurred through his intercession.

He is the patron of separated spouses and childless couples.

Today, October 11th is his feast day. Saint Gummarus, pray for us!

BLESSED CARLO ACUTIS
PATRON OF THE YOUNG

"To always be close to Jesus. That is my life plan." - Blessed Carlo Acutis

He looked like any other teenage boy but he had an extraordinary love for God that touched the hearts of everyone who knew him.

Carlo loved to pray the Rosary since he was young. His parents weren't regular church-goers but after Carlo received his First Communion, he went to Holy Mass as often as he could and spent an hour in prayer either before or after the Mass. He went to confession every week. His example of faith helped his family and relatives to draw closer to God and they started coming to daily Mass as well.

He had the usual hobbies of young boys his age - soccer, comics, video games, and computers. He instilled discipline in himself by limiting his time for video games and instead put his free time to good use. As a gift to the Church, he created a website on Eucharistic miracles.

When he contracted leukemia and was in pain, he did not complain and he consoled and comforted those who were distressed for his condition. He died on October 12, 2006. He is a patron of the young.

Today, October 12th is his feast day. Blessed Carlo Acutis, pray for us!

BLESSED ALEXANDRINA
MARIA DE COSTA

Whenever one saw Blessed Alexandrina Maria de Costa, they were greeted with a joyful smile. She was a well-liked, hardworking farm girl living in Balasar, Portugal who was a devout Christian.

At age 12, Alexandrina contracted a serious infection which almost took her life. She recovered but its effects stayed with her all her life.

When she was 14, it was Holy Saturday and she was sewing at home. Suddenly, 3 men broke into the house and were about to assault her and the other girls. To preserve her purity, Alexandrina jumped out the window and was severely injured. Her condition left her paralyzed. For 5 years, she dragged herself to church where she would sit in prayer, bearing much pain and discomfort.

For the next 30 years, she became totally immobile and she offered up all her tremendous suffering as a "victim soul". She united her pains to that passion of Christ and received mystical visions every Friday. Despite her difficulties, her disposition transmitted a profound peace to all who saw her.

11 years before she died, she subsisted only on the Holy Eucharist. Today, October 13th is her feast day. Blessed Alexandrina Maria de Costa, pray for us!

POPE SAINT CALLISTUS I
PATRON OF CEMETERY WORKERS

Saint Callistus lived as a slave to a Christian. He became a victim of circumstance when he was accused of thievery and had to do hard labor. In time, Pope Victor helped nurse him back to good health. When Pope Victor died, Callistus served his successor.

It was at this time that Callistus was given the duty of cemetery caretaker of the Christians' underground cemetery. Half a million people were buried there - many of whom were martyrs for the faith.

Saint Callistus became the 16th Pope and he was known to have a merciful heart. Others accused him of heresy when he allowed communion for repentant sinners. He was a man of courage for he allowed members of different economic classes to marry despite this being against Roman civil law. He stated that in matters concerning the sacraments, the Church's law mattered more than the state's.

He gave his whole life to God until the very end. He was martyred during the time of Alexander Severus in 223.

He is the patron of cemetery workers.

Today, October 14th is his feast day. Pope Saint Callistus I, pray for us!

SAINT TERESA OF AVILA
PATRON OF PEOPLE IN NEED OF GRACE

Teresa grew up much like other teenagers did. She liked boys, and clothes, and was a bit of a rebel. Since she thought of herself as prone to sin, she decided to enter religious life. Her father and the rest of the family opposed this so when she turned 17, she left home and joined the Carmelites. Eventually, they accepted Teresa's true calling.

After she took on her final vows, she grew ill and this ailment stayed with her for the rest of her life. She started having heavenly visions and wrote about her divine inspirations. She founded several convents and was proclaimed as a Doctor of the Church in 1970.

Saint Teresa of Avila passed away in 1582. Her body was found to be incorrupt and her heart showed signs of "transverberation" (piercing of the heart).

She is the patron of people in need of grace, the sick, people with headaches, the religious, those ridiculed for their piety, those who are praying against the death of their parents, and lace makers. She is also the patron of Spain, Pozega in Croatia, and other places.

Today, October 15th is her feast day. Saint Teresa of Avila, please pray for us!

SAINT HEDWIG OF ANDECHS
PATRON AGAINST JEALOUSY

Dressed in tattered clothes among the poor of Andechs, Bavaria, Germany one would not be able to distinguish a great lady. She was known to many as a living saint. She often clothed herself like a beggar even when she possessed vast earthly riches.

Saint Hedwig lived in a castle and was the daughter of a duke. At the tender age of 12, she was married to Prince Henry I the Bearded of Silesia (he was 18 years old) and together they had 7 children. One of these was Saint Gertrude of Trebnitz.

Together with her husband, Saint Hedwig's deeds promoted the growth of the Christian faith in Germany, Poland, and Central Europe.

Saint Hedwig had a generous heart and spent her days caring for the poor and sick. She used all her wealth to build churches and hospitals. When her husband died, she gave away all she had to the poor and entered monastic life. She joined the Trebnitz nunnery where her daughter was abbess as a lay sister.

She is the patron against jealousy, the death of children, and difficult marriages.

Today, October 16th is her feast day. Saint Hedwig of Andechs, please pray for us!

SAINT MARGARET MARY ALACOQUE
PATRON OF DEVOTEES TO THE SACRED HEART

In 17th century France lived a nun who received the extraordinary grace of seeing Jesus and discovering the depths of His great love for mankind.

Even as a young child, Margaret loved to honor God by spending time with Him in the Blessed Sacrament instead of playing with her friends.

This habit continued until she entered religious life. She spent a "Holy Hour" every Thursday and began experiencing mystical visions. about the Sacred Heart of Jesus.

She said that "He (Jesus) showed me His loving and lovable Heart as the living source of those flames. Then he revealed to me all the unspeakable marvels of His pure love, and the excess of love He had conceived for men from whom He had received nothing but ingratitude and contempt."

She is the patron of devotees to the Sacred Heart of Jesus, those afflicted with polio, and those who are praying for their dying parents.

Today, October 17th is her feast day. Saint Margaret Mary Alacoque, please pray for us!

SAINT LUKE THE EVANGELIST
PATRON OF ARTISTS

Saint Luke was a faithful follower of Jesus and he used his many talents for the glory of God and the building up of His kingdom. He was a physician, writer, and artist and one of the earliest converts to the faith. He was a student of medicine in Antioch and Tarsus and worked as a ship's doctor.

Saint Luke met Saint Paul at Troas and accompanied him on his travels. They brought the Good News to Greece and Rome. He went through many trials and difficulties in spreading Christianity such as being shipwrecked on their way to Rome.

He is one of the Gospel writers who, from his experiences, Saint Paul's writings as well as from the stories of those closest to Jesus, passed down Christian teachings to us.

He is the patron of artists, artists, bachelors, bookbinders, brewers, butchers, doctors, glass makers, glassworkers, glaziers, gold workers, goldsmiths, lacemakers, lace workers, notaries, painters, physicians, sculptors, stained glass workers, surgeons, and unmarried men. He is also invoked by the Worshipful Company of Painters and 2 cities.

Today, October 18th is his feast day. Saint Luke the Evangelist, please pray for us!

SAINT PAUL OF THE CROSS
PATRON OF HUNGARY

When hardened sinners, soldiers, and bandits heard Saint Paul of the Cross preach, they would weep. They turned from their wicked way of life and pursued holiness. Many entered the priesthood.

In 17th-century Italy, the young Paul attended daily mass and received Holy Communion as often as he could. When he was 20, he heard a sermon that became the point of his conversion. The light of truth illuminated in his soul and he was convicted to enter religious life.

Father Paul's apostolic works included serving the poor and sick. He taught catechism to children. He spent time with young men, taking long walks with them to talk about Christ's Passion. He was given the ability to read souls and this brought about many conversions. He became known to all as a living saint.

One day he had a vision that led him to form the organization known as the Passionists. The group was dedicated and deeply devout, spending at least 3 hours of prayer daily. To this day the Passionist congregation continues the work around the world.

He is the patron of Hungary and Ovada, Italy.

Today, October 19th is his feast day. Saint Paul of the Cross, pray for us!

SAINT CORNELIUS THE CENTURION

"Cornelius, God has heard your prayer and remembered your gifts to the poor." - an angel said to Saint Cornelius

There once lived a man in the 1st century called Cornelius. He was a Roman centurion who lived with his family in Caesarea, Palestine. He was what Jews called a "Gentile" and someone they were not allowed to visit or be friends with.

Cornelius and his family were prayerful, generous to the poor, and feared God. One day at 3 o'clock, while Cornelius was praying, a heavenly messenger arrived and instructed him to ask Saint Paul to come to his home.

After the Holy Spirit revealed to Saint Peter in a vision that salvation was now available to the Gentiles through Jesus' sacrifice on the Cross, he went to the home of Cornelius. Upon his preaching, the whole family and all who listened were baptized. They were the first Gentiles who received baptism as Christians. This story is recounted in Acts 10.

Today, October 20th is his feast day. Saint Cornelius, please pray for us!

SAINT HILARION
OF GAZA

He had the usual amusements of every 4th-century citizen - the theatre, circus, and arena but at 15 years old, his life dramatically changed.

Due to the influence of Saint Anthony the Great, he was converted to Christianity. He gave away all his wealth and lived in the desert with Saint Anthony as a hermit. Later when crowds flocked to see Saint Anthony, Hilarion sought to be in a more remote place and traveled to Gaza with his faithful student Saint Hesychius.

To purge himself of temptations and near occasions of sin, he lived a severely ascetic life. He would subsist on a mere 15 figs a day and would only eat after sunset. He shaved his hair only once a year and never washed his clothes. He changed these only when they fell apart.

In the region of Palestine, he founded several monasteries.

He was known to work miracles such as the time when a woman from Eleutheropolis (a Roman city in ancient Syria) was able to conceive after 15 years and when 3 children were cured of near-fatal diseases. He was also known to be able to exorcise demons and whose prayers cured a paralyzed charioteer.

Today, October 21st is his feast day. Saint Hilarion of Gaza, pray for us!

POPE SAINT JOHN PAUL II
PATRON OF WORLD YOUTH DAY

Karol Wojtyla was born on the 18th of May, 1920 in Wadowice, Poland. He was a bright and active young man who participated in theatre, and literature and loved the great outdoors. As a parish priest in Nazi-occupied Poland, he would conduct secret meetings in the forest with young people where he would celebrate the Holy Mass and read from C.S. Lewis' classic "Screwtape Letters" around the campfire.

His ministry was greatly influenced by Saint Louis Marie Montfort and Saint John of the Cross. As Pope, he was instrumental in dismantling communism. He is the most well-traveled Pope in history covering 3x the distance as the earth to the moon - 775,000 miles! He also wrote many books whose royalties went to rebuilding churches in Yugoslavia.

"To go to Mass means going to Calvary to meet Him, our Redeemer. He comes to us in Holy Communion and remains present in the tabernacles of our churches, for He is our friend." - Pope Saint John Paul II

He is the patron of World Youth Day and the World Meeting of Families 2015.

Today, October 22nd is his feast day. Pope Saint John Paul II, please pray for us!

SAINT JOHN OF CAPISTRANO
PATRON OF LAWYERS

"Those who are called to the table of the Lord must glow with the brightness that comes from the good example of a praiseworthy and blameless life." - Saint John of Capistrano

Imagine leading an army of 70,000 soldiers into battle at the age of 70. That is what Saint John of Capistrano did as he was called on to do by Pope Callistus II. It was a fight in defense of Europe against the invasion of the Turks. In 1456, they won the great battle of Belgrade.

In his youth, he studied law in Perugia and practiced in Naples. When war broke out in the region, John worked to establish peace between the two parties but when they broke the agreement, he was imprisoned.

During his incarceration, his vocation became clear. After his release, he entered religious life as a Franciscan friar in 1416. He became known for his sermons and traveled all throughout Europe including Italy, Germany, Bohemia, Austria, and Russia. He preached to tens of thousands and established Franciscan communities.

His prayers for the sick were especially powerful as he only needed to make the sign of the cross over them and they would be healed.

He is the patron of lawyers, jurists, and military chaplains. Today, October 23rd is his feast day. Saint John of Capistrano, please pray for us!

SAINT ANTHONY MARY CLARET
PATRON OF CLARETIANS

"I will be kind to everybody, particularly to those whom I find troublesome." - Saint Anthony Mary Claret

When he was 11 years old, a bishop visited his school and asked him what he wanted to be when he grew up. He said, "a priest".

His father owned a small textile factory though they weren't rich. The young lad helped out in the business as a weaver. By the time he was 28, he was ordained and traveled as a missionary priest to Catalonia and the Canary Islands. In 1850, he established the Congregation of Missionary Sons of the Immaculate Heart of Mary (now known as the Claretians). He became the confessor of Queen Isabela II and preached as many as 10,000 sermons. He also wrote extensively, publishing 200 works.

He evoked in many of his hearers a devotion to the Blessed Sacrament and the Immaculate Heart of Mary. He was known to have the gift of prophecy and was a miracle worker as well.

He is the patron of Claretians, the Catholic press, weavers, and the Missionary Sons of the Immaculate Heart of Mary.

Today, October 24th is his feast day. Saint Anthony Mary Claret, please pray for us!

SAINTS CRISPIN AND CRISPIAN
PATRONS OF SHOEMAKERS

In 3rd century Soissons, France, there lived the shoemakers Crispin and Crispian. Their work supported not just themselves but also the poor.

During the day, they shared God's Word with all they met and at night they worked at their trade. Many witnessed their piety and devotion and were won over to the faith. This caught the attention of Emperor Maximian Herculeus who told them to leave Christianity or die a gruesome death. Their reply was, "Thy threats do not terrify us, for Christ is our life, and death is our gain."

Thus, they were turned over to Rictus Varus, a cruel governor who was the enemy of all believers. He subjected them to various tortures but somehow the pair survived. He had their necks fastened to millstones and they were thrown to the river. Despite this, they were able to swim across to the other side. In desperation, the governor himself ended his life.

The saints were eventually beheaded and entered into their heavenly reward. They are the patrons of shoemakers, cobblers, glove makers, lace workers, leather workers, saddle makers, tanners and weavers.

Today, October 25th is their feast day. Saints Crispin and Crispian, please pray for us!

26
OCTOBER

BLESSED DAMIAN DEI FULCHERI

His parents were distraught. Their baby boy was suddenly kidnapped by a mentally ill man. They did not know where to look. They knew that only God could help them and they prayed fervently and asked for the intercession of the Blessed Virgin Mary.

Soon afterward, those searching for baby Damian were led to where he was hid by a bright miraculous light! He was safe!

Damian dei Fulcheri was born in the 15th century in Liguria, Italy.

He had a strong faith that led him to join the Dominican order at Savona. As a missionary priest, he traveled all around Italy preaching God's Word. He was able to convert hundreds to the faith.

He was also known as a miracle worker and when he passed away, many healings and answered prayers were said to have occurred at his tomb.

Today, October 26th is his feast day. Blessed Damian dei Fulcheri, please pray for us!

SAINT EMILINA
OF BOULANCOURT
PATRON OF SINGLE WOMEN

From far and wide, people came to Sister Emelina for prayers but even before they arrived, God told her of their imminent arrival. She could foresee what God had in store for them and was able to direct them to the good and right path so they could get closer to Him.

She lived in 12th-century France. She spent her days in solemn prayer and silence and patiently attended to her visitors who sought her guidance.

To free herself from worldly attachments and unite herself more closely with Jesus, she fasted 3 times a week. She did not eat nor drink anything during this time. She often wore a hairshirt and walked barefoot during summer and even in winter. She bore everything with kindness and joy.

From the time she passed on, the people kept a perpetual flame to mark her tomb but due to the French Revolutionaries' destruction of Christian relics, her grave is nowhere to be found. Yet the memory of this holy woman inspires us today.

She is the patron of single laywomen and today, October 27th is her feast day. Saint Emilina of Boulancourt, please pray for us!

SAINT JUDE THADDEUS
PATRON OF IMPOSSIBLE CASES

Often mistaken for Judas Iscariot, people did not think to ask for Saint Jude's help so he became the patron for those with lost causes.

Saint Jude was one of the 12 apostles of Jesus. He was the son of martyr Saint Cleophas and Saint Mary who stood by the Blessed Mother at the foot of the Holy Cross. His mother was among those who anointed Jesus' body for burial.

Saint Jude's brother was Saint James the Lesser. Since he was the nephew of the Blessed Virgin Mary and Saint Joseph, he was also a blood relative of our Lord Jesus. They said that Saint Jude looked very much like Jesus. He is often depicted with an image of the Lord.

He was described as a tender-hearted man with a child-like humility. He wrote one of the canonical epistles and preached in Syria, Mesopotamia, and Persia with Saint Peter. He was able to exorcise evil spirits causing pagan idols to crumble and he was also known to heal the sick.

He is the patron of impossible cases, desperate situations, and hospital workers.

Today, October 28th is his feast day. Saint Jude Thaddeus, pray for us!

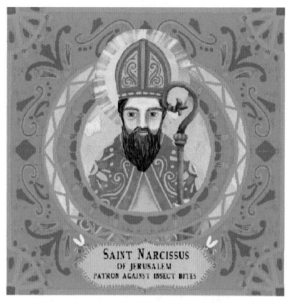

SAINT NARCISSUS
OF JERUSALEM
PATRON AGAINST INSECT BITES

In 3rd-century Jerusalem lived a great bishop called Narcissus. He took on this duty late in life.

One day, he was accused of a crime but no one who knew him believed this. In response, Bishop Narcissus retreated into the desert and lived alone in silence. In time, his name was cleared and he returned to his flock. He was much older by then and roughened by desert living but his spirit and zeal were stronger.

During one Holy Saturday, they did not have any oil for the Easter lamps and Saint Narcissus took a water pitcher and prayed over it. The water turned into oil! Thus the vigil service went on as planned.

He lived to the age of 116. When he died, he was buried in Girona, Northern Catalonia, Spain. When the French invaded the city, they ransacked the church and his tomb somehow came open. From it emerged a multitude of flies and the sheer number drove away the French soldiers, saving the city! This is why you will find the city of Girona peppered with images and artifacts with flies on it.

Saint Narcissus then became the patron against flies and insect bites.

Today, October 29th is his feast day. Saint Narcissus of Jerusalem, please pray for us!

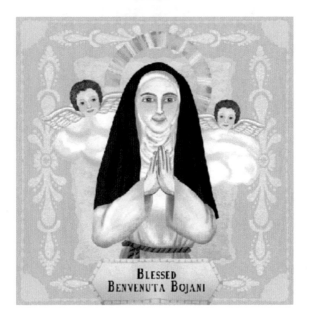

BLESSED
BENVENUTA BOJANI

She was born in Cividale del Fruiuli, Italy in 1254. She was the youngest in the family and had 6 sisters. The family hoped she would be a boy but when she arrived, her father said, "She too shall be welcome!" Thus she was named "Benvenuta" meaning "Welcome".

As a child, she was more inclined to divine things compared to childhood play. By 12 years old, she wore a rope and a hairshirt to remind herself of Christ's sufferings for mankind.

As she matured, the rope belt got embedded into her waist and could not be removed. She prayed over the belt and it dropped to the floor.

As a young lady, she became a Dominican tertiary. She kept her austere way of life and never left home. When she contracted a serious illness, she was bedridden and had to be carried to daily Mass. During one Mass on the eve of the feast of Saint Dominic, she had a vision of him and was miraculously healed!

She developed heavenly sight seeing both angels and demons. By saying the name of the Blessed Virgin Mary, the demons would flee.

Today, October 30th is her feast day. Blessed Benvenuta Bojani, please pray for us!

BLESSED THOMAS BELLACCI
PATRON OF BUTCHERS

In 14th-century Florence, Italy lived a bad boy whom parents warned their sons not to associate with. He lived a rebellious, wild, and dissolute life that led him into trouble with the law. He was wrongly accused of a serious crime and this pushed the young man to wander aimlessly around the streets in search of peace.

He met a kind priest who listened to his story and believed he was innocent. By the grace of God, Thomas' life turned a new leaf and he resolved to become good.

Inspired by the priest's pious ways, Thomas started to pray and do penance. He joined the Franciscans as a lay brother and became an example for the other members. He adopted fasting with joy and kept vigils often. His meditations were so focused that he began to experience heavenly visions. His holiness and simplicity influenced many.

He established several monasteries, built God's kingdom by promoting peace between the Eastern and Western Churches and was also willing to die as a martyr when he was imprisoned for his faith.

He was the son of a butcher so he is the patron of butchers. Today, October 31st is his feast day. Blessed Thomas Bellacci, please pray for us!

NOVEMBER

SAINT MATHURIN
PATRON OF THE MENTALLY ILL

Saint Mathurin's mother Euphemia and father Marinus were unbelievers and did not raise him in the Catholic faith. His father was a government official of Emperor Maximian in 4th-century Larchant, France. His role was to oppress and persecute Christians in the region.

At the age of 12, Mathurin was baptized in secret by Saint Polycarp. He became a devout Christian and grew in wisdom and virtue. He eventually won over his parents by his example and was ordained a priest by the age of 20.

He was zealous in spreading the Word and by his powerful intercession was able to heal and exorcise evil spirits.

When the emperor's daughter Theodora was possessed by a demon, Emperor Maximian sent for Saint Mathurin and asked him to cure her. With great compassion for the girl, he prayed over her and she was instantly cured.

He is the patron of the mentally ill, comic actors, jesters, clowns, sailors, tinmen, plumbers and those who are praying for a child.

Today, November 1st is his feast day. Saint Mathurin, please pray for us!

SAINT WINIFRED OF WALES
PATRON OF UNWANTED ADVANCES

There is a place called Holywell where a church is built around a mountain spring. Since medieval times, pilgrims have flocked there for miraculous cures. This site is where a 7th century lady lived. She was very beautiful and virtuous. She was the daughter of a nobleman who was the king's advisor. She grew so devoted to Christ that she desired to become a nun and never marry.

There was a chieftain called Caradog who was so enthralled by Winifred that he repeatedly asked her to be his wife. Because she repeatedly refused, he attacked her with his sword, decapitating her.

Then a miracle happened! Saint Beuno came and somehow reattached Winifred's head and she was nursed back to health! She later entered the cloister at Cwytherin, Deubighshire, Wales and became its abbess.

The mountain spring where this happened became a source of healing for those with leprosy, skin ailments, and more.

Saint Winifred is the patron of unwanted advances and martyrs.

Today, November 2nd is her feast day. Saint Winifred, please pray for us!

SAINT MARTIN DE PORRES
PATRON OF THE POOR

Since Martin was 10, he started to spend several hours each day in prayer. In 17th-century Peru, no dark-skinned people were ever ordained, he was remained a "donato" (a volunteer lay brother) all his life. Due to his piety, he was allowed to wear the Dominican habit.

Countless miracles are attributed to him. He served both noblemen and slaves with equanimity and could heal with a single glass of water. When an epidemic hit Peru, he was said to have appeared and ministered within sick friars' quarters despite their doors being locked. Light would emanate from him when in prayer. He was seen to levitate and bilocate. He also received divine revelations.

He fed, sheltered, and cared for multitudes of the poor and sick every day. He established an orphanage that taught the children trades so they could earn a living. He loved animals and rats would obey his orders not to chew on the linen. He also nursed sick cats and dogs back to health. He was the first dark-skinned person who was proclaimed a saint of the Catholic Church. When his grave was opened after 25 years, an aroma of roses came from his body.

He is the patron of the poor. Today, November 3rd is his feast day. Saint Martin de Porres, please pray for us!

SAINT CHARLES BORROMEO
- PATRON OF SEMINARIANS

Charles was born in a castle to the powerful, affluent, and influential Medici family. At the age of 21, he was thrust as a cardinal by his uncle Pope Pius IV, without even being ordained. He could have settled into a life of carefree luxury as a well-provided-for cleric and yet he chose to forego worldly comforts and live simply, giving much of his wealth to the poor.

At a time when many believers were lukewarm in the faith, Saint Charles Borromeo shone brightly as one of the forerunners of the Catholic Reformation. He rallied for strict disciplinary measures that some monks found too severe and thus an assassination attempt was plotted against him. Despite being shot at, he was not hit and the attempt to end his life was foiled.

During the plague in Milan in 1576, he served the sick and buried the dead so he is often represented with a cord around his neck which was worn during that time.

He established seminaries, schools for the poor, hospitals for the sick, and practiced what he preached.

He is the patron of seminarians, bishops, and catechists. Today, November 4th is his feast day. Saint Charles Borromeo, please pray for us!

SAINT KEA
PATRON AGAINST TOOTHACHES

In 5th-century Scotland lived Saint Kea. He was the son of a king but had no royal ambitions. He wished to live solely for God and became a bishop. Later in life, he decided to live as a hermit in Wales. He then traveled to Somerset and Devon and established churches. He eventually reached Old Kea in Cornwall where he chose to live. The town was named after him.

When the Cornish King Teudar was hunting one day, the deer he was pursuing took shelter with Saint Kea. Since then the king tried to make the saint's life difficult. He took his oxen so Saint Kea used the deer to plow the land instead.

It is written that Saint Kea journeyed across the Channel to Cleder in Brittany and that is where he passed away. He is called "Saint Quay" in Brittany.

He is the patron to ask for prayers when you have a toothache.

Today, November 5th is his feast day. Saint Kea, please pray for us.

SAINT LEONARD OF NOBLAC
PATRON OF PRISONERS

Leonard who was born into Frankish nobility, desired to renounce his riches and life at court to live a hermit's life dedicated to God. He began preaching, making penance, and practicing austerity. He eventually entered the monastery in Orleans, France. His brother was also deeply touched by Leonard's witness and followed in his footsteps.

During his lifetime, he lived in the Limousin forest and subsisted only on wild herbs, fruits, and spring water. Pilgrims who encountered him were awed at his holy life and desired to live as he did so a monastery was built around his hermitage.

Saint Leonard was known for his devotion to those in prison. He was able to have many of them have reformed lives and be released. Many reported having their shackles fall to the ground after invoking his help. They would then bring their heavy chains and irons to offer it to the saint in gratitude.

After Saint Leonard died, records of 4,000 answered prayers are attributed to his intercession. He is the patron of those in prison.

Today, November 6th is his feast day. Saint Leonard of Noblac, please pray for us!

SAINT PETER OU

Wu Gousheng was born in 1768 in Longping, Guizhou Province, China. He was a married layman who was known to all as a kind-hearted, just man who was generous with the poor and outspoken. When missionaries came to his town, he was one of the first converts and he immediately threw away all his household idols. He was baptized and took on the name of Peter.

He was a successful businessman who owned a large hotel. Whenever he met someone new, he would talk about God and share the richness of the Catholic faith. He volunteered to teach catechism with the missionaries in the area.

When a new emperor took over, he imposed strict rules against Christianity but Saint Peter Ou courageously kept proclaiming the faith so he was arrested. While incarcerated, he conducted prayer sessions within the prison cells thus inspiring many. He is credited with bringing more than 600 people to Christianity.

When he refused to step on the crucifix, he was sentenced to death by strangulation. His last words were, "Heaven, heaven, my true home! I see my heavenly mother and my guardian angel coming to take me home."

Today, November 7th is his feast day. Saint Peter Ou, pray for us.

SAINT ELIZABETH OF THE TRINITY
PATRON AGAINST THE DEATH OF PARENTS

Elizabeth Catez was born in Bourges, France to a captain and his wife. At the age of 7, her father died and yet she grew up to be a lively, popular girl. She was known for her skillful piano playing and how she liked to visit the sick and teach catechism to children.

As a Discalced Carmelite nun, she found the key to happiness in life. In a letter she wrote, "I can't find words to express my happiness. Here there is no longer anything but God. He is All; He suffices and we live by Him alone."

Her closeness to God brought her much spiritual knowledge and insight and she helped many souls find the right path to take. Her many writings became retreat guides and a rich source of wisdom for all of us.

"He is always with you, be always with Him, through all your actions, in your sufferings, when your body is exhausted, remain in His sight, see Him present, living in your soul." - Saint Elizabeth of the Trinity

She is the patron against the death of parents and the sick.

Today, November 8th is her feast day. Saint Elizabeth of the Trinity, please pray for us!

SAINT AURELIUS OF RIDITIO
PATRON AGAINST HEADACHES

When you help out one of God's saints, you may become a saint yourself.

In the year 400 in Milan, Italy the Arians were in pursuit of Saint Dionysius and so he fled to Armenia. There, he encountered Aurelius and they soon became friends.

Aurelius became known as the Bishop of Riditio in Armenia.

When Saint Dionysius passed away, Saint Aurelius traveled to Milan to transport his friend's remains.

In Milan, he formed a close friendship with Saint Ambrose. Saint Aurelius stayed in Milan until his death in 475.

Since ages past, Catholics have been calling on him for prayers when they had a headache, head ailment, or injury.

Today, November 9th is his feast day. Saint Aurelius of Riditio, please pray for us!

POPE SAINT LEO THE GREAT
DOCTOR OF THE CHURCH

In 5th-century Rome, all the people were in great despair and trepidation as reports that Attila the Hun would soon encroach on the city.

Instead of fleeing in fear, Pope Saint Leo came out to meet Attila and spoke to him, calmly asking him to leave. While the pope was speaking, Attila saw a man in priestly garb with a sword and heard him say that he would meet death if he did not obediently leave in peace. Attila chose to leave and the city was safe!

This holy saint did not only protect his people but the whole Church from the heretical beliefs of his day. Nestorianism, Monophysitism, Manichaeism, and Pelagianism all threatened to change doctrine and depart from what Christ taught the disciples. Pope Saint Leo called the Council of Chalcedon together to combat these and was triumphant.

His writings and sermons still encourage the faithful to this day and he was the first Pope that was called "Great". He was declared one of the Doctors of the Church in 1574.

Today, November 10th is his feast day. Pope Saint Leo the Great, please pray for us!

SAINT MARTIN OF TOURS
PATRON AGAINST IMPOVERISHMENT

One day, the young Martin encountered a beggar along the way. He did not have anything to give the man so with his sword, he cut his cloak in two and gave one half to the beggar. Later on, Martin had a vision of Jesus wearing his cloak.

Desiring a holy life, he became a hermit for 10 years. He preached the Gospel, tore down old temples, built churches, and won many over to the faith. Many became attracted to his sanctity and those who wished to live as he did came from all over. In that place was built the Benedictine Abbey of Liguge.

Despite his humility in not wanting to accept the post, he was chosen to be the Bishop of Tours and consecrated in the year 372.

He is the patron against impoverishment and alcoholism. He is also the intercessor for beggars, the cavalry, equestrians, geese, horses, horsemen, hotel-keepers, the Pontifical Swiss Guards, quartermasters, riders, soldiers, tailors, vintners, wine growers, France, and other places.

Today, November 11th is his feast day. Saint Martin of Tours, please pray for us.

SAINT ASTRICUS OF ESZTERGOM
PATRON OF HUNGARY

Bohemia-born Anastasius XIX took on the name Astricus and chose to live as a monk in Rome, Italy. He became the first abbot of Brevnov. His friend Saint Adalbert of Prague was doing missionary work and Astricus supported him.

In the year 997, Christians were persecuted so Astricus fled to Hungary. He began to share God's Word with the Magyars. He became the first abbot of Saint Martin's Monastery which was the first monastery in Hungary. He also became the first archbishop of the Hungarian church.

The wife of Duke Geza wanted to live the faith devoutly and regularly sought the advice of Saint Astricus. She became the mother of Saint Stephen of Hungary. When Saint Stephen was crowned as King by Emperor Otto III, Saint Astricus became his spiritual counselor.

He is the patron of Hungary.

Today, November 12th is his feast day. Saint Astricus of Esztergom, please pray for us!

SAINT HOMOBONUS OF CREMONA
PATRON OF BUSINESS PEOPLE

In 12th-century Cremona, Italy lived a man called Homobonus. His name meant "good man".

He was the son of a wealthy merchant tailor and when he was old enough, he took over the father's business.

He was like many today who married and earned a living for his family but he was no ordinary businessman. He knew that all his material goods were from God as well as his ability to work. He saw his livelihood as a means to help those in need.

He allotted most of his earnings to support the poor. Even his own home was used for works of mercy.

He is the patron of business people, clothworkers, cobblers, shoemakers, tailors, and the city of Cremona, Italy.

Today, November 13th is his feast day. Saint Homobonus, please pray for us!

Saint John Licci
PATRON OF HEAD INJURIES

The young John Licci began the habit of reciting the Daily Offices before he was 10 years old. By the influence of Blessed Peter Geremia took on religious vows as a Dominican priest. He served God for 96 years.

Through a heavenly vision, he received a mission to establish the convent of Saint Zita but he had no money for the construction. A series of miraculous events occurred. A stranger supplying much-needed building materials came with all they needed. When roof beams were cut too short, Saint John would pray over these and they would stretch to the proper length.

When a boy came to watch his uncle set stones, he accidentally fell from the wall and died. Saint John rushed to him and prayed. The boy came back to life! On 3 separate occasions, people's heads were crushed and each of them was saved by the prayers of Saint John Licci! This is why he is the patron of head injuries.

Today, November 14th is his feast day, Saint John Licci, please pray for us.

SAINT ALBERT THE GREAT
PATRON OF NATURAL SCIENCES

"The greater and more persistent your confidence in God, the more abundantly you will receive, all that you ask." - Saint Albert the Great

He was known as someone who was as knowledgeable as Aristotle. He taught theology in Cologne, Germany, and Paris, France. He was not only a teacher but also a preacher and administrator who served as the Bishop of Regensburg, Germany.

He wrote much about the natural sciences and produced illustrated guides about botany, biology, chemistry, astronomy, etc. He is responsible for introducing Greek and Arabic scientific study to medieval Europe.

"The surest and quickest way to attain perfection, is to strive, for purity of heart. Once the obstacles have been removed, God finds a clear path and does wonders, both in and through the soul." - Saint Albert the Great

He is the patron of natural sciences, scientists, medical technicians, philosophers, school children, students, and theology students.

Today, November 15th is his feast day. Saint Albert the Great, please pray for us!

16
NOVEMBER

SAINT GERTRUDE
THE GREAT
PATRON OF NUNS

Since Gertrude was 5 years old, she grew up in the Benedictine Abbey of Saint Mary of Helfta Eisleben, Saxony. She was very diligent in her studies and was highly intelligent especially in philosophy and literature. When she came of age, she took religious vows as a Benedictine nun.

Philosophy filled much of her thoughts and when she was 26 years old, she received a vision of Jesus lovingly teaching her where to direct her mind. It was at that point that she started studying the Bible and writings of the Church Fathers. She continued to receive heavenly revelations and discovered a great many things. All of these, she faithfully recorded for other's edification.

In one vision, Jesus taught her a prayer that if prayed with love and devotion could release a thousand souls in purgatory.

Saint Teresa and Saint Francis de Sales both spoke highly of Saint Gertrude's writings and these are available for us to read until this day.

She helped spread devotion to the Sacred Heart of Jesus.

She is the patron of nuns.

Today, November 16th is her feast day. Saint Gertrude the Great, please pray for us!

SAINT GREGORY THAUMATURGUS
PATRON AGAINST EARTHQUAKES & FLOODS

Gregory embraced a priestly life and was appointed to be bishop of Caesarea. At the time he arrived there, there were only 17 Christians. By the time the good bishop passed away, he had converted almost everyone and it is said that only 17 unbelievers remained. Because God endowed him with the gift of healing, he would only need to lay his hand on the sick and they would be cured instantly as well as converting to the faith!

Saint Gregory began the tradition of commemorating the lives of the Christian martyrs and instituted their feast days. He did countless good works such as attending to the sick during a plague, settling disputes among his flock using his legal training, and opposing heretic beliefs in his day.

When the number of Christians increased rapidly, a new church was needed. However, construction was halted when a huge boulder impeded their progress. Saint Gregory simply ordered the huge rock to move out of the way and it did!

He is the patron against earthquakes, floods, and desperate lost causes.

Today, November 17th is his feast day. Saint Gregory Thaumaturgus, please pray for us!

SAINT MAWES
PATRON AGAINST SNAKES AND WORMS

There once was a hermit who lived in 5th-century Cornwall, England. He was known to all as a good teacher.

When he traveled to Brittany, he wanted to establish a monastery on an island. The trouble was that it was full of snakes, insects, and rats. The saint set the vegetation on fire and all of these left the area so they were able to complete the monastery and it is now known as Maudez.

One day, someone extinguished the last remaining fire on the island and Saint Mawes sent a young boy to the mainland during low tide to fetch a flame. Upon his return, he was caught on a rock with the rising tide threatening to engulf him and the flame. The boy prayed and asked Saint Mawes' intercession. Just then, the rock he was on started to rise higher and higher so the flame was not quenched and he was able to carry it safely to Saint Mawes.

Today you can find that the places where he lived are named after him as well as 60 churches that were built in his honor.

He is the patron against snakebites, worms, vermin, and the intercessor to call when you have a headache.

Today, November 18th is his feast day. Saint Mawes, please pray for us!

SAINT MECHTILDE OF HELFTA
PATRON AGAINST BLINDNESS

Like a princess, Mechtilde was born in a castle in Saxony, Germany in 1241 and yet she knew that her true riches lay in heaven.

Her family was powerful in the land but they were pious and devout Catholics so they raised Mechtilde in a convent since she was 7 years old. Her older sister was a nun so Mechtilde also decided that she had a calling to the religious life as well. By the age of 17, she joined the Helfta Monastery where her sister was the abbess.

She spent her days teaching at the convent school and also served as the choir director. She was known to all as a holy nun and many came to learn from her wisdom and spiritual guidance. She became the novice mistress for Saint Gertrude the Great who later wrote a story about her life.

She was a mystic who experienced divine revelations. She was also given the gift of healing. Once, she was able to intercede for a fellow nun who was blind. She was able to see through the prayers of Saint Mechtilde. This is why she is the patron against blindness.

Today, November 19th is her feast day. Saint Mechtilde of Helfta, please pray for us!

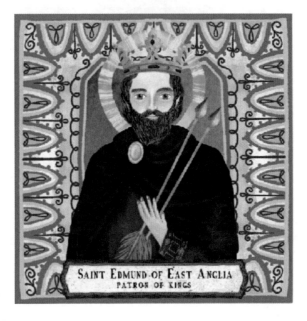

SAINT EDMUND OF EAST ANGLIA
PATRON OF KINGS

Imagine yourself being crowned king at the age of 14. This was the life of King Edward of East Anglia. He was enthroned by Bishop Saint Humbert of Elmham on Christmas day in the year 855.

By all accounts, he was an exemplary ruler who was kind and just. He had a genuine concern for all of his people. He wished to serve God faithfully and spent a year memorizing the Psalter by heart.

Alas, an invasion by the Danish Vikings forced him to lead his army into several battles and was eventually overpowered. His enemies ordered him to give his people over to them but he refused. He bravely defended them until his last breath under the hand of his oppressors. He died before he reached the age of 30.

He is the patron of kings, torture victims, wolves, and against the plague and pandemics.

Today, November 20th is his feast day. Saint Edmund, please pray for us!

BLESSED CLELIA MERLONI
PATRON OF THE APOSTLES OF
THE SACRED HEART OF JESUS

Clelia lived in 19th-century Italy and was born into a wealthy and prominent family. Her father wanted her to take over the business but what her heart really desired was to become a nun. Her father became very hostile to religion and Catholicism in particular because he was totally engrossed in the business and joined the Freemasons. Clelia prayed unceasingly for her father and offered reparation. God heard her prayer as he converted to the faith towards the end of his life.

Upon his death, Clelia was able to pursue a religious vocation. At the time she was very ill with a lung ailment but after doing a novena to the Sacred Heart of Jesus and to the Immaculate Heart of Mary, she was miraculously cured. She also realized her calling to form a new congregation. This was called the Apostles of the Sacred Heart of Jesus. They live by the words, "The love of Christ impels us."

Today, their mission spans 14 countries. Blessed Clelia Merloni is their patron saint.

Today, November 21st is her feast day. Blessed Clelia Merloni, please pray for us!

SAINT CECILIA
PATRON OF MUSICIANS

Cecilia lived in 3rd-century Rome. She desired to be a consecrated virgin but her family arranged for her to wed Valerian of Trastevere. After their wedding, she confided to him that she could see her guardian angel and that if he wished to see him, he needed to have a pure heart and be baptized.

Valerian agreed and was soon baptized. Upon his return from the ceremony, he witnessed Cecilia deep in prayer, and alongside her was an angel who was also praying. The angel then put a crown on Cecilia and Valerian.

The angel turned to Valerian and asked him if there was anything he desired. Valerian's petition was that his brother may be converted. God granted his prayer and he and his brother started to serve the Church by ministering proper burials to martyred Christians.

Since Christianity was a serious offense during that time in history, Cecilia, Valerian and his brother were all martyred for their faith.

She is the patron of musicians and composers.

Today, November 22nd is her feast day. Saint Cecilia, please pray for us!

SAINT COLUMBANUS
PATRON OF MOTORCYCLISTS

Columbanus was an intelligent, rich, and handsome young fellow whom all the ladies wanted to get close to. He could have had an easy life but decided to withdraw from the world and put his spiritual life before worldly pursuits. He studied Scripture and grew in the ways of the saints.

His single-hearted love for the Lord attracted many men and their monastery grew. Those that Saint Columbanus taught were also able to convert many to the faith.

On one occasion, he found the perfect spot to live - a cave. Finding a bear inhabiting it, he asked the bear to let him stay there and it graciously allowed the saint to do so. Another time, the monastery needed help with the harvest and he tamed a bear to help them plow the fields.

When he needed water to live on, he prayed and a spring miraculously appeared nearby. When the brothers were in need of food, he prayed and suddenly their empty storage became filled with grain! Several healings occurred as well through his intercession.

Due to his extensive travel in preaching the Gospel, he is the patron of motorcyclists.

Today, November 23rd is his feast day. Saint Columbanus, pray for us!

SAINT ROMANUS OF LE MANS
PATRON AGAINST SHIPWRECK

He was known to all as a lousy preacher and he was not the outgoing type. He lived in the 4th century and was born in Rome, Italy.

His uncle was Saint Julian, the missionary bishop of Le Mans. He sent for his nephew Romanus who dutifully crossed over the Alps to serve his uncle. Upon arrival, his uncle ordained Romanus and he began serving alongside his uncle in the mission. His sermons were not at all noteworthy and yet, one by one, souls came to him for baptism into the faith.

Saint Romanus was also known to have the gift of healing, exorcising demons, and effectively teaching the faith to unbelievers. He had great influence over the sailors in the region.

When Saint Julian passed away, Saint Romanus, alongside a group of monks, cared for his tomb and the graves of other Christians. They became known as the Grave-Diggers who maintained the churchyard tombs. They gave great consolation to the families of those who passed on.

He is the patron against shipwreck.

Today, November 24th is his feast day. Saint Romanus of Le Mans, please pray for us!

SAINT CATHERINE OF ALEXANDRIA
PATRON OF EDUCATORS AND APOLOGISTS

In 4th-century Alexandria lived Catherine, a woman of noble birth with a brilliant mind trained in science and oratory. Since her conversion to Christianity, she used all her skills and knowledge to teach the faith.

When she was 18 years old, the emperor suppressed Christianity and everyone who professed the faith was instantly condemned to die. Catherine boldly stood out and debated the pagan philosophers. The truth of her arguments were so undeniable that she was able to win many of them over and they were instantly put to death. Catherine was scourged and jailed.

When the empress heard about these events, she visited Catherine in her prison cell along with the leader of the army. Their talk with Catherine was so enlightening that they were both converted to the faith. Thus they were also subsequently martyred.

Catherine herself was sentenced to death by the wheel of torture. When Catherine touched the wheel, it broke so the executioner instead beheaded her and thus she received her heavenly reward.

She is the patron of educators and apologists. Today, November 25th is her feast day. Saint Catherine of Alexandria, please pray for us!

BLESSED GAETANA STERNI
PATRON OF THE SISTERS OF DIVINE WILL

Gaetana was living a comfortable, well-off existence until a series of tragic events came upon her. Her sister Margherita died and then her father passed away soon after. Her brother left home to become an actor so the family had little means to support itself.

Then, when she got married to a widower with 3 children, life seemed to take an upward turn especially when she was found to be pregnant.

Alas her happy days were short-lived. Her husband passed away before Gaetana gave birth and when the baby was born, it too, died a few days later. This was not all. Her in-laws demanded that her 3 step-children live with them. Gaetana was left alone so she returned home to her mother.

The grieving Gaetana did not turn bitter. She did not lose her faith. She joined a Canosian convent for 5 months. She was able to fulfill God's plan for her which she discerned a few years back - "to employ all of herself in the service of the poor".

She spent the rest of her life caring for the poor, aged, sick, and the dying. Together with friends, she formed the Daughters of the Divine Will and is now their patron saint. Today, November 26th is her feast day. Blessed Gaetana Sterni, please pray for us!

SAINT LAVERIUS
PATRON OF GRUMENTO NOVA, ITALY

The 4th-century amphitheatre was packed with spectators and the wild animals were released into the arena. A Roman soldier Laverius stood defenseless in their midst. The crowd was awestruck as the hungry animals did not come close to Laverius. Instead, they knelt down before him.

When Laverius knew the truth of the Gospel of Jesus Christ, could not keep this to himself. Despite Christianity being a serious offense in those days, he started preaching in the streets of Teggiano. Agrippa, the Roman prefect had him arrested and subjected him to torture and public mockery.

He ordered Laverius to make a sacrifice to the pagan gods but Laverius refused. He was returned to his prison cell and an angel appeared to him in the middle of the night. The angel freed Laverius and told him to go to Grumentum. He reached that place on August 15th, 312.

As soon as he arrived, he shared the faith and many were converted and baptized. Agrippa's soldiers soon caught up with him and he was whipped and beaten for his punishment. All the while, he preached to the soldiers until his death.

He is the patron of several places in Italy namely Grumento Nova Today, November 27th is his feast day. Saint Laverius, please pray for us!

SAINT CATHERINE LABOURE
PATRON OF SENIORS

The young Zoe lost her mother when she was only 8 years old. After her funeral, she picked up the statue of the Blessed Virgin Mary and kissed it saying, "Now you will be my mother." Since she was very young, she was drawn to the religious life. After her vision of the priest, she joined the Sisters of Charity who cared for the aged, poor, and sick.

One day on the 18th of July, 1830, Catherine was awakened by a soft whisper. It was the Blessed Virgin Mary! She knelt at Our Lady's feet and described this vision as the "sweetest moment" in her life.

The Blessed Mother told her about the Miraculous Medal which would allow wearers to receive a multitude of heavenly graces. She had it made and many believers started wearing it. This devotion is still known and practiced today because of the beautiful and amazing events that surround it.

Because Saint Catherine devoted her life to tending to the elderly, she is the patron of seniors.

Today, November 28th is her feast day. Saint Catherine Laboure, please pray for us!

SAINT SATURNINUS OF TOULOUSE
PATRON AGAINST DEATH ANXIETY

Saint Saturninus was a holy man who roamed the Pyrenees teaching the faith and converting many. Some of those he preached to became saints who went on mission with him. Many healings took place from their prayers. One time, he and his fellow missionaries were imprisoned by the prefect Rufinus. They were miraculously set free by an angel.

Saint Saturninus became the first bishop of Toulouse, France. When he arrived there, the pagan priests noticed that the evil spirits they were communicating with were no longer there and they blamed Saint Saturninus.

They hatched a horrible plot to murder him. They gathered their followers and seized the saint. They then commanded him to offer sacrifice to their gods. When he was brought before the pagan statues, these simply crumbled in front of Saint Saturninus. When their gods were destroyed, the crowd was enraged and they martyred Saint Saturninus by having a bull drag his body until he died and angels carried his soul to his heavenly reward.

He is the patron against anxiety over one's death. Today, November 29th is his feast day. Saint Saturninus of Toulouse, please pray for us!

· SAINT ANDREW THE APOSTLE ·
PATRON FOR A HAPPY MARRIAGE

Saint Andrew is called "the Protoclete" meaning he was the "first called". He was a fisherman by trade. After Jesus' crucifixion, he traveled to Asia Minor and Greece preaching the Good News. Some say he also reached as far as Russia and Poland.

He held nothing back and loved God with his all. He gave his life martyred on a saltire (x-shaped) cross but still preached for 2 days from it until he passed away.

Down through the ages, Saint Andrew has been called upon for many prayers. He is not only known for his powerful prayers for a happy marriage but a great many other needs. His intercession has been sought out in cases of fever, gout, neck pain, convulsions, sore throat, and whooping cough.

He is also the patron of single women, those who want to have a child, pregnant women, fishermen, butchers, farm workers, miners, rope makers, water carriers as well as Scotland and many other places.

Today, November 30th is his feast day. Saint Andrew the Apostle, please pray for us!

DECEMBER

SAINT ELIGIUS OF NOYON
PATRON OF CRAFTSMEN

7th-century Noyon, France was home to the holy Bishop Eligius whose home was always surrounded by a crowd. The poor and sick flocked there to receive food and care. His charity and kindness won many converts.

He was known for his great skill at metalwork. He was honest, pious, and hard-working. He helped build the Saint Paul Basilica, several other churches, convents, and monasteries. He made reliquaries and inspired others by sharing about the truth of the faith and the lives of the saints.

God granted him gifts of healing, miracles, visions and prophecy. He foresaw the day he was going to die

Saint Eligius bequeathed his horse to a priest upon his passing. The new bishop wanted the horse and took it. As soon as he did, the horse fell ill. When the bishop returned it to the priest that Eligius had chosen, the horse soon recovered. An astonishing story is also known of Eligius removing a horse's leg from its joints to put a shoe on it and returning the leg without difficulty or pain to the horse.

He is the patron of craftsmen and horses and many other things:

Today, December 1st is his feast day. Saint Eligius of Noyon, please pray for us!

SAINT BIBIANA
PATRON AGAINST HEADACHES

It was a crime to be a Christian believer in 4th-century Rome and Bibiana's holy parents Saints Flavian and Dafrosa of Acquapendente were executed for practicing the faith. Babiana and her sister Demetria were apprehended and forced to live with a wicked woman.

The woman tried to get Babiana and her sister to become prostitutes but the sisters refused. Day in and day out, the woman coerced them and tried to get them to comply rather than be punished. Bibiana was steadfast until the very end and protected her purity.

The woman then imprisoned Bibiana with the mentally ill and then she was scourged to death. Upon her passing, the cruel authorities left Bibiana's body to be mangled by dogs but they did not go near it. Two days later, she was buried with fellow martyrs in the catacombs.

Upon her grave, the villagers noticed that a certain herb grew plentifully. This herb proved to be a medicinal cure for those suffering from headaches or epilepsy.

She is the patron against headaches, epilepsy, and mental illness.

Today, December 2nd is her feast day. Saint Bibiana, please pray for us!

SAINT FRANCIS XAVIER
PATRON OF MISSIONARIES, INDIA AND JAPAN

"What profit would there be for one to gain the whole world and forfeit his life?" Matthew 26:16

These words challenged the young Francis and led to his conversion.

The young wealthy nobleman then joined the Society of Jesus and pledged to a live a life of poverty, chastity, and obedience.

Fervently desiring to win souls for Christ, he traveled far to preach the Good News. He would ring a bell in the streets, calling children to learn catechism. In Goa he was said to have converted the whole city!

He spoke out against slavery, journeyed thousands of miles and always served the poor and forgotten. He broke bread with headhunters, washed the sores of lepers in Venice, and oftentimes walked barefoot to his next destination. Throughout his whole mission, he was able to baptize more than 40,000 into Christianity. God imbued him to work many miracles, healings and had the gift of tongues and prophecy.

He is the advocate of prayer for missionaries and navigators.

Today, December 3rd is his feast day. Saint Francis Xavier, please pray for us!

SAINT JOHN DAMASCENE
DOCTOR OF CHRISTIAN ART

In 7th-century Syria, the young well-educated John, through a captured Italian monk, was converted to the faith. Despite being a Christian in a predominantly Muslim country, he was able to live well amongst the Saracens. He even worked as the caliph Abdul Malek's chief financial officer. When Germanus, the patriarch of Constantinople, made laws banning the use of religious icons, Saint John wrote letters to him in defense of them. Germanus in turn hatched a plot to discredit John. He forged a letter as evidence of treason against the caliph.

As a result, the caliph ordered John's writing hand to be chopped off! Afterward, the Blessed Virgin Mary came, and re-attached the hand, miraculously restoring it. This event convinced the caliph of Saint John's innocence.

The orthodox beliefs of the faith were preserved in Saint John's writings such as The Fountain of Wisdom, poems, hymns, and commentaries on Saint Paul the Apostle.

He is the patron of icon painters, pharmacists, and theology students.

Today, December 4th is his feast day. Saint John Damascene, please pray for us!

Saint Sabbas the Great

In 5th-century Cappadocia lived Sabbas who, due to being unhappy at home ran away and decided to become a monk. He soon became the most pious. When he was 30, he lived in a cave by himself. He prayed while weaving 10 willow baskets a day. His exemplary was sought after and he was appointed to be the leader of the monastery. He took care of over 1,000 hermits in the region.

One time, he was looking for a solitary place to pray. He found a cave but a lion lived there. The lion, seeing the holy Sabbas left and let him have the cave.

In obedience to God's will, Saint Sabbas throughout his life traveled around Palestine, preaching the truth of the Gospel. He was able to convert many souls to the faith.

A time came when the bishops of Palestine came under religious persecution by Anastatius I. Saint Sabbas organized a peaceful protest wherein 10,000 monks marched in their defense.

He is one of the founders of Eastern Monasticism.

Today, December 5th is his feast day. Saint Sabbas, please pray for us!

SAINT NICHOLAS of MYRA
The Miracle Worker

In 4th-century Turkey was a man so desperately poor that he was contemplating selling his daughters to the brothel. Saint Nicholas rushed to their aid and in the middle of the night threw 3 bags of gold into their window, saving the whole family from starvation. Since then, the symbol for pawn shops became 3 golden balls.

On another occasion, three young boys were murdered and were hidden in a barrel of brine. Saint Nicolas heard of this dastardly deed and prayed over the dead boys. Miraculously, they came back to life! This is why he became a patron of children and barrel makers.

Even hardened criminals changed their lives because of Saint Nicholas. He disturbed their consciences, and robbers would return their loot to the owners. This is why he became the patron against theft and robbery.   In times past, thieves were known as the Knights of Saint Nicholas

He is also known as a patron of sailors because his prayers saved a sinking ship.

He is the patron of many people such as newlyweds, sweethearts, maidens, paupers, and pilgrims. He is also an intercessor in cases of fires and robberies. Today, December 6th is his feast day. Saint Nicholas of Myra, please pray for us!

355

7
DECEMBER

SAINT AMBROSE OF MILAN
THE HONEY TONGUED DOCTOR

When the bishop of Milan passed away during the 4th century, trouble erupted. Quarrels rapidly violent and amidst this chaos, the city's governor Ambrose stepped in to bring peace to the warring factions. Everyone recognized him as the one who would be able to set everything right. He was unanimously voted to become Milan's next bishop - even when he was not even a baptized Christian!

Ambrose came from a noble Roman family and was the brother of Saints Marcellina and Satyrus. He was well-educated, knowledgeable in philosophy, and a skilled orator. Despite feeling unworthy to be a bishop, Ambrose consented and was baptized, ordained and consecrated in the year 374. He then gave away all his possessions to the poor.

He was so eloquent in his sermons that many flocked to hear him and even the Emperor Theodosius was converted and did public penance for his sins. His most famous convert was Saint Augustine of Hippo, formerly an athiest who turned away from his worldly life to become a saint and Doctor of the Church.

He is the patron of Milan, bees, beekeepers, bishops, and candlemakers. Today, December 7th is his feast day. Saint Ambrose of Milan, please pray for us!

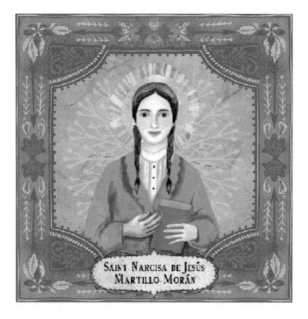

SAINT NARCISA DE JESÚS
MARTILLO-MORÁN

There was once a beautiful young lady who was loved by everyone. She was always sweet, kind, and cheerful. Her blue eyes constantly reflected the happiness within her heart.

She was hard-working and very good at sewing. This is how she supported her younger siblings when their parents passed away. She was always generous and thoughtful of others' needs, giving away what she could to the poor.

She dedicated a room in their home for prayer and it became a little chapel. Her prayers often turned into songs of praise.

Every day, she spent 8 hours in prayer and meditation and oftentimes God allowed her to experience divine ecstasies in His presence.

Since she was very young, she would find time to be alone with God in the woods. The tree of Guayabo where she prayed is now a pilgrimage site where many would still come to grow closer to the Lord.

She passed away on December 8th, 1869 in Lima, Peru. Today is her feast day. Saint Narcisa de Jesús Martillo-Morán, please pray for us!

SAINT JUAN DIEGO

On December 9th, 1531, Juan Diego was surprised to encounter a most beautiful lady. She told him that she was the mother of all of his people and that she wished to have a chapel built on Tepeyac Hill where they were.

Mother Mary also said, "Am I not here, I who am your mother?" She said this to reassure him because of his sick uncle who was later healed.

She then instructed him to collect flowers on the hill and he gathered them on his cloak (called a "tilma"). He showed this to the Blessed Mother and she arranged these for presentation to the bishop. ```

In front of the bishop, he opened his tilma and an image of the Blessed Virgin Mary was imprinted on it! No one could fathom how this image came to be. Even scientists have studied it and have concluded that it could not have been made by ordinary means.

Many cures and amazing conversions have occurred through the prayers of the Blessed Virgin Mary at the church of Our Lady of Guadalupe. Saint Juan Diego is the first Roman Catholic indigenous saint from the Americas. Today, December 9th is his feast day. Saint Juan Diego, please pray for us!

SAINT JOHN ROBERTS

John lived in 16th-century England where practicing Catholicism was punishable by death. A year after his conversion, he entered religious life with the Benedictines in Spain and was ordained when he was 23 years old.

He believed in his heart that he was called to minister to the remnant of Catholics in England. So, he journeyed to England where, after a year of being on mission, he was arrested. Afterward, he was exiled.

The following year, he returned to England and served the victims of the plague in 1604. He was arrested and then banished once again. He repeatedly returned to England and was arrested and exiled. At times he was able to escape and another time he was pardoned.

Finally, while celebrating Holy Mass on December 2, 1610, he was arrested, convicted, and executed for the crime of being a priest. He was martyred with Blessed Thomas Somers and is known as one of the 40 Martyrs of England and Wales.

Today, December 10th is his feast day. Saint John Roberts, please pray for us!

POPE SAINT DAMASUS I
PATRON OF ARCHEOLOGISTS

If you have a Bible in your home, it is in large part because of the efforts of Pope Saint Damasus I. It was during his papacy that the Council in Rome decreed which books were to be part of sacred scripture. He commissioned Saint Jerome to finish the Vulgate translation. That was the year 382.

It was a time of great confusion in the Church with many opposing views being pushed forward such as Arianism and Apollinarianism. Arianism was advocated by Arius which falsely stated that Jesus was not divine but a created being. Apollinarianism was a heretical view by Apollinaris that Jesus had a divine mind but a human body.

Pope Saint Damasus was faithful to his duty as the 37th pope in defending the faith. His reign saw the establishment of Christianity as the official religion of the Roman state.

He honored the saints and martyrs by restoring their graves, catacombs, and shrines. He also wrote poetry dedicated to them.

He is the patron of archeologists.

Today, December 11th is his feast day. Pope Saint Damasus I, please pray for us!

SAINT SPYRIDON OF CYPRUS
PATRON OF POTTERS

Spyridon was born a shepherd in the year 270. Since his youth, he lived righteously. He married and had one daughter. He was a kind and just man and his family so loved our Lord that they decided to each serve God more fully. Spyridon's wife and daughter entered the convent and became nuns. He became a monk at Mount Carmel and in time accepted the role of Bishop of Tremithus. One of his students was Saint Tryphillius of Leucosia. He upheld the doctrine of the Church against Arianism.

During the reign of Galerus, Christians came under severe persecution. Spyridon was apprehended and tortured. His right eye was gouged out and his left calf was cut off. He was also subjected to slave labor in the Spanish mines until the edict of Milan set him free.

Saint Spyridon was known to be a miracle worker. One day when he was trying to convince a philosopher about the trinity, he used the properties of a clay pot. He exclaimed that despite its being made of earth, fire and water, it was still one object. While he was explaining this to the man, water poured out from under the shard and fire appeared on top of it. This is why he is the patron of potters.

Today, December 12th is his feast day. Saint Spyridon of Cyprus, please pray for us.

SAINT LUCY OF SYRACUSE
PATRON FOR EYE DISEASES

Lucy had a secret prayer. Her mother had arranged a marriage for her with a man called Paschasius but Lucy wanted only to live for God. Her prayer was answered but the jilted suitor became enraged.

He exposed Lucy as a Christian and as a punishment, she was sentenced to become a prostitute. The guards came to apprehend Lucy and to the amazement of all, they could not move her. They tied her to a team of oxen to cart her away and yet she would not budge.

Lucy said, "The chaste are the temple of God, and the Holy Spirit dwells in them." The governor ordered her to be executed instead. She was subjected to horrendous pains including having her eyes torn out and yet she remained steadfast to her faith. Then the guards surrounded her with wood and planned to set her on fire but the fire would keep dying out. Her death was made final with a dagger.

When she was being prepared for burial, they saw that her eyes were fully restored!

She is the patron in all cases of eye ailments and spiritual blindness

Today, December 13th is her feast day. Saint Lucy, please pray for us!

SAINT JOHN OF THE CROSS
PATRON OF CONTEMPLATIVES

"The endurance of darkness is the preparation for great light." - Saint John of the Cross

In 1567, at the age of 21, John responded to God's call for him to be a Carmelite priest. He was influenced by Saint Teresa of Avila to establish the Discalced (barefoot) order and took the name "John of the Cross".

Together with Saint Teresa, he sought to bring reform to the order but many thought him to be too severe and his austerities too difficult to follow. They rebelled and imprisoned him for 9 months in a room with only a prayerbook and an oil lamp. He lived only on bread and water and was subjected to cruel lashings every week. His cell was so small that he could hardly lie down but a friar smuggled small pieces of paper where he was able to write some of the most beautiful mystical poetry there ever was.

Upon his release, he continued the mission of reformation and with the help of Saint Teresa was able to establish monasteries all over Spain.

He is the patron of contemplatives, mystics, and Spanish poets.

Today, December 14th is his feast day. Saint John of the Cross, please pray for us!

Saint Virginia
Centurione Bracelli

Arranged marriages were the custom in 17th-century Genoa and though drawn to religious life, Virginia consented to her parent's wishes.

She wed Gasparo Grimaldi Bracelli in 1602 but he turned out to be prone to gambling and drinking. They had 2 daughters and Virginia raised them as best as she could without much support from her husband. After only 5 years, he passed away. Virginia led a quiet life caring for her daughters until they were fully grown and married. Afterward, she devoted her time to caring for the sick, aged, and needy.

In 1625, a war broke out, and many orphans and refugees were in town. Virginia housed the children and extended her help and resources to them. After 4 years a severe plague and famine occurred and her place was overrun with the sick and homeless so she rented a vacant convent and took in 300 patients.

She worked for the good of others unceasingly and had the gift of visions and interior locutions during her later years.

She is the patron of the Sisters of Our Lady of Refuge in Mount Calgary. Today, December 15th is her feast day. Saint Virginia Centurione Bracelli, please pray for us!

Saint Adelaide & Burgundy
PATRON FOR IN-LAWS

A princess' life is not always easy. It was a challenging one for Adelaide who was the daughter of the King of Upper Burgundy (found in ancient France) in the year 931. Her life was mapped out by the age of 2. To solidify alliances, she had an arranged marriage at 16 years old with Lothair (the future king of Italy). Their union did not last long as Lothair was found to be poisoned presumably by his successor Berengarius.

Berengarius forced Adelaide to marry his son but she refused. For this, she was held captive in prison but was set free by King Otto of Germany who defeated Berengarius.

Adelaide married King Otto who was enthroned as the Emperor of Rome. Their reign lasted 20 years. All the while, Queen Adelaide was known for her generosity to the poor. She used her influence and wealth to bring the Christian faith to the people, building and repairing monasteries and churches.

Sadly, her stepson and his wife did not like her and were often unkind to her. Eventually, Saint Adelaide who was prayerful and pious, won them over. She is the patron for those with troubles with their in-laws. Today, December 16th is her feast day. Saint Adelaide, please pray for us!

17
DECEMBER

SAINT LAZARUS OF BETHANY

Imagine awakening from a long sleep and finding yourself bound and encased in darkness. A commanding voice calls out your name and instantly you are brought to your feet and realize that you have just come back from the dead!

Lazarus was in his tomb for 4 days and the Lord Jesus performed a miracle for all to see that He had the power over life and death. He was reunited with his ecstatic sisters Martha and Mary.

We know from tradition that Saint Lazarus' resurrection was made known to all in the region and after Christ's own passion and rising, he went on to become a missionary in Gaul. He gave his life as a martyr during the Domitian persecution.

He is the patron of the dioceses of Autun and Marseille, France.

Today, December 17th is his feast day. Saint Lazarus, please pray for us!

SAINT WINEBALD OF HEIDENHEIM
PATRON OF CONSTRUCTION WORKERS

Indeed saintly parents produce saintly families. Today's saint was born a prince in 8th-century England. His parents were Saint Richard the King and Saint Wunna of Wessex. His siblings were Saint Willibald and Saint Walburga. His uncle was also a holy man, Saint Boniface.

Saint Winebald wished to serve the Lord and his uncle Saint Boniface ordained him in the year 739. He traveled with his uncle to Germany as a missionary and shared the Good News with everyone as much as they could.

Saint Winebald is often represented with a trowel because he helped build many churches and monasteries in England. In fact, the country's Christian heritage is largely due to pious men like him who converted many souls to the faith. He also traveled throughout France, Holland, Austria, Belgium and Luxembourg.

He established a Benedictine monastery at Heidenheim and served as the first abbot. His grave has become a place of pilgrimage.

He is the patron of construction workers and engaged couples.

Today, December 18th is his feast day. Saint Winebald, please pray for us!

POPE BLESSED URBAN V

It was the year 1362 and a new pope was to be installed. Guillaume de Grimoard was chosen, the Apostolic Nuncio in Italy. His reason for choosing the name Urban was, "all the popes who have borne this name were saints".

Though he had a brilliant mind as a canon lawyer, and his position as pope was surely that of power and influence, and yet he lived simply and modestly, adhering to the Benedictine rule. He often served ordinary people and brought reformation to churches and monasteries. He continuously sought to unite the Eastern and Western churches.

With the encouragement of Saint Bridget of Sweden and Saint Catherine of Siena, he returned to the papacy to Rome.

Today, December 19th is his feast day. Pope Blessed Urban V, please pray for us!

SAINT DOMINIC OF SILOS
PATRON OF PREGNANT WOMEN

In the olden days, pregnant queens in Spain put the staff of Saint Dominic of Silos beside their beds to ensure a safe delivery.

It was Saint Dominic's prayers that helped the Blessed Joan of Aza to conceive. When she gave birth, she named her son Dominic in his honor.

Dominic was born to a poor peasant family and grew up tending sheep. He entered into religious life as a Benedictine monk and in time became the monastery's prior.

King Garcia III wanted to take possession of the monk's lands but Dominic refused. They were forcibly banished and were given a new home at the San Sebastian monastery in Silos. The place was in disrepair and housed only 6 monks.

Under his leadership, the monastery flourished and became a spiritual center for arts and literature. The place was also where the poor came to receive nourishment and care. The mission grew prosperous so they used the funds to free Christians enslaved by the Moors.

He is the patron of pregnant women, shepherds, and captives, and against hydrophobia or rabies. Today, December 20th is his feast day. Saint Dominic of Silos, please pray for us!

SAINT PETER CANISIUS
PATRON OF GERMANY

Saint Peter Canisius once thought of himself as lazy. In retrospect, his 76 years were anything but. He was a most accomplished saint in his day and was second to Saint Boniface in reviving the Catholic faith in all of Germany. He was a man of many talents, knowledge and abilities. He used all of these for God's glory. He was ordained in 1546.

His days were never dull for he taught at university, helped found the first Jesuit house in the city and eventually traveled on mission with Saint Ignatius of Loyola. Whenever he finished his many duties, he ministered to the poor and imprisoned. Oftentimes, he would teach catechism to young children and hear their confessions.

During one day at Holy Mass, he received a vision of the Sacred Heart of Jesus. From then on, he offered all his work to the Sacred Heart.

When many abandoned the faith, Saint Peter worked to bring them back. He restored Catholicism to Germany. His books on catechism, known as "Canisi" had 200 editions and was translated into 12 languages. He established several schools and seminaries.

He was proclaimed a Doctor of the Church in 1925. He is the patron of the Catholic press. Today, December 21st is his feast day. Saint Peter Canisius, please pray for us!

SAINT FRANCES XAVIER CABRINI
PATRON AGAINST MALARIA

In 1850, Francesca was born into a large Italian family and grew up on a farm. She was constantly in poor health and yet always served God.

She started to teach at the House of Providence Orphanage, a school for girls. When she was 27, her desire to become a nun was fulfilled and she added "Xavier" to her name in honor of the famous missionary saint. Caring for others, specially orphans was her special gift. The bishop assigned her to establish the Missionary Sisters of the Sacred Heart which ministered to poor children in schools and hospitals.

Pope Leo XIII heard of the holy Saint Frances and commissioned her to serve in New York in 1889. There, she was able to take care of many immigrants many of whom were Italians like herself.

In time, she was able to establish 67 institutions such as schools, hospitals and orphanages in the United States, Europe and South America.

She passed away when she fell ill with malaria.

She is the patron of malaria patients, orphans, immigrants and hospital administrators. Today December 22nd is her feast day. Saint Frances Xavier Cabrini, please pray for us!

SAINT MARGUERITE D'YOUVILLE
PATRON OF DIFFICULT MARRIAGES

When Marguerite was 21, she married Francois de Youville. They decided to live with Francois' mother. Soon they had 6 children but 4 of them died soon after they were born. Both the remaining sons chose to become priests later in life.

Marguerite's husband was an adulterous alcoholic who paid no attention to his children. After only 7 years of marriage, he died leaving the family steeped in debt. She set up a small shop to care for her family and generously gave to the poor.

She was always thinking of others and never let her own hardships in life stop her from serving the needy around her. With the guidance of a priest and 3 other women, she established the Sisters of Charity of the General Hospital of Montreal, also known as the Grey Nuns. They then restored the old General Hospital in the city and there Marguerite lived for the rest of her days as its director. The order still operates today around Canada, the United States, Africa, and South America.

She is the patron of difficult marriages and in-law troubles.

Today, December 23rd is her feast day. Saint Marguerite d'Youville, please pray for us!

ADAM AND EVE
THE PATRIARCH AND MATRIARCH

The day before Christmas and it is the time that the Church honors all of the holy ancestors of Jesus whose birthday we celebrate tomorrow.

God formed Adam and Eve out of the dust of the earth and they are man's first parents.

"Now the Lord God had planted a garden in the east, in Eden; and there he put the man he had formed. The Lord God made all kinds of trees grow out of the ground—trees that were pleasing to the eye and good for food. In the middle of the garden were the tree of life and the tree of the knowledge of good and evil." - Genesis 2:8

"So the Lord God caused the man to fall into a deep sleep; and while he was sleeping, he took one of the man's ribs and then closed up the place with flesh. Then the Lord God made a woman from the rib he had taken out of the man, and he brought her to the man.

The man said, 'This is now bone of my bones and flesh of my flesh; she shall be called 'woman', for she was taken out of man.'" - Genesis 2:8

They are the patrons of tailors and gardeners. Today, December 24th is their feast day. Saints Adam and Eve, please pray for us!

LOVE BEYOND ALL TELLING, GOODNESS BEYOND IMAGINING, LIGHT OF INFINITE INTENSITY GLOWS IN MY HEART.

BLESSED JACOPONE DA TODI

"Love, infusing with light all who share Your splendor, You teach us the true light is not to be found in the light of this world." - Blessed Jacopone da Todi

A tragic event happened in the year 1268. During a public tournament in Bologna, Italy, a certain part of the stands gave way, and one of the casualties was a married woman named Vanna di Guidone. Her husband Jacopone was devastated. He was the one who insisted that she come to this event. His wife was a pious woman who was praying for the greedy and worldly Jacopone to change his ways

That was a turning point in the life of Jacopone. He set aside his successful career as a lawyer and became a Franciscan tertiary. Furthermore, he gave away all his wealth to the poor and dressed in rags, thus earning the name "Crazy Jim" from his former colleagues.

Jacopone wrote beautiful poetry and hymns in his love for God. His most famous work is the Latin hymn, Stabat Mater.

Christmas day on December 25th is his feast day. Blessed Jacopone da Todi, please pray for us.

SAINT STEPHEN
PATRON AGAINST HEADACHES

"Look," he said, "I see heaven open and the Son of Man standing at the right hand of God." - Saint Stephen

There was trouble in first-century Jerusalem. The young Christian deacon Stephen who preached the Good News of salvation through Jesus Christ was being questioned by members of the Sanhedrin. The religious leader's arguments were no match for the truth that Saint Stephen proclaimed.

They could no longer refute him so they accused him of blasphemy. During that time, the Jewish penalty for such an act was death by stoning. That is when he had a vision of heaven.

While they were stoning him, Stephen prayed, "Lord Jesus, receive my spirit." Then he fell on his knees and cried out, "Lord, do not hold this sin against them." When he had said this, he fell asleep. - Acts 7:59

He is he is the first martyr of the Christian church. He is the patron of headache sufferers, bricklayers, casket makers, deacons, horses, stonemasons, and several dioceses.

Today, December 26th is his feast day. Saint Stephen, please pray for us!

SAINT JOHN THE BELOVED APOSTLE
PATRON OF FRIENDSHIPS

Saint John is one of the most well-known apostles of the Lord Jesus. He was the only one of the 12 who was present during the Lord's passion. Jesus entrusted His beloved Mother Mary to his care. He wrote the fourth Gospel.

Because Christianity was banned during that time, the Roman Emperor Dometian sentenced him to a gruesome death. He was beaten, given poison, and then thrust into a cauldron filled with boiling oil. He came out unscathed! Since he was unharmed, he was exiled to the island of Patmos.

In one of his travels, their ship encountered a fierce storm and sank. Everyone except Saint John was swept onto the shore and everyone thought he didn't make it. Two weeks later, Saint John was found alive on the beach.

One story recounts when Saint John preached against praying to stone idols. The followers of the false god Artemis stoned him but somehow, the rocks hit them instead of Saint John! Once a year, the site where Saint John was buried gave off a lovely fragrant dust that when sprinkled on the sick, cured them.

He is the patron of friendship and many other things.

Today, December 27th is his feast day. Saint John, please pray for us!

SAINT ANTHONY of LERINS

In 6th-century Italy lived a hermit on an island on Lake Como. He was a holy an pious man and his prayers wrought many miracles. The people came from far away to live with him for his life inspired them to love God and live for Him.

His name was Anthony and he was tutored by Saint Severinus of Norichelle when his father died at the age of 8. When he became a teenager, Saint Severinus passed away and he was put in the care of his uncle, the Bishop of Lorsch.

Upon reaching adulthood, he decided to live as a monk and his life and vocation served as a good witness to all.

Today, December 28th is his feast day. Saint Anthony of Lerins, please pray for us!

SAINT THOMAS BECKET
PATRON OF THE CLERGY

Your friend can sometimes be your greatest foe. This was the case for Thomas who was the friend of King Henry II.

He lived in 12th-century Canterbury, England and was a civil and canon lawyer, soldier and officer. When he was appointed as Archbishop of Canterbury, his life changed. He put God first in all that he did. He became known as a generous benefactor of the poor.

The king wished for him to sign a document that would curtail the Church's freedom. Thomas refused to sign. This enraged the king - once his closest ally, now his worst enemy. Thomas fled and was in exile for 2 years. Upon his return, the people rejoiced but the king muttered, "Will no one rid me of this turbulent priest!" These words led to the murder of Thomas.

His last words were, "For the name of Jesus and the protection of the Church, I am ready to embrace death."

"Wait the end with joy. It is the end which characterizes everything and which tests a man's expectations." - Saint Thomas Becket

He is the patron of the clergy. Today, December 29th is his feast day. Saint Thomas Becket, please pray for us!

BLESSED GIOVANNI
MARIA BOCCARDO
PATRON AGAINST CANCER

There was once a blind beggar who needed care. Someone took notice of the poor man and cared for his basic needs. The man was Blessed Giovanni Maria Boccardo who was later known as the "Father of the Poor".

He was born in 1848 in Turin, Italy and grew up in a devout Catholic family. Out of the 10 children, 4 of the boys grew up to join the priesthood. Blessed Giovanni Maria was one of them and his brother Blessed Luigi was another. In 1817, he was ordained and proceeded to work in the seminary as the spiritual director of young seminarians. He was friends with Saint John Bosco, Saint Leonard Murialdo, and Blessed Joseph Allamano.

He spent his days caring for his parishioners and he was well-loved by all. He tended the poor and the sick by setting up a hospice. He taught children the faith and also organized a prison ministry. He established the Poor Daughters of Saint Cajetan whose work spans several countries and still operates today.

An 80-year-old woman was miraculously cured of cancer through his intercession. That is why he is the patron against cancer.

Today, December 30th, is his feast day. Blessed Giovanni Maria Boccardo, please pray for us!

SAINT JOHN FRANCIS REGIS
PATRON OF EMBROIDERERS

Saint John Francis Regis traveled from town to town sharing simple yet powerful words of salvation. Many farmers, workers and country folk were converted through his preaching! Every day, he was busy living out his mission of hearing confessions in the morning and visiting prisons and hospitals in the afternoon. He did not spend much time for himself but kept busy serving his flock. He usually ate only apples and black bread and whatever else was available.

To save desperately poor women and reformed prostitutes, he helped them learn embroidery and put up hostels for them called the "Daughters of Refuge". He inspired the rich to use their wealth to uplift the poor.

Miraculous multiplication of food in the granary occurred through his prayers. The sick were also cured but he said, "Every time God converts a hardened sinner, He is working a far greater miracle."

He is the patron of embroiderers, lace makers, medical social workers, and against the plague.

Today, December 31st is his feast day. Saint John Francis Regis, please pray for us!

You have made us for Yourself, O Lord, and our heart is restless until it rests in You.

SAINT AUGUSTINE

Made in the USA
Las Vegas, NV
03 December 2024

13308620R00228